Best Hikes Sedona

Best Hikes Sedona

The Greatest Views, Desert Hikes, and Forest Strolls

Bruce Grubbs

GUILFORD, CONNECTICUT

An imprint of The Rowman & Littlefield Publishing Group, Inc.
4501 Forbes Blvd., Ste. 200
Lanham, MD 20706
www.rowman.com
Falcon and FalconGuides are registered trademarks and Make Adventure Your Story is a trademark
of The Rowman & Littlefield Publishing Group, Inc.

Distributed by NATIONAL BOOK NETWORK

Photos by Bruce Grubbs unless otherwise noted
Maps by Melissa Baker

British Library Cataloguing in Publication Information available

Library of Congress Cataloging-in-Publication Data available

ISBN 978-1-4930-3453-6 (paperback)
ISBN 978-1-4930-3454-3 (e-book)

∞™ The paper used in this publication meets the minimum requirements of American National
Standard for Information Sciences—Permanence of Paper for Printed Library Materials, ANSI/NISO
Z39.48-1992.

Contents

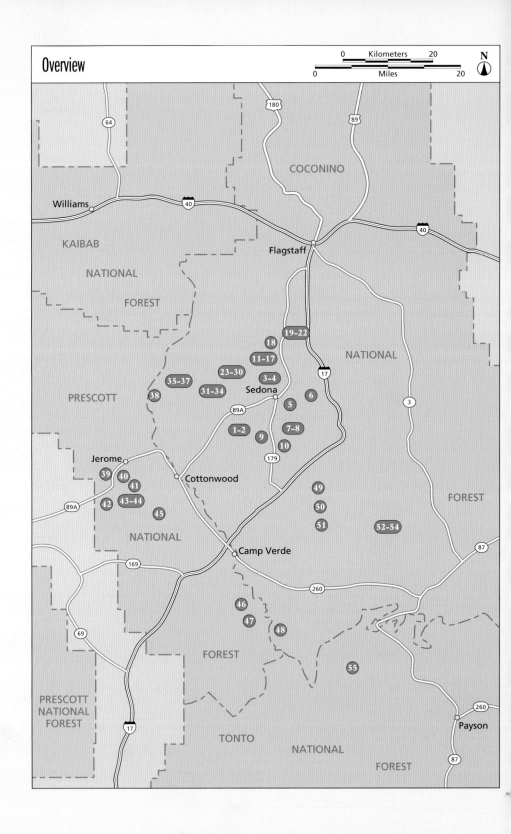

Overview

Kilometers 0 — 20
Miles 0 — 20

N

COCONINO

Williams

KAIBAB
NATIONAL
FOREST

Flagstaff

NATIONAL

PRESCOTT

19-22
18
11-17
23-30
3-4
35-37
31-34
Sedona
38
6
5
1-2
7-8
9
10

Jerome
39
40
41
43-44
42
45

Cottonwood

49
50
51
52-54

FOREST

NATIONAL

Camp Verde

FOREST

46
47
48

55

PRESCOTT
NATIONAL
FOREST

TONTO
NATIONAL

FOREST

Payson

Acknowledgments

I'd like to thank all the USDA Forest Service and other agency personnel who made valuable comments and suggestions. Warm thanks to Duart Martin for encouraging this project, not to mention hiking with me. Thanks to Marvin and Sharon Baur for doing shuttles and hikes, and thanks to all my other hiking companions over the years. It wouldn't have been nearly as much fun without you. Thanks to David Legere and my other editors for working with me to make this the best possible book. I really appreciate Melissa Baker and her staff cartographers for the excellent maps. Finally, I greatly appreciate the production people at Rowman & Littlefield, who worked hard to turn my rough manuscript into another fine FalconGuide.

Introduction

This book is based on the Sedona portion of my book *Hiking Northern Arizona*, but since I have more room in this full-size FalconGuide, I have used the luxury of space to greatly expand the trail descriptions for the fifty-five trails in this book. I've also included far more trail tips and techniques, as well as local knowledge of the flora, fauna, and geology. The more you know, the more fun it is to hike and explore, and I aim to help you get there.

Canyons and Rims

Sedona is located in the northeast side of the Verde Valley, under a spectacular portion of the Mogollon Rim. The Verde Valley is drained by the Verde River, one of the last free-flowing perennial rivers remaining in the American Southwest. On the southwest, the Verde Valley is bounded by the Verde Rim. Elevations range from 2,800 feet along the lower Verde River to 7,726 feet atop Mingus Mountain on the Verde Rim and 8,058 feet at Baker Butte on the Mogollon Rim. This varied region, mostly within an hour's drive of Sedona, creates a hiker's paradise of deep, shady canyons; high rims with stunning views; and a climate that lets you hike and explore all year.

Plant Communities

The highest portions of both rims are forested with ponderosa pine, while the lowest areas are part of the Sonoran Desert, marked by its signature plant, the towering saguaro cactus. At intermediate elevations, typified by Sedona itself, grows a miniature woodland of juniper trees, pinyon pines, and, in some of the secret canyons, the beautiful Arizona cypress. Riparian zones, such as along Oak and Sycamore Creeks, feature water-loving trees including Arizona sycamore, Arizona walnut, Arizona alder, Fremont cottonwood, and several others.

Wildlife

Common larger wildlife includes mule deer, coyotes, and bobcats, found everywhere from low deserts to the highest mountains. The largest animal found in the area is the Roosevelt elk, which was imported from the Yellowstone region in the 1950s. The native Merriam's elk had unfortunately been hunted to extinction by 1900. Elk are mainly found on the Mogollon Rim in summer, moving down to the less-snowy pinyon-juniper woodland in the winter—but still preferring the plateau country rather than the canyons. Mountain lions are the largest remaining predators; they tend to be secretive, preferring remote rugged mountains and canyons. Black bears can occasionally be spotted, most often in the ponderosa pine forests but sometimes at lower elevations.

Geology

The Mogollon Rim begins northwest of Sedona and runs east nearly 200 miles into New Mexico, marking the boundary between the high Colorado Plateau to the north, and the Basin and Range Province to the south. The Colorado Plateau is formed on the top of layers of sedimentary rocks laid down over millions of years. Some of the rocks were formed underwater; others were deposited in Sahara-like deserts. Mountain-building forces have raised the plateau 1 to 2.5 miles above sea level, warping and fracturing the rocks. Running water from rain and snowmelt has eroded these weaknesses into thousands of canyons. Sedona, located right at the foot of the Mogollon Rim, features unique red rock formations and canyons eroded out of the sedimentary rock.

The northernmost portion of the vast Basin and Range Province lies just south of the Mogollon Rim and is known as the Central Mountains. Here, rugged mountain ranges border deep valleys and canyons, as typified by the Verde Valley and Mingus Mountain, and downstream along the Verde River, the Verde River canyons, Pine Mountain, and the exceptionally rugged and remote Mazatzal Mountains.

History

As you hike Arizona's backcountry, you will see artifacts left by the state's prehistoric peoples. The first human inhabitants were Paleo-hunters, who arrived at least 11,000 years ago, in the waning years of the last glacial period. Arizona's weather was considerably cooler and wetter than it is today, and small glaciers graced the summits of the San Francisco Peaks and the White Mountains.

Using a spear-throwing device called an atlatl, these hunters stalked mammoths, ground sloths, giant bison, Harrington's mountain goats, tapirs (piglike mammals), camelids, and other relics of the Pleistocene era. Over several thousands of years of gradual warming and drying, and perhaps further decimated by overhunting, the great ice-age mammals disappeared. The hunters turned their attention to other game, such as deer, elk, bighorn sheep, and pronghorns; rabbits, squirrels, and other rodents; and birds. A greater emphasis was also placed on the gathering of wild plant foods. These people had to be opportunists to survive in this unforgiving environment.

Although maize and squash were introduced into Arizona from Mexico perhaps as long as 4,000 years ago, not until about 2,000 years later did the hunter-gatherers become serious farmers. As agriculturalists, they tended to remain in one area to work and guard their small farming plots. Permanent homes were constructed. These were usually pit houses—structures that were partially subterranean, with vertical poles running around the perimeter of the hole to support a roof. Later, aboveground stone-and-mud houses replaced the pit houses, sometimes with attached rooms and several stories. A few dwellings were located in south-facing caves or on hilltops.

Around AD 600, Arizona's native people acquired several other new items from people to the south in Mexico. Beans—pinto, lima, and tepary—were introduced, as were the technique of pottery making and the bow and arrow. These new foods, ways of preparing them, and more efficient hunting implements apparently allowed the population to increase dramatically.

Three major and distinct Indian cultures developed, along with a number of smaller groups. People in the southern part of the state, whom archaeologists call the Hohokam, engineered complex irrigation canals to carry river water onto the hot desert plains. The Anasazi (sometimes called the Ancestral Puebloans) lived on the Colorado Plateau and relied on rainstorms to water their crops. The Mogollon people lived throughout the Central Highlands and practiced both irrigation and dry farming.

After six or seven centuries of prosperity, the Anasazi began to abandon their lands. What caused their departure is not fully understood, but it was probably a combination of drought, overuse of natural resources, overpopulation, and perhaps disease and warfare. By the mid-1400s the Mogollon and Hohokam peoples had also left their villages.

Where did everybody go? Some probably moved out of the Arizona region entirely; others resumed a hunting-and-gathering lifestyle. A few, such as the Hopi (who are likely direct descendants of the Anasazi), found different locations favorable to their dry-farming methods and continued their agricultural tradition. About this same time, new people from the north entered the American Southwest, including the Navajo and Apache.

Arizona's historic period begins in 1539 with Estevanico (Little Esteban), a black Moor slave who was with the Spaniard Fray Marcos de Niza exploring north toward the American Southwest. Estevanico had gone ahead of the padre and sent back word of "seven very rich great cities." Unfortunately, Zuni Indians killed Estevanico. Hearing this news, Niza retreated to Mexico, where his report of a collection of cities of unbelievable riches led Francisco Vásquez de Coronado to mount an expedition the next year to find the Seven Cities of Cíbola. The Spaniards were disappointed to discover that legendary Cíbola was in reality the stone-and-mud pueblos of the Zuni. However, a small detachment of Coronado's men led by García López de Cárdenas is credited with being the first Europeans to see the Grand Canyon, in 1542. Not long after this foray, Spanish padres came seeking Indian souls instead of gold. Some Native Americans fared better than others under the Spanish invasion.

By the 1820s, fur trappers such as James Ohio Pattie, Jedediah Smith, Bill Williams, Pauline Weaver, and Kit Carson were traipsing along Arizona's streams and rivers, even though the land was under Spanish and then Mexican rule. After the Mexican War of 1847–1848, Arizona north of the Gila River was ceded to the United States. Within a few years, prospectors, ranchers, and settlers followed, displacing the original Indian residents. In 1854 the Gadsden Purchase completed the acquisition of present-day Arizona. Originally part of New Mexico Territory, Arizona became a separate territory in 1863.

Conflict erupted as these different groups fought over Arizona's limited natural resources. However, by the end of the nineteenth century, the Old West was quickly becoming a memory. On Valentine's Day 1912, Arizona became the nation's forty-eighth state.

Preserving Arizona's Heritage

Arizona is fortunate to have some of the best-preserved prehistoric structures and artifacts in the world. Unfortunately, many of these sites have been vandalized to some degree. Disturbing archaeological sites or collecting artifacts not only lessens their scientific value but also deeply upsets Native Americans whose ancestors left these things behind.

Two federal laws, the American Antiquities Act and the Archaeological Resources Protection Act, forbid removal or destruction of archaeological and historical resources on federal land. The Arizona State Antiquities Act provides similar protection on state lands. Failure to comply with these laws can result in stiff fines and imprisonment, not to mention many years of bad luck and terrible nightmares inflicted by ancient spirits. Any vandalism should be immediately reported to the nearest federal or state resource office or law enforcement agency.

Climate

Because of the 5,000-foot elevation range in the Sedona area, temperatures and climate vary greatly across the region. The wet seasons are December through March, when winter storms are common, and July through mid-September, when summer thunderstorms are prevalent. Fall and late spring are usually dry and cool and are the best overall hiking seasons, but hiking is delightful year-round.

Starting in late November, snow storms can be frequent, and there is often several feet of snow along the Mogollon Rim and the highest part of the Verde Rim. But Arizona's climate is extremely variable, and occasionally the first snowfall is delayed into January or even later. Many high-elevation areas then remain open for hiking well into winter, but the late-season hiker should be prepared for possible winter snowstorms. The lower desert areas may experience occasional snowfall, but the snow doesn't usually stay on the ground for more than a day or two. Between storms the weather is bright and sunny. Winter rain turns normally dry, stony desert into a hiker's paradise of running streams and lush, green grass.

Spring weather is changeable as the storm track starts its seasonal swing to the north. By April the weather is usually dry but still cool, making spring a very good time to hike. Springs, water pockets, and streams are often full, which makes it easier to plan backpack trips into the remotest areas. In wet years, the desert often becomes a riot of wildflowers during spring.

In May the weather usually takes a serious turn toward the summer's heat. Desert temperatures over 100°F are common by June. During high summer, plan your hikes for the morning hours. This is also a good time to explore desert canyons that require wading and swimming to progress through their narrow depths.

By early July, moisture moves in from the southeast, marking the onset of the North American monsoon. Late-summer mornings usually dawn cool and clear, but by noon masses of cumulus clouds form over the high country. In a short time the innocuous cumulus clouds develop into full-blown thunderstorms, which lash the countryside with lightning, heavy rain, hail, and high winds. Get an early start, and plan to be off high ridges and peaks by noon. Heavy rain from thunderstorms runs off quickly, creating flash floods in normally dry washes and canyon bottoms. Stay out of narrow canyons during the monsoon, and never camp or park a vehicle in a dry wash. On the plus side, the summer rains bring a resurgence of flowers to the forest country and are a welcome change from the hot, dry days of June.

The monsoon usually ends by mid-September, and autumn is clear, cool, and dry. The fine weather and changing fall colors make hiking at all elevations an absolute delight. Dry weather usually continues into late November, but late-fall and winter hikers should keep a close eye on the weather. The first winter storm is sometimes a large one, dropping several feet of snow on elevations above 5,000 feet.

Wildfires

In recent years Arizona has suffered a number of unusually large and destructive wildfires. While fire has always been part of the natural forest ecology in Arizona, a combination of long-term drought, tree-killing insect epidemics, and over-dense forests caused by more than a century of poor management practices has led to fires not only burning hundreds of thousands of acres of forest but also large areas of desert. A number of the hikes in this book have been affected by recent large fires, and more will be affected in the future. Always call or e-mail the land management agency before your hike, or at least check their website, for current conditions and possible area or trail closures.

Tips for Hiking in the Red Rock Country

Ten Essentials

Always make sure you have the ten essentials. The concept of the ten essentials was started by The Mountaineers, a Seattle-based mountaineering club, in the 1930s. The following list is modified for Arizona's arid climate:

1. Water—as much as 2 gallons per person per day in very hot weather
2. Sun protection—sunhat and sunscreen of at least SPF 15
3. Navigation—map, compass, GPS device, personal locator beacon (PLB)
4. Snacks—high-energy food such as trail mix and energy bars
5. Headlamp—LED with fresh batteries
6. Knife—a Swiss Army knife or multi-tool
7. Fire—disposable lighter
8. First aid kit—one designed for wilderness sports
9. Extra clothes—at least an insulating layer, such as fleece, and a rain shell
10. Shelter—a Mylar emergency blanket

Hazards

Wilderness can be a safe place—if you are willing to respect your limitations. You'll safely gain confidence and self-reliance if you start out with easy hikes and progress to more difficult adventures.

Trip Planning

Individuals or parties pushing too hard often suffer wilderness accidents. Instead, set reasonable goals, allowing for delays caused by weather, deteriorated trails, unexpectedly rough country, and dry springs. Remember that your group moves at the speed of the slowest member. Be flexible enough to eliminate part of a hike if your original plans appear too ambitious. Do not fall into the trap of considering a trip plan "cast in stone"—instead, take pride in your adaptability. Plan your trip carefully using maps, guidebooks, websites, blogs, and information from reliable sources, such as experienced hikers and backcountry rangers.

When backpacking, consider alternatives to traditional campsites. Dry camping—that is, away from water sources—virtually eliminates the possibility of contaminating wilderness streams and lakes. You can also avoid heavily used campsites and their camp-robbing animal attendants such as skunks, mice, rock squirrels, jays, and insects. The technique is simple: Use collapsible water containers to pick up water at the last reliable source of the day, and use minimal water for camp chores. With practice, dry camping will become second nature, and you'll be able to enjoy many beautiful, uncrowded campsites.

Water Essentials

Backcountry water sources are not safe to drink. Infections from contaminated water are uncomfortable and can be disabling. Giardiasis, for example, is a severe gastrointestinal infection caused by cysts that can result in an emergency evacuation of the infected hiker. Purify all backcountry water sources. The newer chlorine dioxide tablets are effective against viruses, bacteria, and cysts, but they are slow to work. Iodine tablets work faster but are not effective against cryptosporidia. Either tablet system is far lighter than a filter.

Water filters remove bad tastes as well as bacteria and cysts, but most do not remove viruses. Filters labeled "water purifier" have an active iodine element that does kill viruses.

You can also purify water by bringing it to a rolling boil. This technique produces safe water at any altitude. After boiling, pour the water back and forth between containers to cool it and improve its taste.

Backcountry Navigation

Maps are essential for finding your way in the backcountry. Don't depend on trail signs, which are often missing or misleading.

Topographic maps are the most useful type of map for backcountry navigation because they show the elevation and shape of the land using contour lines. All of

Arizona is covered by the 7.5-minute quadrangle series published by the US Geological Survey, available for sale from the USGS and retailers. You can download these maps for free directly from USGS at usgs.gov. Each hike description in this book lists the USGS topographic maps that cover the hike. Keep in mind that USGS maps are not updated very often, so man-made details such as trails and roads may be inaccurate.

The USDA Forest Service and several private companies publish recreational and wilderness-area topographic maps with more up-to-date trail information. The forest service and the Bureau of Land Management (BLM) publish a series of road maps that cover national forests and other public lands. These maps are useful for navigating roads and finding the trailhead.

The most useful of the privately produced maps are the Trails Illustrated series, published by National Geographic Maps (natgeomaps.com/trail-maps/trails-illustrated-maps/). These maps are printed on waterproof plastic and cover most of the trails in this book. The hike description lists the Trails Illustrated map covering the hike.

Among the many digital maps available, my current favorite is Gaia GPS. Available both as a web page (gaiagps.com) and apps for Android and iPhone, Gaia GPS has many different map layers to choose from. These include USGS topo maps, satellite imagery, and Trails Illustrated maps. It has great tools for creating waypoints, routes, and tracks, and all your data is saved to the Gaia cloud. For example, if you use your phone to record a track, it automatically shows up on the Gaia GPS web page.

Before entering the backcountry, study the maps to become familiar with the general lay of the land. This is a good time to establish a baseline—a long, unmistakable landmark such as a road or highway that borders the area. In the rare event that you become totally disoriented, you can always use your compass to follow a general course toward your baseline. Although hiking to your baseline will probably take you out of your way, it's comforting to know you can always find a route back to known country.

Refer to the map often while hiking, and locate yourself in reference to visible landmarks. Use trail signs to confirm your location. If you do this consistently, you will never become lost.

The satellite-based Global Positioning System (GPS) is very useful in areas where landmarks are few, such as pinyon-juniper flats, dense forest, and when bad weather hides landmarks. GPS works especially well in combination with computer-based topographic maps such as Gaia GPS. With computer and online maps, you can plot GPS waypoints on the computer and then download them to your GPS receiver. You can also use a variety of on-screen tools to measure distances and elevations, which can be of great help in planning your hike. You can then print custom maps for your trip. You can also share your hike with others, even make it public if you wish. Although GPS makes it possible to find your location nearly anywhere, a GPS receiver is no substitute for a good map and a reliable compass. With GPS alone, you'll know your coordinates to within a few feet but still not know where you are, let alone where you need to go. You'll need a map and compass to plot your location and determine the route you need to travel. Also, as with any other mechanical or electronic device, a GPS unit can fail. Bring spare batteries. GPS works especially well in combination with computer-based topographic maps such as Gaia GPS. With computer and online maps, you can plot GPS waypoints on the computer and then download them to your GPS receiver.

The GPS coordinates given for all the trailheads and selected points in the "Miles and Directions" sections of the hike descriptions use latitude and longitude (lat/long) because it is the most universal coordinate system. Unfortunately lat/long is difficult to use on printed maps without a special plotter. The Universal Transverse Mercator (UTM) coordinate system is much easier to use in the field, and all GPS receivers and many printed maps use it. You can convert between UTM and lat/long using a number of websites, including geoplaner.com. If this site is down, search for "UTM conversion."

Most computer-based maps are based on the WGS84 datum, which is the standard for GPS land navigation; the coordinates in this book use WGS84. Most printed USGS topo maps use the older NAD27 datum. Since the datum provides the reference points on which the maps are drawn, using the wrong datum can cause large errors—miles in some cases. Be sure to set your GPS receiver accordingly before using the coordinates in this book or from a paper map.

A number of sources on the web provide GPS data, including waypoints, routes, and tracks, for trails and hiking routes. Use caution, and don't rely on such data as your only means of navigation in the backcountry. There's no way to tell how reliable GPS data is unless you collected it yourself or it comes from a source that you know you can trust; always cross-check with a topo map and a written trail description.

Also, don't walk along with your face buried in your GPS or cell phone screen, following a detailed track or route. That's a really good way to blunder into a cactus or, worse, a sunbathing rattlesnake! Leave your GPS off while walking, and take it out at rest stops to check your location and progress. Doing so also greatly extends the battery life.

Trail Courtesy

Don't cut switchbacks. It takes more effort and erodes the trail and landscape. Give horses and pack animals the right-of-way by stepping off the trail on the downhill side. Avoid sudden movements or loud noises, and follow any instructions given by the wrangler. You will encounter mountain bikes outside designated wilderness areas. Since they're less maneuverable than you, it's polite to step aside so that the riders can pass without having to veer off the trail, even though you have the right-of-way.

Smokers should stop at a bare spot or rock ledge, then make certain that all smoking materials are extinguished before continuing. Due to fire hazard, it may be illegal to smoke while traveling on public land. Never smoke or light any kind of fire on windy days or when the fire danger is high—wildfires can start easily and spread explosively.

Dogs are not allowed on trails in state parks, including Red Rock and Slide Rock State Parks. Dogs are allowed in the national forests and designated wilderness in this book, but it is your responsibility to keep them from bothering wildlife or other hikers. Dogs must be under verbal control or on a leash.

Don't cut live trees or plants of any kind, carve on trees or rocks, pick wildflowers, or build rock campfire rings, rock cairns, rock stacks, or any other rock structures. Leave the backcountry just as you found it.

Motorized vehicles and bicycles, including mountain bikes, are prohibited in all designated wilderness areas. State parks and other areas may also have restrictions.

Camping

Choose campsites on durable, naturally drained surfaces, such as forest duff, sand, gravel, or rock. In the forest look above you for dead branches that could break off. Do not camp on grass, and avoid fragile meadows and sites next to springs and creeks. Never dig drainage ditches or make other "improvements." Rangers sometimes close specific areas to camping or entry to allow them to recover from heavy use—please obey such restrictions.

Campfires

Don't build campfires except in an emergency. There are far too many fire scars in Arizona's backcountry. If you have good equipment, you'll be warmer without a fire.

Campfires are prohibited in certain areas at all times and during periods of high fire danger in other areas. Be aware that when fires are prohibited, the fire danger is so extreme that fires will spread explosively. Check with the land management agency listed with each hike for current regulations.

Trash

If you carried it in, you can also carry it out. Do not bury food or trash—animals will always dig it up. Don't feed wild creatures. They become dependent on human food, which can lead to unpleasant encounters and cause the animals to starve during the off-season.

Sanitation

A short walk in any popular recreation area will show you that few people seem to know how to answer the call of nature away from facilities. Many diseases such as giardiasis are spread by poor human sanitation. If facilities are available at places such as trailheads or campgrounds, always use them. In the backcountry, select a site at least 100 yards from streams, lakes, springs, and dry washes. Avoid barren, sandy soil, if possible. Dig a small "cat hole" about 6 inches down into the organic layer of the soil. (Some people carry a small plastic trowel for this purpose.) When finished, refill the hole; carry out used toilet paper in double zipper bags. Baking soda reduces the odor.

Weather

Summer heat is a serious hazard at the lower elevations covered in this book. Protection from both the heat and the sun is important: A lightweight sunhat is essential. During hot weather, hike in the shady canyons or along flowing creeks, and hike early in the day to avoid the afternoon heat.

Afternoon thunderstorms, which bring high winds, heavy rain and hail, and lightning, are common from July through mid-September but may occur any time of year. When thunderstorms form, stay off exposed ridges and mountaintops and away from lone trees. Also avoid camping or parking your vehicle in dry washes and drainages. Flash floods can appear suddenly from heavy rains falling many miles away. Never try to cross a flooded wash, either by vehicle or on foot.

Hypothermia is a life-threatening condition caused by continuous exposure to chilling weather. Rainy, windy weather causes an insidious heat loss and is especially dangerous. Snowfall and blizzard conditions can occur at any time of year at the higher elevations covered in this book. Extended wet weather occasionally occurs during winter. Hypothermia may be prevented by adjusting your clothing layers to avoid chilling or overheating and by eating and drinking regularly so that your body continues to produce heat.

Insects and Their Kin

A few mosquitoes may appear in the desert after wet spring weather and in the high country during late-summer rains. Since Arizona mosquitoes are known to carry West Nile virus, use repellent and sleep in a tent when mosquitoes are out.

Although most scorpions can inflict a painful sting, only the bark scorpion—a small, straw-colored scorpion found in the lower deserts—is dangerous. Black widow and brown recluse spiders can also be a hazard, especially to young children and adults who are allergic. Susceptible individuals should carry insect-sting kits prescribed by their doctors. Kissing bugs and other obnoxious insects are dormant during cool weather but active in warm weather. Use a net tent to keep nighttime prowlers away when camping in warm weather in the deserts. You can avoid most scorpion and spider encounters by never placing your hands or bare feet where you can't see. Kick over rocks and logs before picking them up.

Aggressive Africanized bees are found throughout the state and are indistinguishable from domesticated honeybees. The best way to avoid being stung is to give all bees a wide berth. If attacked, drop your pack, protect your eyes, and head for dense brush or a building or vehicle if one is nearby. Don't swat at the bees.

Snakes

Arizona boasts more species of rattlesnakes than any another state—eleven species and several varieties. Rattlesnakes are most common at lower elevations but may be encountered anywhere. Since rattlesnakes can strike no farther than approximately half their body length, avoid placing your hands and feet in areas that you cannot see, and walk several feet away from rock overhangs and shady ledges. Because bites often occur on feet, ankle-high hiking boots and loose-fitting long pants offer some protection. Snakes, which are cold-blooded, prefer surfaces at about 80°F, so during hotter weather watch for snakes in shady places. In cool weather be alert for snakes sunning on open ground.

Wildlife

Wild animals normally leave you alone unless molested or provoked. Black bears, mountain lions, wolves, and coyotes are shy around people and usually not a problem. Do not feed any wild animal—they rapidly get accustomed to handouts and will then vigorously defend their new food source. Around camp, rodent problems can be avoided by hanging your food from rocks or trees.

Plants

Poison ivy grows along streams and canyon bottoms in the Sedona area. Poison ivy is easily recognized by its leaves, which grow in groups of three. Contact with the leaves, stems, and berries sometimes causes a rash that later starts to blister. Unless large areas of skin are involved, or the reaction is severe, no specific treatment is required other than calamine lotion to relieve the itching. Cacti and other spiny plants occur at all but the highest elevations. Some cacti, especially cholla, have tiny barbs on their spines, which cause them to cling ferociously. Use a pair of sticks to quickly pluck the burr or joint from your skin or clothing. A pair of tweezers is essential for removing spines.

Never eat any wild plant unless you know its identity. Many common plants, especially mushrooms, are deadly.

Rescue

Most of the hikes in this book are popular and well-traveled, but a few are remote. Anyone entering remote country should be self-sufficient and prepared to take care of emergencies such as equipment failure and minor medical problems. Very rarely, circumstances may create a life-threatening situation that requires a search effort or an emergency evacuation. Always leave word of your hiking plans with a reliable individual. For backpack trips, you should provide a written itinerary and a map. In your instructions, allow extra time for routine delays, and always make contact as soon as you are out. The responsible person should be advised to contact the appropriate authority if you become overdue. County sheriffs are responsible for search and rescue. Calling 911 is the best way to initiate a rescue in all areas.

If you have a cell phone, it's worth trying to use it in an emergency situation. It may work, especially if you are on a ridge or other high point, but don't count on a cell phone for communications in the backcountry. The cellular system is designed to cover populated areas such as major highways and cities.

A better option is to carry a personal locator beacon (PLB). These lightweight devices use the same satellites as the emergency beacons on aircraft. Your PLB must be registered to you before you can use it. When activated, it uses GPS satellites to determine your exact location then signals the rescue authorities via satellite. The rescue center first calls your contact numbers (given when you register your PLB) to make sure the activation isn't a false alarm then dispatches rescuers directly to your location (by helicopter if necessary.) This means rescue in a matter of hours rather than days, weather permitting.

How to Use This Guide

Hike number and name: The hike number is also shown on the locator map to help you visualize the general location of the hike. I've used the official, or at least the commonly accepted, name for a trail or hike wherever possible. Loop hikes or other routes that use several trails are usually named for the main trail or for a prominent feature along the way.

Each hike is introduced with a **general description**, including special attractions. Next are the hike specs, which give you specific information about the hike in an at-a-glance format so that you can see if the hike suits your desires.

Distance: This indicates the total distance of the hike in miles. Distances were carefully measured using digital topo maps, which is the most accurate method of measuring trail distances short of physically rolling a trail wheel over the route. Both methods are more accurate than measuring distance with the odometer in a GPS receiver. Hikes may be loops, which use a series of trails so that you never retrace your steps; out and back, which return along the same trails used on the way out; point-to-point hikes, which normally require a car shuttle between trails; and lollipop, which are hikes with an out-and-back section leading to a loop.

Hiking time: This time in hours is based on average hiking times for a reasonably fit person. Non-hikers will take longer; very fit, seasoned hikers will take less time.

Difficulty: All the hikes are rated as easy, moderate, or strenuous, along with the reason for the rating. This is a subjective rating, but in general, easy hikes can be done by nearly anyone and take a few hours at most. Moderate hikes take all or most of a day and require moderate physical abilities and/or wilderness route-finding skills. Strenuous hikes are long with significant elevation change, requiring a full day or several days to accomplish, and may involve cross-country hiking and route finding. These hikes should be attempted only by experienced hikers in good physical condition.

Seasons: This is the recommended season to do the hike. The season may be longer or shorter in some years. "Year-round" hikes may be hot in summer; you may want to hike early in the morning. Remember that individuals vary in their tolerance to heat or cold. A temperature that may be comfortable for one hiker may be unpleasant for another.

Trail surface: Paved, dirt and rocks, sand, etc.

Water: Since this is generally arid country, you should always be aware of water sources along the trail, even for day hikes on which you'll normally carry all the water you'll need from home. Dehydration occurs quickly in the low-humidity conditions that are common here, and running out of water can quickly result in a medical emergency, especially during the hotter half of the year. Backpackers must plan their entire trip around water sources. This section lists known sources, including springs, creeks, rivers, and natural water tanks and pockets. Very few water sources in this dry country can be considered absolutely reliable. Don't ever depend on a single water source, no matter how reliable it has been in the past. And remember: *All backcountry water should be purified.*

Other trail users: Inside the wilderness areas, you may encounter horses. On trails outside the wilderness areas, you may also encounter mountain bikes or all-terrain vehicles.

Canine compatibility: This section tells you if dogs are permitted or not and, if permitted, whether they must be on a leash.

Land status: Most of the trails in this book are in the Coconino National Forest. A few are in the Prescott National Forest, state parks, or the city of Sedona

Fees and permits: This section lists if a fee is required for trailhead parking or backcountry travel and whether a permit is required.

Maps: The appropriate Trails Illustrated map and USGS 7.5-minute topographic quadrangles are listed. The Trails Illustrated map is the best map for most of the hikes in the book because they are updated frequently. If you plan to hike cross-country, you may want the more-detailed USGS maps.

Trail contacts: This section lists the name and contact information for the land management agency that has jurisdiction over the hike. It's always a good idea to contact the agency before you head out to learn of trail closures or other unusual conditions.

Finding the trailhead: These driving directions are given in miles from the nearest large town for all the hikes, followed by the GPS coordinates of the trailhead. To use these coordinates with a map, you must set your GPS to the datum used by your map. For paper USGS topo maps, use NAD27. For most other maps, use WGS84. The coordinates are in latitude and longitude—if you prefer UTM, you can convert from lat/long to UTM at a number of websites, including rcn.montana.edu/resources/converter.aspx. These sites seem to come and go—to find more, use your web browser to search for "convert lat/long to UTM."

The Hike: This narrative describes the hike in detail, along with interesting natural and human history. The description uses references to landmarks rather than distances wherever possible, since distances are listed under key points. Many summits remain unnamed but are useful as landmarks. I refer to these by their official elevations as shown on the USGS 7.5-minute topographic maps; for example, "Peak 1,234."

Miles and Directions: This is a listing of key points along the hike, including trail junctions and important landmarks. You should be able to follow the route by reference to this section; however, the key points are not a substitute for thoroughly reading the hike narrative before taking the trip. Distances are given from the start of the hike in miles.

Enjoy and Respect This Beautiful Landscape

As you take advantage of the spectacular scenery offered by the Sedona area, remember that our planet is very dear, very special, and very fragile. All of us should do everything we can to keep it clean, beautiful, and healthy, including following the Green Tips you'll find throughout this book.

Trail Finder

Use this table to quickly find the best hike for your interests.

Hike #	Name	Best Hikes for Families	Best Hikes for Water	Best Hikes for Views	Best Hikes for Dogs	Best Hikes for Easy Access	Best Hikes for Canyons	Best Hikes for Avoiding Crowds	Best Hikes for History	Best Hikes for Photos
1	Eagles Nest Trail	•	•	•		•			•	•
2	Apache Fire Trail	•	•	•		•			•	•
3	Mormon Canyon	•				•	•			
4	Jim Thompson Trail			•		•				•
5	Huckaby Trail		•		•	•	•			•
6	Munds Mountain			•	•	•		•		•
7	Little Horse Trail			•	•	•				•
8	Courthouse Butte	•		•	•	•				•
9	House Mountain				•		•	•		
10	Jacks Canyon	•			•	•		•		
11	Wilson Canyon				•	•	•			
12	Wilson Mountain Trail			•		•				•

#	Trail									
13	Allens Bend Trail	•				•	•		•	•
14	Casner Canyon Trail	•	•			•	•	•		
15	North Wilson Mountain Trail	•		•	•	•	•	•		
16	Sterling Pass Trail	•			•	•	•	•		
17	AB Young Trail	•	•	•		•	•	•		
18	Thomas Point Trail	•	•	•		•	•			
19	West Fork Trail	•			•	•			•	
20	Harding Spring Trail	•		•		•	•	•		
21	Cookstove Trail			•		•	•	•		
22	Pumphouse Wash	•		•	•	•			•	
23	Devils Bridge	•					•	•		•
24	Brins Mesa	•					•	•		•
25	Secret Canyon			•			•	•	•	
26	Vultee Arch		•				•			•
27	Dry Creek	•			•		•	•		•
28	Bear Sign Canyon	•			•		•	•		•
29	Long Canyon	•			•	•	•	•		•

Hike #	Name	Best Hikes for Families	Best Hikes for Water	Best Hikes for Views	Best Hikes for Dogs	Best Hikes for Easy Access	Best Hikes for Canyons	Best Hikes for Avoiding Crowds	Best Hikes for History	Best Hikes for Photos
30	Boynton Canyon	•		•	•	•	•			•
31	Fay Canyon Arch	•		•	•	•				•
32	Doe Mountain			•	•	•				•
33	Bear Mountain			•		•		•		•
34	Loy Canyon Trail				•		•	•		
35	Robber's Roost	•		•	•			•	•	•
36	Mooney-Casner Loop			•				•		•
37	Taylor Cabin Loop		•	•			•	•		•
38	Parsons Trail		•	•			•	•		•
39	Woodchute Trail			•	•	•		•		
40	North Mingus Trail			•	•			•		•
41	Mingus Rim Loop			•	•	•		•		•
42	Yaeger Canyon Loop				•	•		•		
43	Gaddes Canyon Trail				•	•		•		
44	Coleman Trail			•	•			•		•

#	Trail	1	2	3	4	5	6	7	8	9
45	Black Canyon Trail	●		●			●	●		
46	Chasm Creek Trail	●		●			●	●		
47	Cold Water Spring	●		●			●	●		
48	Towel Creek			●			●		●	
49	Bell Trail	●			●	●	●		●	
50	Walker Basin Trail	●		●			●	●		
51	Buckhorn Trail	●		●			●	●		
52	Tramway Trail	●	●	●	●				●	●
53	Maxwell Trail	●	●	●	●				●	●
54	Willow Crossing Trail			●	●		●			●
55	Fossil Springs Trail	●			●		●	●	●	

Map Legend

Transportation

≡(17)≡ Freeway/Interstate Highway

—(87)— State Highway

≡[231]≡ Forest Road

──── Other Road

= = = = Unpaved Road

- - - - Unimproved Road

Trails

■■■■■■ Featured Route

- - - - - - Trail

••••••••• Featured Off-Trail Route

••••••••• Off-Trail Route

Water Features

⬭ Body of Water

∿ River or Creek

⌇⁄⁚⁖ Intermittent Stream

⚬⌐ Spring

Symbols

‿ Bridge

■ Building/Point of Interest

🅰 Campground

∩ Cave/Arch

▲ Mountain/Peak

🅿 Parking

‿⁀ Pass

🌐 Picnic Area

🖼 Scenic View/Overlook

🎋 Tower

○ Towns and Cities

① Trailhead

❓ Visitor Center/Information

Land Management

▭▭ National Forest

▭ State/Local Park

Sedona

The early ranchers and cowboys referred to the Sedona area as Hell's Hole because of its color and the difficulty of travel by horse before trails and roads were constructed. Settlers were attracted to Oak Creek because of its permanent water. Originally called Oak Creek Crossing, the tiny settlement changed its name to Sedona after the postmaster general balked at the length of the name. Sedona Schnebly, the town's namesake, was the wife of an early rancher. Modern Sedona, easily reached via good highways, is a mecca for tourism and retirement. The town is surrounded by the spectacular red rock area of the Coconino National Forest, and there are many excellent hiking trails.

1 Eagles Nest Trail

A day hike along lower Oak Creek through a historic property that is now an Arizona state park.

Distance: 2.0-mile lollipop
Hiking time: About 1 hour
Difficulty: Easy
Seasons: Year-round
Trail surface: Dirt and rocks
Water: Visitor center
Other trail users: None
Canine compatibility: Dogs not allowed in order to protect wildlife

Land status: Red Rock State Park
Fees and permits: Entrance fee
Maps: Trails Illustrated Flagstaff and Sedona; USGS Sedona; Red Rock State Park brochure
Trail contacts: Red Rock State Park, 4050 Red Rock Loop Rd., Sedona 86336; (928) 282-6907; azstateparks.com/red-rock

Finding the trailhead: From Sedona, go west on AZ 89A to the lower Red Rock Loop Road, which is signed for Red Rock State Park. Turn left (south) and continue 2.9 miles, then turn right on the Red Rock State Park road. Continue past the entrance station to the end of the road at the visitor center. GPS: N34 48.703' / W111 49.732'

The Hike

From the visitor center, follow the main trail downhill toward Oak Creek. Turn right at a junction, and cross Oak Creek on a low bridge at Sentinel Crossing. Notice the flood debris piled up from the huge flood that roared down the creek in the winter of 1993. Geologists once thought such floods were very rare and called them 1,000-year events. Today it's commonly accepted that such large floods occur every few decades and are responsible for much of the erosion that takes place in the desert. Not surprisingly, the plants that grow in and along canyon bottoms such as Oak Creek are adapted to floods. Many of the larger trees survive the floods, and smaller plants that are swept away quickly regenerate from their roots.

On the far side of the creek, turn right (west) on the signed Kisva Trail. Continue a short distance then turn left (south) on the signed Eagles Nest Trail. This trail crosses an irrigation ditch then climbs away from the creek via several short switchbacks. At the signed junction with the Coyote Ridge Trail, turn right (south). The Eagles Nest Trail eventually turns northwest and works its way onto a ridge with a fine view of Oak Creek in the foreground and Cathedral Rock in the distance. Continue north as the trail descends to Oak Creek, crosses the ditch, and meets the Ridge Trail. Stay right here on the Kisva Trail. The Kisva Trail turns southeast to follow the creek. At the junction with the Eagles Nest Trail Trail, you've completed the loop. Turn left and retrace your steps to return to the visitor center.

Riparian meadow along the Eagles Nest Trail

History

Dedicated in 1991, Red Rock State Park is one of the newest additions to Arizona's state park system. Originally the area was part of a working ranch. In 1941 Jack and Helen Frye purchased the Smoke Tree Ranch and built the House of Apache Fire, which still stands on the bluffs south of Oak Creek. The Fryes, whose primary home was on the East Coast, used the Smoke Tree Ranch as a vacation escape from Jack's duties as president of Trans World Airlines. In the 1970s, after Jack's death, a developer purchased 330 acres of the ranch from Helen Frye but had to sell the property when plans to develop a resort fell through. Another portion ended up being owned by Eckankar, a religious group, which intended to develop a retreat for their members.

Things came to a head in 1980 when then-governor Bruce Babbitt was hiking in the area with friends; advised that he was trespassing on private land, he was asked to leave. Impressed with the area's beauty and its potential for public recreation, the governor approached the Arizona State Parks Board about the possibility of the state buying the land for a park. This was complicated by the fact that there were two

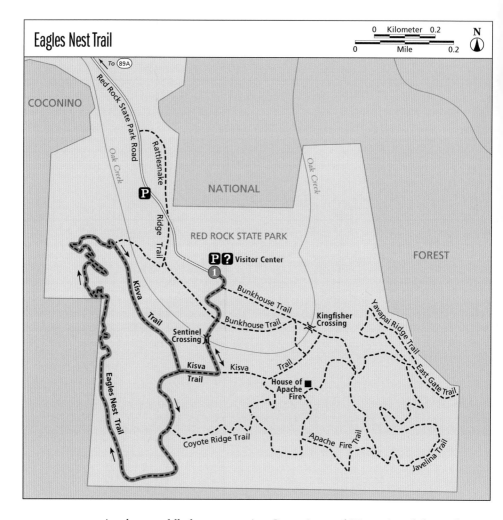

separate properties that straddled two counties, Coconino and Yavapai, and the parks board didn't have the authority to buy land across county lines. Over a period of eleven years, complex negotiations took place that involved one private owner buying another of the parcels; ultimately a bill was passed through the state legislature to authorize the various purchases and land trades. This bill also specified how the future park would be developed.

One of the key features of the bill was the requirement that existing structures be used as much as possible for the new park's facilities, partly to preserve them for historic purposes and also to lower the cost of creating the park.

Red Rock State Park was finally dedicated on October 19, 1991. The Miller Visitor Center was named for Duane Miller, who served on the Arizona State Parks Board for twenty-five years, in recognition of his and his family's service to the state park system.

Visitor Center

Be sure to check out the Miller Visitor Center before or after your hike. Two movies are shown continuously unless preempted by special events: *The Natural Wonders of Oak Creek* and *Oak Creek Loved to Death*. Total running time for the two movies is 62 minutes. *Natural Wonders* is 44 minutes and includes stunning aerial views of the red rock country.

Also have a look at the visitor center's educational exhibits, which are hands-on and focus on the biotic communities of Oak Creek and the surrounding area. These displays bring to life the variety of ecosystems that the permanent water of Oak Creek makes possible in what would otherwise be a dry desert. Wildlife and the earliest human residents of the red rocks are also featured.

If you're hungry or thirsty, snacks and drinks are available at the visitor center, as well as maps and gifts related to the Sedona area. Most Sedona trailheads don't provide any amenities, so enjoy these while you have the chance!

Group Events

Red Rock State Park is a great place to host group events of fifty to seventy-five people. Weddings and birthday parties are among the popular events held here. There are three separate ramadas that can be reserved six to twelve months in advance, depending on the event. If not reserved, the ramadas are available on a first-come, first-served basis.

Miles and Directions

0.0 Start at the visitor center .

0.1 Cross bridge at Sentinel Crossing and turn right on the Kisva Trail.

0.2 Turn left on Eagles Nest Trail.

1.4 Ridge Trail; turn right on Kisva Trail.

1.8 Eagles Nest Trail; turn left to rejoin the Kisva Trail and tetrace your steps to the visitor center.

2.0 Arrive back at the visitor center.

2 Apache Fire Trail

An easy, scenic hike to a historic site near lower Oak Creek.

Distance: 1.8-mile loop
Hiking time: About 1 hour
Difficulty: Easy
Seasons: Year-round
Trail surface: Dirt and rocks
Water: Visitor center
Other trail users: None
Canine compatibility: Dogs not allowed

Land status: Red Rock State Park
Fees and permits: Entrance fee
Maps: Trails Illustrated Flagstaff and Sedona; USGS Sedona; Red Rock State Park brochure
Trail contacts: Red Rock State Park, 4050 Red Rock Loop Rd., Sedona 86336; (928) 282-6907; azstateparks.com/red-rock

Finding the trailhead: From Sedona, go west on AZ 89A to the lower Red Rock Loop Road, which is signed for Red Rock State Park. Turn left (south) and continue 2.9 miles, then turn right on the Red Rock State Park road. Continue past the entrance station to the end of the road at the visitor center. GPS: N34 48.703' / W111 49.732'

The Hike

From the visitor center follow the left fork of the Bunkhouse Trail southeast (downhill) toward Oak Creek; cross Oak Creek on the bridge at Kingfisher Crossing. On the far side of the creek, turn left (east) on the signed Apache Fire Trail. A side trail goes to the House of Apache Fire.

Back on the Apache Fire Trail, continue a short distance past the junction with the Javelina Trail. The trail works its way along the foot of the steeper bluffs above, then encounters another signed junction. Turn left (west) on the Coyote Ridge Trail, which continues to contour west. There are good views of Oak Creek and its lush habitat of Fremont cottonwood trees and other riparian vegetation. At the Eagles Nest Trail junction, turn right (north) and follow the trail down toward Oak Creek.

WHY ARE THE ROCKS RED?

Rust. Many of the sandstones and shales that form the rock formations along Oak Creek and in the Sedona area contain tiny amounts of iron oxide, which is the same reddish mineral that forms on the surface of unprotected iron. In this case, there is just enough iron oxide present in formations such as the Schnebly Hill and Supai Formations to color the rocks striking shades of red. In contrast, the Coconino Sandstone, visible to the distant north and east below the Mogollon Rim, contains almost no iron oxide and is buff colored rather than red.

The House of Apache Fire in Red Rock State Park, seen from Oak Creek

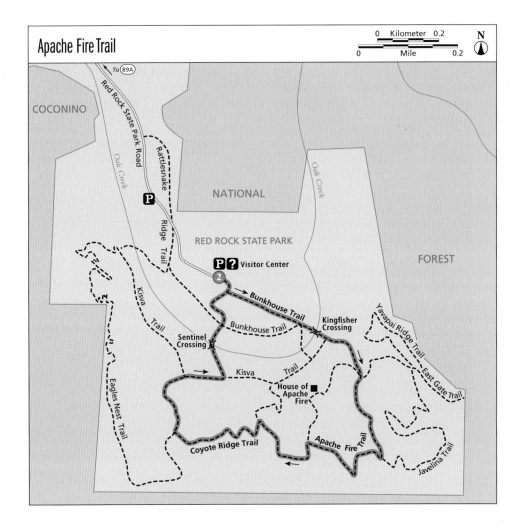

0   Kilometer   0.2

0   Mile   0.2

N

To 89A

COCONINO

Red Rock State Park Road

Oak Creek

Rattlesnake Ridge Trail

P

NATIONAL

Oak Creek

RED ROCK STATE PARK

FOREST

P ? Visitor Center

2

Bunkhouse Trail

Kisva Trail

Bunkhouse Trail

Kingfisher Crossing

Yavapai Ridge Trail

East Gate Trail

Sentinel Crossing

Kisva

Trail

House of Apache Fire ▪

Eagles Nest Trail

Coyote Ridge Trail

Apache Fire Trail

Javelina Trail

After crossing an irrigation ditch, turn right (east) on the Kisva Trail. Next, turn left (north) and cross Oak Creek on the low bridge at Sentinel Crossing. Here there is an excellent view of the House of Apache Fire reflected in the creek. On the north side of Oak Creek, turn right on the Smoke Trail then left on the main trail to the visitor center.

History

The House of Apache Fire got its name from the smoke of the campfires of the local Apache Indians that the Fryes employed in the building of their house. The natives camped along Oak Creek.

Ecology

The park includes about 1.4 miles of Oak Creek, a rare permanent stream. In a desert landscape, the riparian (streamside) habitat formed by creeks is extremely important habitat for both plants and animals. The semidesert slopes above Oak Creek are home to plants and animals adapted to the arid climate, creating an astonishing diversity of wildlife in a relatively small area.

Along the creek, the major trees are Arizona sycamore, Fremont cottonwood, velvet ash, and Arizona alder. The creek is home to several species of rare fish and frogs, as well as the Sonoran mud turtle. There are also several species of snakes and lizards.

On the slopes above, velvet mesquite, netleaf hackberry, and juniper trees are common. The park is part of the Lower Oak Creek Important Bird Area and is home to both rare and common birds, such as the common black hawk, wood duck, and common merganser.

Large animals roam the creekside and the slopes above, including otter, mule deer, javelina, coyote, and mountain lion. Most of these larger animals are shy of people and tend to come down to the creek for a drink at night, when the park is closed.

Miles and Directions

0.0 Start at the visitor center and take the Bunkhouse Trail to Kingfisher Crossing.

0.3 Kingfisher Crossing; turn left on the Apache Fire Trail.

0.5 Pass trail to the House of Apache Fire.

0.9 Pass junction with the Javelina Trail.

1.2 Turn left on the Coyote Ridge Trail.

1.3 Turn right on the Eagles Nest Trail.

1.5 Turn right on the Kisva Trail.

1.6 Cross bridge at Sentinel Crossing. Turn right on the Smoke Trail and then left toward the visitor center.

1.8 Arrive back at the visitor center.

A short hike to the towering, spectacular Coconino Sandstone cliffs and spires of the Schnebly Hill Formation on the west side of Wilson Mountain offers a feeling of remote wilderness remarkably close to uptown Sedona.

Distance: 4.2 miles out and back, including on-trail and cross-country
Hiking time: About 3 hours
Difficulty: Moderate
Seasons: Year-round
Trail surface: Dirt and rocks
Water: None
Other trail users: Horses
Canine compatibility: Dogs under control allowed

Land status: Red Rock–Secret Mountain Wilderness, Coconino National Forest
Fees and permits: None
Maps: Trails Illustrated Flagstaff and Sedona; USGS Wilson Mountain; Coconino National Forest
Trail contacts: Coconino National Forest, 1824 S. Thompson St., Flagstaff 86001; (928) 527-3600; fs.usda.gov/coconino

Finding the trailhead: From the junction of AZ 89A and AZ 179 in Sedona, drive north on AZ 89A about 0.4 mile; turn left onto Jordan Road. After 0.8 mile turn left on Park Ridge Road; continue to the trailhead at a locked gate (the last 0.2 mile is dirt). GPS: N34 53.291' / W111 46.098'

The Hike

Go past the gate and continue past the old shooting range on the Brins Mesa Trail. This trail works its way through the Arizona cypress forest along the west side of Mormon Canyon. As the trail starts to climb toward Brins Mesa, visible on the skyline to the north, watch for a cairned (piles of rock marking the way) route that turns off to the right (northeast). Leave the trail and follow the cairns across the red sandstone ledges of the Schnebly Hill Formation. The route descends into the bed of Mormon Canyon and follows it upstream. Without much difficulty you can get very close to the beautiful, buff-colored Coconino Sandstone cliffs of Wilson Mountain. The head of Mormon Canyon offers a surprisingly remote feeling, considering its proximity to Sedona.

Walking Cross-Country

The pinyon-juniper woodland that covers much of the Sedona area is both tough and fragile. Tough in that pinyon pines and especially juniper trees are able to survive in arid conditions with long periods between rainfall, yet live for hundreds of years. Junipers over a thousand years old have been recorded. Yet the sandy soil that supports these hardy trees is fragile. Because desert rain, when it comes, tends to come all at once—several inches of rain in an hour is common, especially during the

An aerial view of Mormon Canyon, in the center of the photo below the white cliffs of Wilson Mountain

late-summer thunderstorm season—unprotected desert soil is easily washed away. But look between the isolated trees and brush and you'll see a strange-looking gray to almost black spongy-looking crust on the ground. This is cryptobiotic crust—literally, a crust of hidden life. Common on sandy soils throughout the medium- and high-altitude desert and semidesert of the Southwest, cryptobiotic crust is composed of a number of microscopic organisms, including algae, cyanobacteria, and fungi. The bacteria in particular release a gelatinous substance that helps bind the organic and inorganic components together, forming a hard crust. This crust not only resists erosion of the underlying sand but also works just like a sponge, absorbing rainfall that would otherwise run off in a flood. The crust also acts as a mulch, retarding evaporation and keeping the soil moisture higher.

The cyanobacteria and some of the lichens that grow in or on the crust are nitrogen-fixers, which enrich the soil so that it can support other plants, including mosses. In fact, moss and lichens often cover the cryptobiotic crust entirely. All this biotic activity helps create enough soil nutrients to support grasses, flowering plants, and shrubs, all of which further stabilize the soil.

The crust itself is fragile, especially during the drier seasons. Human footprints easily shatter the crust (as do cattle and sheep), exposing the loose sand beneath. Tires from mountain bikes and off-road vehicles are even worse, breaking the crust and at the same time creating channels for erosion. Once disturbed, cryptobiotic crusts take anywhere from a few years to many decades to reform, taking longer in drier areas. As desert hikers, we have a serious responsibility to help preserve cryptobiotic crusts, which, after all, have helped create the landscapes we love.

First, keep to established trails as much as possible. If hiking cross-country, as in the last part of this hike, follow use trails made by other hikers, if there are any. If not, as much as possible walk on surfaces that are less susceptible to erosion, such as bare rock, open sand, gravel, dry grasses, or snow. If you have to walk through an area of cryptobiotic soil, step on sandy areas between the patches of crust. Groups should spread out instead of walking single file.

Stacking Rocks and Cairning Trails

In thinly forested areas such as Sedona, the time-honored method of marking trails with tree blazes isn't practical, so trails and routes are often marked with cairns—stacks of rocks. When done responsibly, cairns are very useful. Not only do they help you find faint trails and established cross-country routes, they also concentrate human use into one route rather than many. Though there are times when cross-country hikers should spread out and not walk single file (as through areas of cryptobiotic soil), most of the time it's better to follow the same route so that when a use trail becomes established, there's only one trail instead of a confusing multitude.

Cairns are best built by trail crews working (or volunteering) for the land management agency, in this case the Coconino National Forest. Professional trail crews know best how to route a trail for the easiest passage through the landscape, as well as to minimize erosion and impact on fragile vegetation and wildlife.

Popular cross-country routes such as Mormon Canyon are usually cairned by other hikers—hopefully hikers who have the same skills as the professionals and can mark the best route. Unfortunately, it's difficult to tell whether a cairn was built by people who knew what they were doing or someone who thinks he or she has found the best route but actually hasn't a clue.

Speaking of clues, one clue to the accuracy of a cairned route is the quality of the cairn. The clueless also tend to be lazy, so a precarious stack of three little rocks a few inches tall is a sign that the cairn may be useless. Trail crews build cairns to last, usually out of large, flat rocks—of which they have plenty from digging rocks out of the trail tread. Such cairns tend to be a couple of feet tall and take a lot more work to build.

So use caution following a cairned route, especially off-trail. Constantly evaluate the route to make sure it makes sense and wasn't made by hikers who were lost themselves. Well-cairned routes always have the next cairn in sight of the previous one. If you fail to find the next cairn, cast around while keeping the last cairn in sight, thinking about where the route should logically go to avoid rough terrain, thick brush, and

ROCK STACKING

This practice is exploding on public land and wilderness areas throughout the American West. Rock stacking is the practice of building random piles of rock in random places that serve no route-finding purpose, apparently for religious, spiritual, or personal reasons. I've revisited places that have always been free of rock stacks, only to find dozens of such stacks, sometimes in places that used to make good rest stops or campsites. While I totally support freedom of religion, I also feel that religion and personal belief must respect the law and other people. By building rock stacks on public land, especially in national parks and wilderness areas, the builders are disrupting my enjoyment of the wilderness as a place untrammeled by humans—and they are breaking the law, which specifically limits man-made structures in designated wilderness to a few things such as trails and trail signs.

Rock stacking can lead other hikers astray if they think the stacks are cairns marking a route or the stacks obscure the existence of true cairns. Building rock stacks churns up fragile desert soil and cryptobiotic crust, increasing erosion.

Note: I am not speaking here of artistic stone balancing. Artists who engage in this creative practice build seemingly impossibly balanced structures from stones of every possible shape, but they never leave them behind on public land, nor do they build them in areas where they are prohibited, such as national parks and wilderness areas.

the like. If you decide to continue beyond the end of a cairned route, make certain you have sufficient wilderness navigation skills with map, compass, and GPS to find your own way—and your way back.

Why do three rocks make a cairn? Because stacks of two rocks are very common in nature, while three rocks are rare. Larger stacks of rocks are extremely rare, which is why well-made cairns are stacks of four or more rocks. And well-made cairns use flat rocks, which create a structure not easily toppled by high winds or even hikers.

So what's the lesson? In well-traveled areas such as Sedona, **don't build cairns. Period.** All the popular cross-country routes, as well as new trail construction, are already cairned as necessary, either by experienced hikers or professional trail crews. If you're exploring a seldom-traveled area, leave it uncairned so that others can have the same sense of exploration.

Arizona Cypress

Tucked away in Mormon Canyon are a few stands of Arizona cypress, easily recognizable by its gray to reddish curling bark. Found only in the American Southwest, in Arizona this cypress prefers intermediate altitudes in the Mogollon Rim country

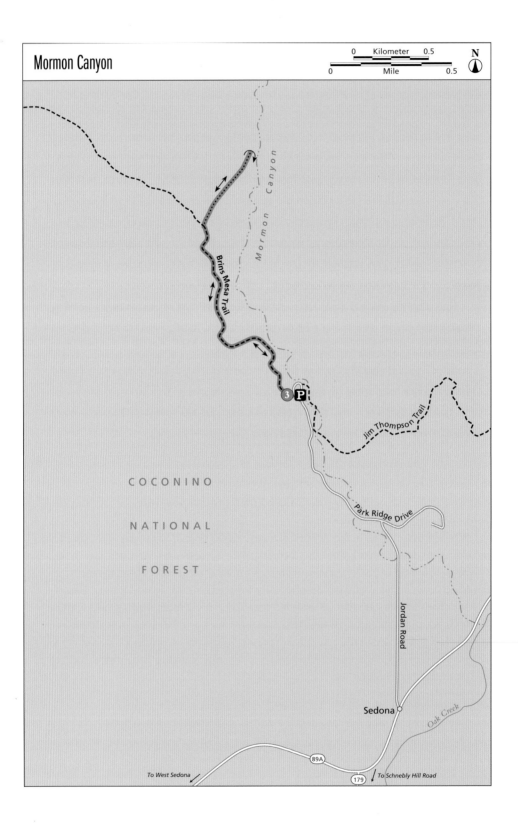

Mormon Canyon

0 Kilometer 0.5
0 Mile 0.5
N

Mormon Canyon

Brins Mesa Trail

③ P

Jim Thompson Trail

COCONINO

NATIONAL

FOREST

Park Ridge Drive

Jordan Road

Sedona

Oak Creek

89A

179

To West Sedona

To Schnebly Hill Road

as well as the central mountains just south of the rim. Arizona cypress tends to form isolated but sometimes dense stands within the pinyon-juniper forest community. It's the tallest tree in the community, reaching as high as 80 feet in favored locations, but usually about 30 to 50 feet in height. Even from a distance, Arizona cypress is easily distinguished from its juniper and pinyon pine companions. Stands of Arizona cypress have a noticeable blueish-green tint, and the taller crowns are conical or spire shaped. Close up, its evergreen needles are scaly and strongly resemble juniper needles, but they are more rounded rather than flat like juniper.

Like the better-known lodgepole pine of the central and northern Rocky Mountains, Arizona cypress is a fire-dependent tree. The cones stay closed for many years and only open after a wildfire kills the parent tree. This means that Arizona cypress is the first tree to reappear after a stand-destroying wildfire, and it helps pave the way for junipers and pinyon pines to regenerate.

Arizona cypress is widely planted as an ornamental tree, not only because of its striking appearance but also because it is highly resistant to the fungus-caused cypress canker, which readily attacks the endangered Monterey cypress.

Miles and Directions

0.0 Start at the trailhead at the locked gate.

1.4 Leave the trail and hike northeast.

2.1 Reach the head of Mormon Canyon; return the way you came.

4.2 Arrive back at the trailhead.

GREEN TIP
Car shuttles on point-to-point hikes add to the carbon load; loop hikes just take foot power.

4 Jim Thompson Trail

This is another fairly short and easy hike south of Wilson Mountain with spectacular views of uptown Sedona, Steamboat Rock, lower Oak Creek Canyon, and Mitten Ridge.

Distance: 4.0 miles out and back
Hiking time: About 2.5 hours
Difficulty: Easy
Seasons: Year-round
Trail surface: Dirt and rocks
Water: None
Other trail users: Horses
Canine compatibility: Dogs under control allowed

Land status: Red Rock–Secret Mountain Wilderness, Coconino National Forest
Fees and permits: None
Maps: Trails Illustrated Flagstaff and Sedona; USGS Wilson Mountain, Munds Park; Coconino National Forest
Trail contacts: Coconino National Forest, 1824 S. Thompson St., Flagstaff 86001; (928) 527-3600; fs.usda.gov/coconino

Finding the trailhead: From the junction of AZ 89A and AZ 179 in Sedona, drive north on AZ 89A about 0.4 mile; turn left onto Jordan Road. After 0.8 mile turn left on Park Ridge Road; continue to the trailhead at a locked gate (the last 0.2 mile is dirt). GPS: N34 53.291' / W111 46.098'

The Hike

Go through the gate then turn right on the Jim Thompson Trail, which crosses the bed of Mormon Canyon then swings northeast. You'll be heading directly for Steamboat Rock, the southernmost ridge of Wilson Mountain. When the trail reaches the base of the red sandstone cliffs, it turns east and contours along ledges. After passing the eastern end of Steamboat Rock, the trail reaches a viewpoint overlooking Wilson Canyon and lower Oak Creek. This is a great ending for an easy hike, though the trail does continue to the bottom of Wilson Canyon. You can hike to the Wilson Mountain Trailhead at the W. W. Midgley Bridge on AZ 89A in Oak Creek Canyon, and also connect to the Wilson Mountain Trail.

Ancient Sand Dunes, Tidal Flats, and Ocean Deeps

As you follow the Jim Thompson Trail, you are walking on the Schnebly Hill Formation, the mostly sandstone rock layer responsible for the majestic red rock formations that make Sedona world famous. Just above you are the towering, buff-colored cliffs of the Coconino Sandstone. At the end of the hike, you are looking down into Wilson Canyon at the layered sedimentary rocks of the Supai Formation. In these layers you can read the story of ancient oceans, tidal flats, and vast seas of restless sand dunes in an ancient desert.

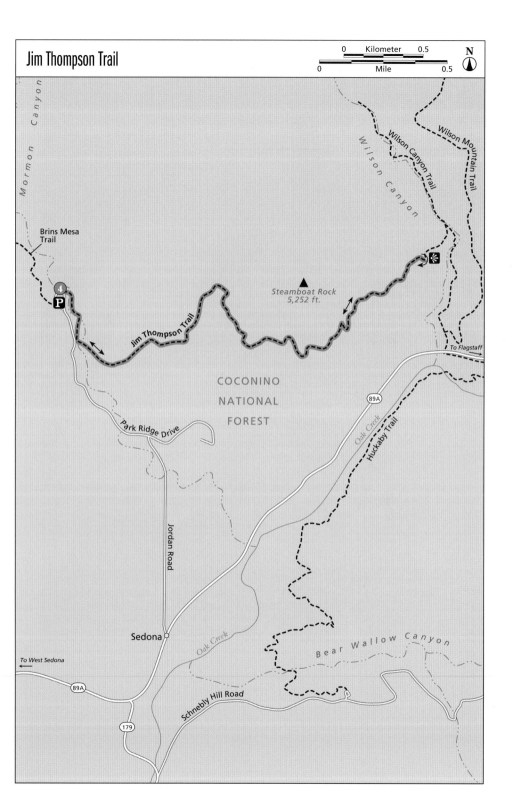

Jim Thompson Trail

Mormon Canyon

Wilson Canyon Trail

Wilson Mountain Trail

Wilson Canyon

Brins Mesa
Trail

4
P

Steamboat Rock
5,252 ft.

Jim Thompson Trail

To Flagstaff

COCONINO

NATIONAL

FOREST

89A

Oak Creek

Huckaby Trail

Park Ridge Drive

Jordan Road

Sedona

Oak Creek

Bear Wallow Canyon

To West Sedona

89A

Schnebly Hill Road

179

0   Kilometer   0.5

0   Mile   0.5

N

You won't notice this cactus until it blooms!

Like the Schnebly Hill Formation, most of the rocks that outcrop in the Sedona area and underlie the Colorado Plateau are sedimentary. These rocks are usually formed when water erodes mountains and streams and rivers transport the resulting silt and sand to the ocean. In the still waters of the ocean, the silt and sand settles to the seafloor. Over time, these layers of sediment thicken and become deeply buried. In the depths of the Earth, heat and pressure gradually compress the sediments into solid rock. The type of rock formed depends on the sediments—sand eventually forms sandstone, while fine particles of mud form siltstone and shale. A mixture of coarse and fine pebbles and silt forms conglomerate, evidence of violent floods in the past.

Not all sedimentary rocks are deposited underwater. The Coconino Sandstone, which forms the massive buff-colored cliffs of the Mogollon Rim above Sedona, was formed from sand deposited on land. The entire southwestern portion of the Colorado Plateau, including the Sedona and Grand Canyon areas, was once covered by an extensive field of sand dunes, forming a desert comparable to today's Sahara Desert. All this sand came from the erosion of the ancestral Rocky Mountains, located to the northeast of northern Arizona.

A fundamental tenet of geology is that younger rocks are laid down on top of older rocks, and in neat horizontal layers. So early geologists were shocked to find evidence that sedimentary rocks in the Alps were upside down—the oldest rocks were on top. Yet in other areas, the same rocks were in the correct order, with the youngest rocks on top. Connecting the dots solved the mystery—the violent forces that built the mountains had tilted the rocks and even thrust older rocks on top of newer ones, but then erosion stripped away much of the layers as the mountains were formed, erasing the connections between outcrops of sedimentary rocks.

Miles and Directions

0.0 Start at the trailhead and turn right on the Jim Thompson Trail.

0.7 Pass the base of Steamboat Rock.

2.0 Reach the Wilson Canyon overlook; return the way you came.

4.0 Arrive back at the trailhead.

5 Huckaby Trail

This is an easily reached, fine day hike on a unique trail that follows Oak Creek for almost half the trail's length. Due to the prevalence of private land along Oak Creek, most access to the creek is at specific points, such as USDA Forest Service recreational sites. At the northern end of the hike, you're treated to a fine overlook where you can see the section of Oak Creek you just hiked.

Distance: 5.0 miles out and back
Hiking time: About 3 hours
Difficulty: Easy
Seasons: Year-round
Trail surface: Dirt and rocks
Water: Oak Creek
Other trail users: Mountain bikes and horses
Canine compatibility: Dogs under control allowed

Land status: Coconino National Forest
Fees and permits: None
Maps: Trails Illustrated Flagstaff and Sedona; USGS Munds Park, Munds Mountain, Sedona, Wilson Mountain; Coconino National Forest
Trail contacts: Coconino National Forest, 1824 S. Thompson St., Flagstaff 86001; (928) 527-3600; fs.usda.gov/coconino

Finding the trailhead: From the junction of AZ 89A and AZ 179 in Sedona, go south 0.4 mile on AZ 179, across Oak Creek Bridge, then turn left on Schnebly Hill Road. Drive 1.9 miles then turn left into the Margs Draw/Huckaby Trailhead (GPS: N34 51.981' / W111 51.981'). To reach the north trailhead from the junction of AZ 89A and AZ 179 in Sedona, drive 1.6 miles north on AZ 89A, cross the W. W. Midgley Bridge, and park on the left at the Wilson Canyon Trailhead and viewpoint. GPS: N34 53.128' / W111 44.493'

The Hike

At first the trail goes west through a confusing area of rehabilitated jeep trails. After the Margs Draw Trail junction, the Huckaby Trail turns right and follows an old road down into Bear Wallow Canyon. This is the canyon north of the trailhead. With time, the route should become more distinct. Once you've found the old road, the rest of the trail is easy to follow. Follow the old road across normally dry Bear Wallow Canyon and out the north side. Here the newly constructed foot trail leaves the old road and contours northeast above the canyon. Soon a switchback takes you to the north as the trail begins to work its way toward Oak Creek. This is a delightful traverse through pinyon-juniper forest, though it would be hot on a summer afternoon. Soon you'll start to descend, and the trail finally switchbacks down to Oak Creek. For more than 0.5 mile the trail stays on the east side of the creek, then it crosses to the west side below the W. W. Midgley Bridge, the impressive structure spanning Mormon Canyon on AZ 89A. Now it follows an old wagon road that climbs steeply out of the canyon and switchbacks up to the north end of the bridge. Follow the trail past the viewpoint, under the bridge, and up to the Wilson Mountain Trailhead.

Steamboat and Wilson Mountains from the Huckaby Trail

Options

This hike can be done one way with a shuttle. You can also hike farther on either the Wilson Canyon or Wilson Mountain Trail.

Encroaching Seas

As the trail gradually descends toward Oak Creek, it works its way down through small cliffs and along steep slopes carved from the Supai Group, the oldest rocks exposed in the Sedona area. The rocks of the Supai Group were formed during the Permian geologic period, about 275 million years ago.

The small cliffs are formed from limestone and sandstone, which are resistant to erosion. The slopes are shale and mudstone, relatively soft rocks that erode out into slopes, undermining the cliffs above and causing them to retreat. This creates the classic cliff-and-terrace canyon walls present here, at other places along the foot of the Mogollon Rim, and throughout the Grand Canyon. The alternating layers of rock reveal that the sediments were deposited during a time when the sea was generally retreating, but sometimes returning for short periods of time.

Studies show that the western edge of the North American continent was located along a north–south line from the present Salt Lake City area down through central Arizona. When the sea was temporarily winning the battle, sediments that eventually formed limestone were deposited. When the sea became shallower, fine silt brought in by rivers was deposited on the seafloor. These fine sediments eventually hardened

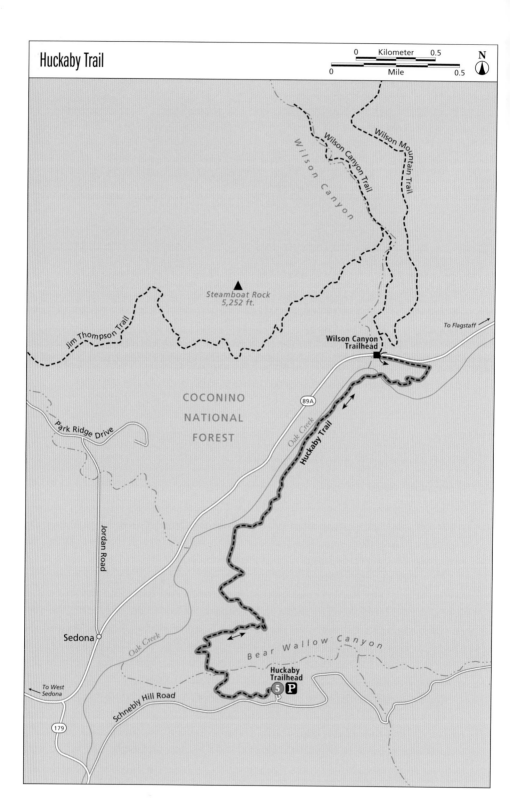

Huckaby Trail

0 — Kilometer — 0.5
0 — Mile — 0.5

N

Wilson Canyon

Wilson Canyon Trail

Wilson Mountain Trail

Jim Thompson Trail

▲ Steamboat Rock
5,252 ft.

Wilson Canyon Trailhead

To Flagstaff →

COCONINO

NATIONAL

FOREST

Park Ridge Drive

89A

Oak Creek

Huckaby Trail

Jordan Road

Sedona

Oak Creek

Bear Wallow Canyon

Huckaby Trailhead
5 P

← To West
Sedona

Schnebly Hill Road

179

into siltstone and shale. Closer to shore and along the beaches, the rivers and stream deposited layers of sand, which eventually became the sandstone members of the Supai Group.

Marine fossils are common throughout the varied layers of the Supai Group; you can also find petrified ripples, showing where ancient streams flowed gently over streambeds of sand and silt.

Miles and Directions

0.0 Start at the Margs Draw/Huckaby Trailhead and go left (west) on the Huckaby Trail.

0.3 Cross Bear Wallow Canyon.

1.5 Reach Oak Creek and continue along its east side.

2.1 Cross Oak Creek.

2.5 Reach the Wilson Mountain Trailhead; return the way you came.

5.0 Arrive back at the trailhead.

GREEN TIP

For rest stops, go off-trail so that others won't have to get around you. Head for resilient surfaces without vegetation. On this hike, take a walk over to the creek.

he Munds Mountain Wilderness takes you up a historic road and offers excellent views of Mitten Ridge, Bear Wallow Canyon, Munds Mountain, and Sedona.

Distance: 4.2 miles out and back
Hiking time: About 3 hours
Difficulty: Moderate
Seasons: Spring through fall
Trail surface: Dirt and rocks
Water: None
Other trail users: Horses
Canine compatibility: Dogs under control allowed

Land status: Munds Mountain Wilderness, Coconino National Forest
Fees and permits: None
Maps: Trails Illustrated Flagstaff and Sedona; USGS Munds Park, Munds Mountain; Coconino National Forest
Trail contacts: Coconino National Forest, 1824 S. Thompson St., Flagstaff 86001; (928) 527-3600; fs.usda.gov/coconino

Finding the trailhead: From the junction of AZ 89A and AZ 179 in Sedona, go south 0.4 mile on AZ 179, cross Oak Creek Bridge, then turn left on Schnebly Hill Road. Drive 4.3 miles, and park at the unsigned trailhead where the road passes through a saddle between the red buttes to the west and the brushy slope on the right. GPS: N34 52.932' / W111 42.655'

The Hike

From the parking area, look across the road and up. You will see an old road descending the slopes from the left (southeast). It comes nearly down to the present road then does a switchback to the right and parallels the road just above it. Walk south down the main road about 100 yards until you can climb up to reach the old road. Follow the old road back to the left (north), around the switchback, and then southward. This is the old Schnebly Hill Road, originally built as a wagon road from Sedona to the Mogollon Rim and on to Flagstaff. It is now closed to motorized vehicles and makes a fine hiking trail with a panoramic view. Because of the west-facing slope, the dominant vegetation is chaparral brush. Near the top there is a dense stand of Gambel oak, a small slender deciduous tree which grows about 10 to 20 feet high. Gambel oaks often favor the slopes just below escarpments or rims. The trail reaches the Mogollon Rim after 0.9 mile, and the old road turns sharply north.

Take the foot trail, which continues south along the rim through tall ponderosa pines, climbing gradually. About 0.7 mile from the old road, the trail reaches a high point along the rim and crosses a grassy section with scattered juniper trees where the view opens out to the southeast. The long ridge of Munds Mountain dominates the view ahead to the southwest. The trail drops down a short ridge to a saddle where there is a signed junction with the Hot Loop Trail to the left. Continue straight ahead about 50 yards to another saddle where there is a signed junction with the Jacks Canyon Trail.

Camping on the red rocks near the Munds Mountain Trailhead. Note: this area is now closed for camping.

Stay right and follow the Munds Mountain Trail as it climbs steeply up the northeast slopes. Several switchbacks lead to a ridge, where the grade moderates. This section is interesting for the extreme contrast in vegetation on the two sides of the ridge. Douglas firs growing on the north slopes meet pinyon, juniper, and Arizona cypress growing on the south slopes. The trail reaches the rim of Munds Mountain about 0.4 mile from the junction at the saddle. According to the map, the actual high point is about 100 yards south along the east edge of the clearing, but it's more rewarding to walk about 200 yards west to the rim for a sweeping view of Sedona and the red rock country. You can also walk about 100 yards to the north rim for a superb view of lower Oak Creek Canyon—and nearly the entire trail you just came up.

More Red Rocks

Above the layers of the Supai Group lie the deep red shales of the Hermit Formation, a rock layer also found in the Grand Canyon. Averaging around 300 feet thick in the Sedona area, the Hermit Formation is soft and erodes into steep slopes. It forms the pedestals of many of the towering rock formations around Sedona. The Hermit shale formed later in the Permian period than the Supai Group and dates to about 270 million years ago. The shale layers formed in a nearshore environment of tidal flats and river deltas.

WHO WAS SCHNEBLY?

Schnebly Hill Road was named for Carl Schnebly, who with his wife, Sedona, were among the first people to settle in the Sedona area. Schnebly built an imposing two-story house on the site of the present-day Los Abrigatos Resort and operated a ranch and an inn. Schnebly saw the need for the tiny village, then called Oak Creek Crossing, to have a post office, but the postmaster general didn't like the first names that Schnebly proposed—Oak Creek Crossing and Schnebly Station. He then suggested his wife's name; the postmaster liked it, so the town of Sedona got its name.

Many people think that Sedona is an Indian or local name, but apparently Sedona's mother, Amanda Miller, just made up the name because she liked the sound.

Oddly enough, Schnebly didn't build the road that is now named for him, although he surely had a hand in maintaining and improving it. Before Schnebly Hill Road was constructed, it took four days to reach Flagstaff via existing dirt roads. Since Flagstaff was on the Santa Fe Railroad and a major market and source of supply for the ranchers and settlers on Oak Creek, the locals wanted a shorter, faster route.

The first route up Bear Wallow Canyon was a trail pioneered by Jim Mund. Joy Loy started work to improve the trail into a wagon road in 1896, but real progress started to be made in 1902, when Coconino County awarded $500 to local J. J. Thompson to build a road up the canyon. Laborers were paid $1 per day to chip and blast the road out of the bedrock, and within six months the road was complete. Connecting to an existing dirt road on the Mogollon Rim that connected Flagstaff to Phoenix, the new road cut the travel time to Flagstaff to two days. When first completed, the road was called Mund's Road, but as Schnebly was the most prominent user of the road, within a few years people started calling it Schnebly Hill Road.

By 1914 a much shorter wagon road had been completed up Oak Creek Canyon. Climbing to the rim at the head of the canyon via a series of steep switchbacks, this road further cut travel time to Flagstaff to one day, and the Schnebly Hill Road was no longer the favored route.

At the lower contact with the Supai Group, ancient stream channels filled with Hermit shale show that there was a period of erosion before the Hermit shale sediment began to be deposited. Some of these ancient stream channels are as much as 60 feet deep, showing that the landscape was somewhat rough and drainages were vigorous.

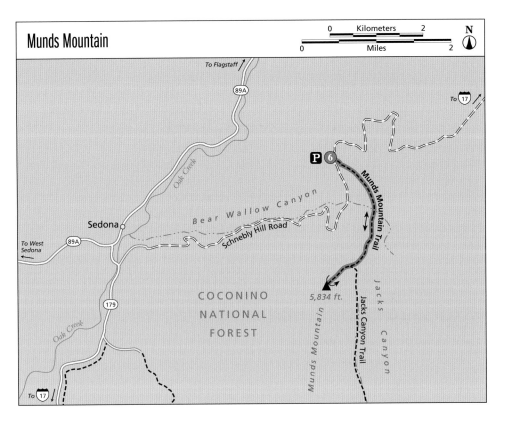

Miles and Directions

0.0 Start at the trailhead and walk about 100 yards; climb to meet the old road.

0.9 Continue south on the foot trail.

1.8 Come to the junction with the Jacks Canyon Trail at a saddle. Keep right.

2.1 Reach the rim of Munds Mountain; walk west and then north for views. Return the way you came.

4.2 Arrive back at the trailhead.

GREEN TIP

Carry a reusable water container that you fill at the tap. Bottled water is expensive, lots of petroleum is used to make plastic bottles, and they're a disposal nightmare.

7 Little Horse Trail

This beautiful walk starts from an easily reached trailhead and climbs past the dramatic Chapel Rocks to a scenic overlook.

Distance: 3.6 miles out and back
Hiking time: About 2 hours
Difficulty: Easy
Seasons: Year-round
Trail surface: Dirt and rocks
Water: None
Other trail users: Mountain bikes and horses
Canine compatibility: Dogs under control allowed

Land status: Coconino National Forest
Fees and permits: None
Maps: Trails Illustrated Flagstaff and Sedona; USGS Sedona; Coconino National Forest
Trail contacts: Coconino National Forest, 1824 S. Thompson St., Flagstaff 86001; (928) 527-3600; fs.usda.gov/coconino

Finding the trailhead: From the junction of Arizona 89A and AZ 179 in Sedona, go 3.5 miles south on AZ 179. Park at the North Bell Rock Trailhead, on the left. GPS: N34 49.457' / W111 46.542'

The Hike

This short but scenic hike uses part of the new urban trail system in Sedona. From the trailhead, turn right on the Bell Rock Pathway. After 0.3 mile, turn left on the Little Horse Trail. This new trail is marked with rock cairns in wire cages. Ignore any side trails, and follow the cairns to Chicken Point, which is actually the pass between the Chapel Rocks and Gibraltar Rock.

And—Wait for It—Even More Red Rocks

On this hike you are literally surrounded by dramatic red rock buttes and cliffs. The Schnebly Hill Formation is responsible for nearly all the impressive red rock forms in the Sedona area. This is another series of layers composed mostly of sandstone from the Permian period. After the underlying Hermit shale was deposited, a short period of erosion took place when the Sedona area was above sea level, but then the seas encroached again and the Schnebly Hill Formation was laid down.

Unlike the rock layers above and below, the Schnebly Hill Formation does not appear in the walls of the Grand Canyon to the north—or anywhere else on the Colorado Plateau except the Sedona area. This is because the conditions that created the Schnebly Hill Formation were simply not present anywhere else. Essentially, Sedona lay at the margins of a shallow sea bordered by extensive desert sand dunes for most of this period. Sand blown into the sea was reworked by tidal action into layers of sand, which were later buried deeply and compressed into rock. During the deposition

Cathedral Rock from the Little Horse Trail

period, the layers of sand were repeatedly exposed to the air (when the tide was out), and trace amounts of iron present in the sand oxidized to form iron oxide—the same mineral that forms rust on man-made iron objects. The result is some of the most strikingly red to orange rocks found anywhere in the world. Especially at sunset, Sedona's rocks seem to glow red as if lit from inside.

The Mogollon Rim, which forms the cliffs above Sedona, extends about 50 miles to the west and nearly 200 miles to the east—all the way into New Mexico—but nowhere else along its ramparts can you find rock formations as striking as those around Sedona.

Trail Markers

When the Little Horse Trail was constructed, the trail builders marked sections of the trail with rock cairns stacked up inside chicken-wire enclosures to ensure that the cairns would be durable. Elsewhere I've encountered cairns that were built from rocks cemented together around a steel pile driven into a hole in the ground. People who try to kick over one of these cairns are in for some sore toes. Though I strongly feel that random cairns and rock stacks that serve no purpose in marking a trail or established route should be destroyed (in the same spirit as picking up others' litter), cairns

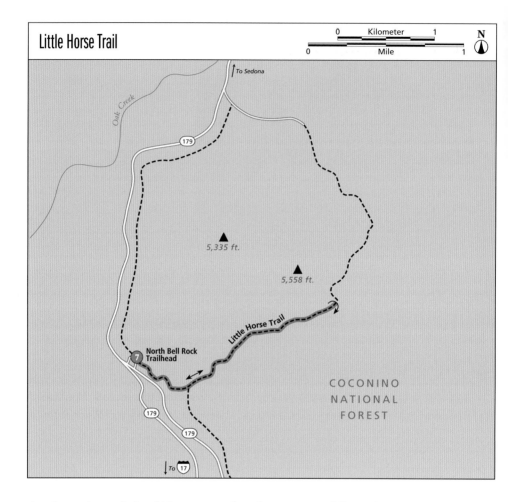

Little Horse Trail

0   Kilometer   1

0   Mile   1

N

To Sedona

Oak Creek

179

5,335 ft.

5,558 ft.

Little Horse Trail

North Bell Rock
Trailhead

7

COCONINO
NATIONAL
FOREST

179

179

To 17

that do mark a trail should be preserved so that everyone follows the same route and avoids creating multiple trails.

Miles and Directions

0.0   Start at the North Bell Rock Trailhead.

0.3   Turn left onto the Little Horse Trail.

1.8   Reach Chicken Point; return the way you came.

3.6   Arrive back at the trailhead.

8 Courthouse Butte

This day hike offers close-up views of Bell Rock and Courthouse Butte.

Distance: 4.3-mile lollipop
Hiking time: About 2.5 hours
Difficulty: Easy
Seasons: Year-round
Trail surface: Dirt and rocks
Water: None
Other trail users: Mountain bikes and horses outside the wilderness
Canine compatibility: Dogs under control allowed

Land status: Munds Mountain Wilderness, Coconino National Forest
Fees and permits: None
Maps: Trails Illustrated Flagstaff and Sedona; USGS Sedona; Coconino National Forest
Trail contacts: Coconino National Forest, 1824 S. Thompson St., Flagstaff 86001; (928) 527-3600; fs.usda.gov/coconino

Finding the trailhead: From the junction of AZ 89A and AZ 179 in Sedona, go 6 miles south on AZ 179. Turn left into the South Bell Rock Trailhead. GPS: N34 47.491' / W111 45.712'

The Hike

Don't let the crowds of windshield tourists at the trailhead put you off. You'll soon leave them and the roar of the highway behind. Follow the broad Bell Rock Pathway north toward Bell Rock. The trail squeezes between Bell Rock and the highway. Before you reach Bell Rock, the Courthouse Loop Trail joins from the right—this will be our return loop, but for now, stay left on Bell Rock Pathway.

After passing between Bell Rock and the highway, turn right on Courthouse Loop Trail, which turns east along the north base of Bell Rock. There are numerous use trails along this hike—stay on the main trail, which skirts the base of Bell Rock and then Courthouse Butte, the massive formation east of Bell Rock. After passing along the north side of Courthouse Butte, the trail turns southeast and climbs gradually toward the pass east of Courthouse Rock. From the pass follow the trail as it descends the drainage to the southeast. At the junction with the Dairy Springs Trail, stay right on the Courthouse Loop Trail. As the trail heads west along the open flat at the south base of Courthouse Butte, two trails fork south; stay right at each junction. Back near the highway, you'll pass the cottonwood trees marking Bell Rock Spring (not reliable) and then meet the Bell Rock Pathway. Turn left to return to the trailhead.

Ancient Oceans and Deserts

Most of the rocks that form the buttes and cliffs around Sedona came from sediments deposited underwater—generally on the floor of an ocean or a sea. Sedona lies more

Rain pocket below Courthouse Butte

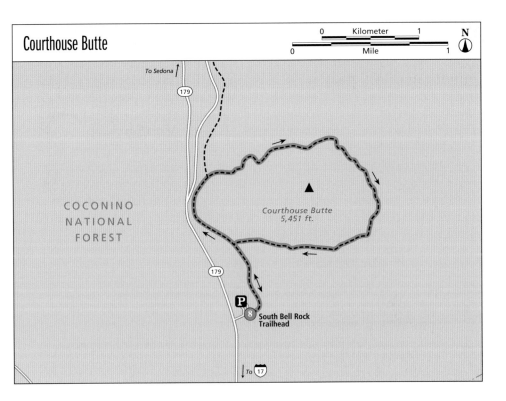

Kilometer
0   1

Mile
0   1

N

To Sedona

179

COCONINO
NATIONAL
FOREST

Courthouse Butte
5,451 ft.

179

P

8 South Bell Rock
Trailhead

To 17

than 4,000 feet above sea level. Does this mean, as many people seem to think, that the oceans were once 4,000 feet deeper? No. It shows that the Sedona area was once more than 4,000 feet lower. Even the tallest mountains in the world, the Himalayas, have sedimentary layers near their summits that were deposited underwater. The ocean was not 29,000 feet higher—the Himalayas were once more than 29,000 feet lower.

This still seems pretty fantastic. How could the elevation of the Earth's surface change so much? The answer lies in plate tectonics. If you look at a map of the world, you may notice that the edges of some continents match up strikingly well with some of their neighbors on the other side of the oceans. An especially good example is the east coast of South America and the west coast of Africa. They are so similar that it's pretty apparent they were once joined together in a single landmass.

When geologists first proposed that continents could drift around like giant rafts on the world's oceans, other geologists scoffed at the idea. How could something as massive as a continent, composed of solid rock, move anywhere? The Earth's crust, or lithosphere, which is composed of plates anywhere from 10 miles thick under the oceans to 150 miles thick for the continental plates, is actually a thin skin of less-dense rock floating on the semiliquid asthenosphere, the next deeper layer.

Current theory holds that slow convective currents (the same currents the help cool off your scalding-hot cup of coffee in the morning) in the asthenosphere cause the tectonic plates to move as much as 2 or 3 inches a year. Over the millions of years of geologic time, this adds up to a lot of movement. It's now pretty clear that all the world's continents have been joined together into giant supercontinents at least twice.

As the ocean and continental plates move, they inevitably scrape past each other or ram directly together. Ocean plates, which are the newest plates, are typically formed from basalt, a type of volcanic rock that is denser than the granitic rocks that make up the bulk of the continental plates. So when an oceanic plate collides with a continental plate, the oceanic plate tends to slide under the continental plate. As the oceanic plate subducts under the continental plate, it pushes the continental plate higher, raising and crumpling the rocks into high mountains. That's why you can final fossil fishes on the highest peaks of the Alps, and rocks made from seafloor sediments around Sedona. The ocean never came to Sedona—instead, the Sedona area went to the ocean, and not just once, but many times.

Miles and Directions

0.0 Start at the Bell Rock Vista Trailhead and turn left on the Bell Rock Pathway.

0.5 Courthouse Loop Trail joins from the right—this will be our return from the loop, but for now, stay left on the Bell Rock Pathway.

1.1 Turn left on the Courthouse Loop Trail. There are multiple trail junctions; stay on the main trail which skirts the base of Courthouse Butte.

2.8 Dairy Springs Trail joins from left; stay right on the Courthouse Loop Trail.

3.3 Trail 135A on left; continue straight ahead on the Courthouse Loop Trail.

3.4 Trail 135B on left; continue straight ahead on the Courthouse Loop Trail.

3.8 Turn left on the Bell Rock Pathway.

4.2 Arrive back at the Bell Rock Vista Trailhead.

GREEN TIP
When hiking in a group, walk single file on established trails to avoid widening them. If you come upon a sensitive area, spread out so that you don't cut one path through the landscape. Don't create new trails where there were none before.

9 House Mountain

A hike near lower Oak Creek with unusual views of the red rock country.

Distance: 6.0 miles out and back
Hiking time: About 3.5 hours
Difficulty: Moderate
Seasons: Year-round
Trail surface: Dirt and rocks
Water: None
Other trail users: Mountain bikes and horses
Canine compatibility: Dogs under control allowed

Land status: Coconino National Forest
Fees and permits: None
Maps: Trails Illustrated Flagstaff and Sedona; USGS Sedona; Coconino National Forest
Trail contacts: Coconino National Forest, 1824 S. Thompson St., Flagstaff 86001; (928) 527-3600; fs.usda.gov/coconino

Finding the trailhead: From the junction of AZ 89A and AZ 179 in Sedona, go south 6.8 miles on AZ 179; turn right at the traffic signal onto Verde Valley School Road. Continue 4.2 miles (the road turns to maintained gravel after 3 miles), then turn left onto FR 9126B, the unmaintained road to the Turkey Creek Trail. Go 0.6 mile and park at the unsigned trailhead on the left, marked by a turnaround circle and small parking area. GPS: N34 48.578' / W111 49.070'

The Hike

Follow the unsigned Turkey Creek Trail, which begins as an old jeep road, north through pleasant pinyon-juniper forest. Stay right where a well-used but unmarked trail branches left. The Turkey Creek Trail crosses a wash and turns more to the southwest. The trail roughly parallels the north rim of House Mountain, visible to the southeast. Now the trail climbs over a low pass between red rock formations then descends a long gentle meadow to reach Turkey Creek Tank. The trail skirts the right (north) side of the tank, where a metal sign marks the Turkey Creek Trail, then continues southwest around the north end of a red rock ridge. It turns south and follows a drainage though dense pinyon-juniper forest then climbs steeply to reach a saddle on the north rim of House Mountain.

Leave the trail at the saddle and hike cross-country directly east, up the ridge 0.3 mile to the top of the rocky peak on the skyline. This is a false summit, and another 0.1 mile of easy walking leads to the end of the hike at the top of a gentle hill. At 5,024 feet, this unnamed rise is the second-highest point on House Mountain. (The highest point is about 1.5 miles west.) It offers panoramic views of House Mountain, a large mesa that slopes gradually to the south, the Sedona area, and the red rock country to the north. In the middle distance, lower Oak Creek winds past Red Rock State Park.

A view of the Mogollon Rim from House Mountain

Volcanos

Much of House Mountain is covered by lava that flowed from nearby volcanoes. Sedona is located at the southern edge of the San Francisco volcanic field, which surrounds the Flagstaff area to the north and contains around 800 extinct volcanoes. (Well, we can hope they are all extinct.) Sunset Crater, a volcanic cinder cone located a few miles northeast of the San Francisco Peaks, erupted in AD 1066 and continued off and on for around 300 years. Seismographs at the base of Sunset Crater still record micro earthquakes, signs that liquid volcanic rock (known as magma) is still rumbling around deep beneath the volcano and that another eruption could occur.

Volcanic activity built at least three different types of volcanic features in the San Francisco volcanic field. The most prominent feature of the volcanic field is the San Francisco Peaks, a shield volcano. This type of volcanic feature is formed when repeated lava flows and cinder eruptions pile up to form a relatively gently sloped mountain.

Most of the volcanoes in the field are cinder cones, steep-sided hills or mountains formed mostly from cinders blasted into the air from volcanic vents. These cinders fall to earth close to the vent and pile up into a steep-sided cone. One of the most striking cinder cones in the world is located north of the San Francisco Peaks. SP Crater is 800 feet tall and has an almost perfectly symmetric 400-foot-deep crater.

Liquid rock, or magma, also poured out of the ground from volcanic vents, which were located at many places in the volcanic field but commonly found at the base of cinder cones. Both SP and Sunset Craters feature such lava flows. Depending on

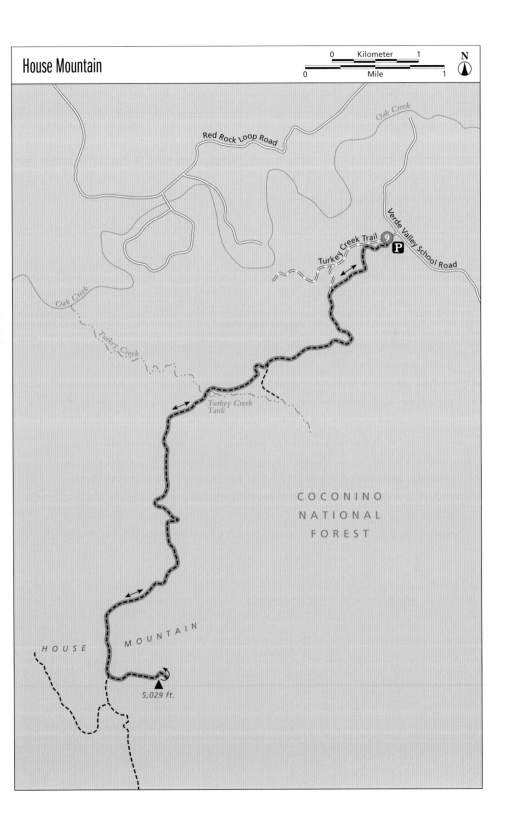

House Mountain

0 Kilometer 1
0 Mile 1

N

Oak Creek

Red Rock Loop Road

Oak Creek

Verde Valley School Road

Turkey Creek Trail

9

P

Turkey Creek

Turkey Creek
Tank

COCONINO

NATIONAL

FOREST

HOUSE   MOUNTAIN

5,029 ft.

the viscosity of the magma and the slope of the terrain, lava flows ran downhill for anywhere from a few miles to 50 miles or more.

It's easy to determine where the younger lava flows came from; but lava flows have been occurring in the area for several million years, while erosion has continued to strip away cinder cones and ancient volcanic vents, making it hard to discover the origins of lava flows such as the one atop House Mountain.

Miles and Directions

0.0 Start at the unsigned trailhead.

0.4 Stay right at an unsigned junction.

1.4 Come to Turkey Creek Tank.

2.6 Reach the north rim of House Mountain.

3.0 Reach the summit; return the way you came.

6.0 Arrive back at the trailhead.

GREEN TIP

Observe wildlife from a distance. Don't interfere in their lives, and never feed them—you both will be better for it. You can make animals sick by giving them human food because their digestive systems are not accustomed to it, and handouts lead to animals hanging around campgrounds and picnic areas hoping for more easy meals instead of foraging on their own and storing up food for the winter—a winter they may not survive because humans and their free lunches are gone and natural food is scarce. Also, feeding makes wildlife lose their fear of humans and become camp nuisances. In a nutshell (pun intended), feeding wild animals doesn't help them—it kills them.

10 Jacks Canyon

A little-used trail into a remote red rock canyon. If you want an all-day hike away from the crowds, you'll like this trail.

Distance: 13.6 miles out and back
Hiking time: About 8 hours
Difficulty: Strenuous
Seasons: Year-round
Trail surface: Dirt and rocks
Water: None
Other trail users: Horses
Canine compatibility: Dogs under control allowed

Land status: Munds Mountain Wilderness, Coconino National Forest
Fees and permits: None
Maps: Trails Illustrated Flagstaff and Sedona; USGS Munds Mountain; Coconino National Forest
Trail contacts: Coconino National Forest, 1824 S. Thompson St., Flagstaff 86001; (928) 527-3600; fs.usda.gov/coconino

Finding the trailhead: From Sedona, drive about 7 miles south on AZ 179 to the Village of Oak Creek; turn left at the traffic light onto Jacks Canyon Road. Go 0.9 mile then turn right to remain on Jacks Canyon Road. After another 1.1 miles, turn right into the trailhead. GPS: N34 47.048' / W111 43.945'

The Hike

The first mile or so of trail parallels the Jacks Canyon Road as it heads northeast to skirt a subdivision. As the canyon starts to swing north, you'll pass an old stock tank, Jacks Canyon Tank, about 2.4 miles from the trailhead. Unlike many of the canyons in the Sedona area, Jacks Canyon is open and spacious. This route also gets less use than the shorter trails. As you continue north, the canyon gradually narrows. At its head, a short, steep climb leads to the saddle between the Mogollon Rim and Munds Mountain. Turn left on the Munds Mountain Trail and climb another 0.4 mile to the summit. The best views are from the west rim of this broad mesa.

Cracked Up

What makes a canyon? Canyons are loosely defined as having closer, steeper walls than valleys. Valleys tend to form where the climate is wet and erosion from water takes place more evenly across the landscape. Canyons tend to form in arid climates, where erosion from occasional floods takes place rapidly along stream courses but much more slowly across the landscape as a whole. So the floods deepen the canyons more rapidly than general erosion can widen them.

Canyons don't appear just at random but rather tend to form along faults. A fault is a break in the rocks caused by rocks on one side of the fault moving in a different direction than the rocks on the other side. As the two rock masses grind against each other, they create a shatter zone, where the rocks are broken and weakened along the

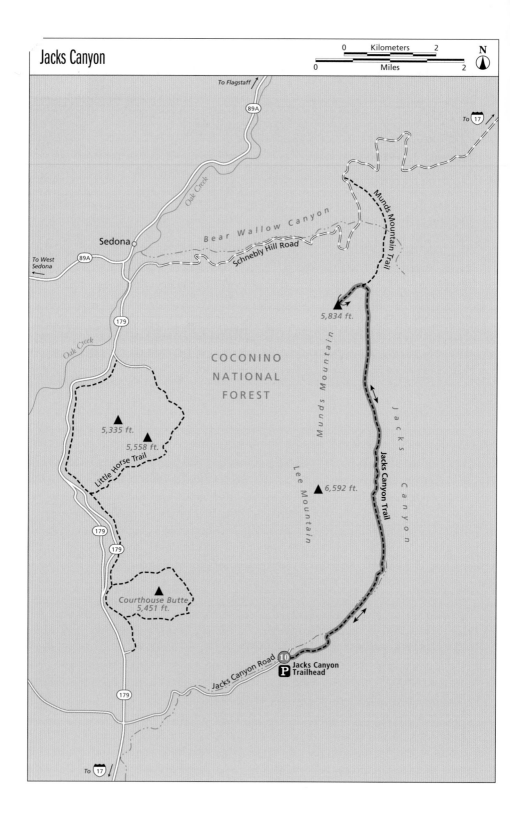

Jacks Canyon

To Flagstaff

89A

To 17

Oak Creek

Bear Wallow Canyon

Munds Mountain Trail

Sedona

89A

Schnebly Hill Road

To West Sedona

Oak Creek

179

COCONINO
NATIONAL
FOREST

5,834 ft.

Munds Mountain

Jacks Canyon

▲ 5,335 ft.

▲ 5,558 ft.

Little Horse Trail

Lee Mountain

▲ 6,592 ft.

Jacks Canyon Trail

179

179

Courthouse Butte
5,451 ft.

179

Jacks Canyon Road

P Jacks Canyon
Trailhead

To 17

Mountain lions still roam the remote backcountry around Sedona.

fault. Water readily exploits the weak zone and carves out a canyon along the fault. Both Jacks and Oak Creek Canyons are formed along the Oak Creek Fault, where vertical movement along the fault raised the rocks on the west side of the fault about 500 feet higher than the rocks on the east side.

As you walk up Jacks Canyon, you can easily see that the rocks on the west side of the canyon have been lifted higher than the same rocks on the east side. The shatter zone created by movement along the Oak Creek Fault are obvious along the AZ 89A switchbacks, where the highway climbs out of Oak Creek Canyon at its north end. You can spot the shattered rocks about halfway up the switchbacks. They are obvious even from your moving car.

Miles and Directions

0.0 Start at the trailhead off Jacks Canyon Road.

2.4 Pass the Jacks Canyon Tank.

6.0 Reach the head of Jacks Canyon.

6.4 Come to a saddle and turn left on Munds Mountain Trail.

6.8 Reach the summit of Munds Mountain; return the way you came.

13.6 Arrive back at the trailhead.

Oak Creek Canyon

Sliced out of the Mogollon Rim, Oak Creek Canyon is very accessible from AZ 89A, which traverses its 20 mile length from Sedona to Flagstaff. The year-round flow of Oak Creek adds to its charm. Numerous USDA Forest Service campgrounds, picnic areas, and private resorts can be found along the highway. In the pioneer days, travel along the canyon was much more difficult. The easiest route to Flagstaff, the nearest source of supplies, was via the canyon rims, so early settlers built several horse trails up the steep walls of the canyon. Once on the rim, the horse would be hitched to a wagon (left there from the last trip), and the all-day journey would resume. Many of these trails survive today, providing hikers with a variety of routes. Other hikes in Oak Creek Canyon explore the side canyons.

11 Wilson Canyon

This is an easy, popular walk up a red rock canyon near Sedona. As with many Sedona area trailheads, and especially trails accessible from paved roads, this trailhead fills up quickly, so arrive early.

Distance: 2.0 miles out and back
Hiking time: About 1.5 hours
Difficulty: Easy
Seasons: Year-round
Trail surface: Dirt and rocks
Water: None
Other trail users: None
Canine compatibility: Dogs under control allowed

Land status: Red Rock–Secret Mountain Wilderness, Coconino National Forest
Fees and permits: None
Maps: Trails Illustrated Flagstaff and Sedona; USGS Munds Park; Coconino National Forest
Trail contacts: Coconino National Forest, 1824 S. Thompson St., Flagstaff 86001; (928) 527-3600; fs.usda.gov/coconino

Finding the trailhead: From Sedona, drive 1.6 miles north on AZ 89A, cross the W. W. Midgley Bridge, then turn left into the Wilson Canyon Trailhead and viewpoint. GPS: N34 53.128' / W111 44.493'

The Hike

The Wilson Canyon Trail starts from the north end of the parking area and stays near the rim of the inner canyon. After this gorge ends at a high, dry waterfall, the Jim Thompson Trail branches left. The trail wanders another 0.5 mile up the canyon, though fine stands of Arizona cypress, before fading out.

Wilson Canyon is a small one as canyons on the Colorado Plateau go, but it's still impressive. It's about 200 feet deep where Midgley Bridge crosses the mouth of the canyon. The walls of Wilson Canyon are eroded from layers of sandstone, limestone, and shale—the main components of the Supai Group.

Points of View
Nearby Midgley Bridge tempts many tourists to walk out on the bridge for photos. Don't do it. There is no pedestrian walkway, and the traffic is fast and dense—and many of the drivers are oblivious, gawking at the scenery and not watching the road. You really don't want to add to the list of those killed on the bridge. As a much safer alternative, walk down the steps to the viewpoint constructed specifically to avoid the hazards of the bridge while providing an even better view. From the parking lot next to the bridge, steps lead down to a very short trail that goes under the bridge and out to a viewpoint overlooking Oak Creek Canyon.

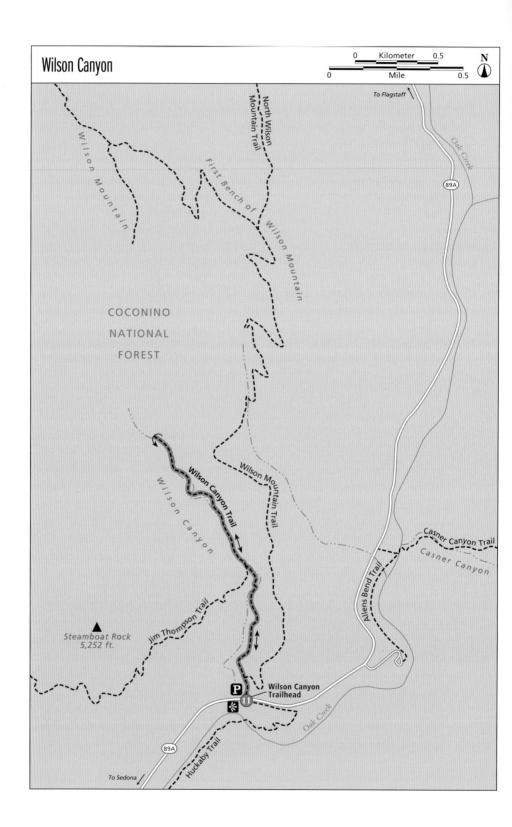

0   Kilometer   0.5

0   Mile   0.5

N

To Flagstaff

Oak Creek

89A

Wilson Mountain

North Wilson Mountain Trail

First Bench of Wilson Mountain

COCONINO

NATIONAL

FOREST

Wilson Canyon Trail

Wilson Mountain Trail

Wilson Canyon

Casner Canyon Trail

Casner Canyon

Allens Bend Trail

Jim Thompson Trail

▲
Steamboat Rock
5,252 ft.

Wilson Canyon
Trailhead

P

11

Oak Creek

89A

To Sedona

Huckaby Trail

An aerial view of Wilson Canyon, tucked below the imposing white cliffs of Wilson Mountain

Bridges to Somewhere

Listed on the National Register of Historic Places, the W. W. Midgley Bridge was completed in 1938 as the last link in the new paved highway connecting Sedona and Flagstaff. The steel-arch bridge is about 200 feet long, spans the mouth of Wilson Canyon, and rises about 200 feet above Oak Creek. It was named for Major W. W. Midgley, who was a strong advocate for better roads in the Sedona area. Before the highway up Oak Creek Canyon was completed, the only road to Flagstaff, the nearest city, was the dirt Schnebly Hill Road up Bear Wallow Canyon. Travel in Oak Creek Canyon itself was even more difficult—the main access was a narrow dirt road, a former wagon track, that wound its way up the canyon. At Wilson Canyon the dirt road wound around the head of canyon. The first part of the Wilson Canyon Trail follows this old road.

Miles and Directions

0.0 Start at the Wilson Canyon Trailhead.

1.0 The trail ends; return the way you came.

2.0 Arrive back at the trailhead.

GREEN TIP

Pack out your dog's waste or dispose of it in a trash can or a hole dug into the ground.

12 Wilson Mountain Trail

This popular trail climbs the south slopes of Wilson Mountain. Your reward for the effort is one of the best views of the Sedona area.

Distance: 6.4 miles out and back
Hiking time: About 5 hours
Difficulty: Strenuous
Seasons: Year-round
Trail surface: Dirt and rocks
Water: None. The trail faces south and is hot in summer; bring plenty of water.
Other trail users: None
Canine compatibility: Dogs under control allowed

Land status: Red Rock–Secret Mountain Wilderness, Coconino National Forest
Fees and permits: None
Maps: Trails Illustrated Flagstaff and Sedona; USGS Wilson Mountain, Munds Park; Coconino National Forest
Trail contacts: Coconino National Forest, 1824 S. Thompson St., Flagstaff 86001; (928) 527-3600; fs.usda.gov/coconino

Finding the trailhead: From Sedona, drive 1.6 miles north on AZ 89A; cross Midgley Bridge, then turn left into the Wilson Canyon Trailhead and viewpoint. GPS: N34 53.128' / W111 44.493'

The Hike

The Wilson Mountain Trail starts climbing immediately, but then the climb moderates for a bit as the trail goes north through open pinyon-juniper forest. The climb starts in earnest as the trail starts switchbacking up the steep, south-facing slopes. The view opens out as the pygmy forest is replaced by the chaparral brush that favors this sunbaked slope. The trail reaches the First Bench of Wilson Mountain then continues north past the junction with the North Wilson Mountain Trail. Stay left here, and continue as the trail swings west and climbs onto the summit plateau. At a trail junction in a saddle, turn left and walk 0.4 mile to the south rim of Wilson Mountain. This great spot has a sweeping view of the Sedona area.

Wildfire

The summit plateau of Wilson Mountain shows the effects of several recent wildfires. In this arid and semiarid country, wildfire was a common event before settlement by Europeans. Most wildfires were caused by lightning, although Native Americans often deliberately set fires for various purposes, including hunting, improving habitat for game, and clearing areas for farming.

The pinyon-juniper woodland that covers most of the Sedona area was not very susceptible to wildfire in its natural, pre-settlement state. The small trees grew in open stands, and the understory of grass and brush was sparse. Anglo settlement changed that with the introduction of cattle and sheep, and especially with the introduction

Wilson Mountain as seen from the Mogollon Rim

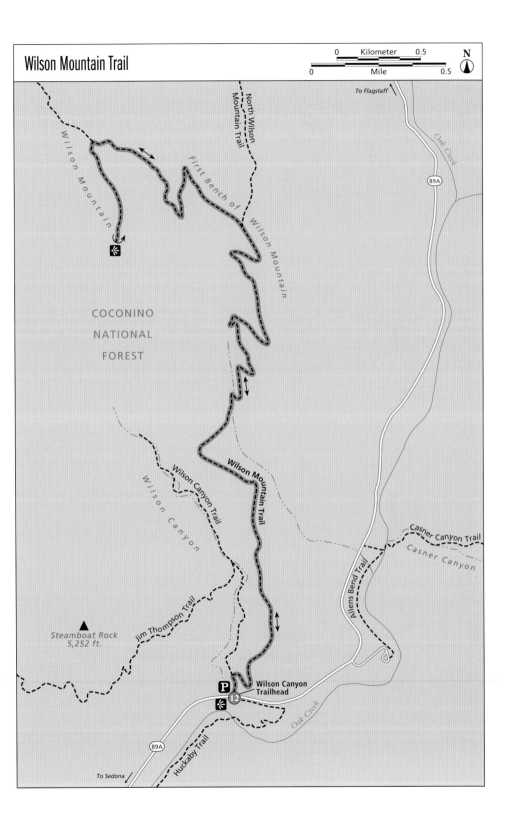

Wilson Mountain Trail

To Flagstaff

Oak Creek

89A

North Wilson Mountain Trail

First Bench of Wilson Mountain

Wilson Mountain

COCONINO

NATIONAL

FOREST

Wilson Canyon Trail

Wilson Canyon

Wilson Mountain Trail

Casner Canyon Trail

Casner Canyon

Allens Bend Trail

Jim Thompson Trail

▲ Steamboat Rock
5,252 ft.

P

12

Wilson Canyon Trailhead

Oak Creek

89A

Huckaby Trail

To Sedona

0   Kilometer   0.5

0   Mile   0.5

N

of exotic (nonnative) plant species such as cheatgrass. In many areas these factors have resulted in denser stands of pinyon pines and junipers, as well as more grass and understory, so that wildfires, whether natural or human-caused, tend to burn hotter and cover larger areas.

In recent years, more and more fires have been started by careless people, usually from abandoned or illegal campfires. One such human-caused fire started on Brins Mesa, at the western base of Wilson Mountain, and rapidly burned over the top of the mountain and down to Oak Creek Canyon. Only hard work by fire crews stopped that fire along the west side of the highway, averting—that time at least—a fire burning in Oak Creek Canyon.

Firefighters' worst nightmare is a fire starting in lower Oak Creek Canyon on a hot, dry, windy day. Such conditions would cause the canyon to act like a chimney, funneling the fire up the canyon with its numerous homes and recreation sites. That's why you see signs along the highway, advising what to do if you hear emergency sirens.

You can do your part to protect this beautiful, unique canyon. Observe all fire restrictions. In Oak Creek Canyon itself, you can only build a campfire in designated recreation sites—campgrounds and day use areas. Building a fire anywhere else on public land in Oak Creek Canyon is illegal. Campfires must always be completely extinguished before you leave the site by mixing the coals with water until the ashes are cold to the touch.

If you smoke outdoor on national forest lands, the law requires you to stop, clear a 2-foot-diameter area to bare ground, and smoke there. This rule applies no matter the fire danger level.

Miles and Directions

0.0 Start at the Wilson Canyon Trailhead.

0.1 Bear right on the Wilson Mountain Trail.

2.2 Reach the First Bench of Wilson Mountain.

2.8 Turn left at the summit trail junction in a saddle.

3.2 Reach the south rim of Wilson Mountain; return the way you came.

6.4 Arrive back at the trailhead.

GREEN TIP
Pack out what you pack in, even food scraps,
which can attract wild animals.

13 Allens Bend Trail

This is one of the few trails along Oak Creek itself. Although short, it's an easy, pleasant walk. It's especially fine in the fall when the colors are changing.

Distance: 0.6 mile out and back
Hiking time: About 0.5 hour
Difficulty: Easy
Seasons: Year-round
Trail surface: Dirt and rocks
Water: Oak Creek
Other trail users: None
Canine compatibility: Dogs under control allowed

Land status: Coconino National Forest
Fees and permits: Fee for parking at Grasshopper Point Picnic Area
Maps: Trails Illustrated Flagstaff and Sedona; USGS Munds Park; Coconino National Forest
Trail contacts: Coconino National Forest, 1824 S. Thompson St., Flagstaff 86001; (928) 527-3600; fs.usda.gov/coconino

Finding the trailhead: From Sedona, drive about 2 miles north on AZ 89A; turn right (east) into the Grasshopper Point Picnic Area. GPS: N34 53.244' / W111 43.897'

The Hike

The unsigned trail, which is not shown on the topographic map, starts from the north end of the parking lot and follows the west bank of Oak Creek. There are several sections of elaborate trail construction near the beginning, then the trail comes out onto a wider bench. Watch for poison ivy, which is very common along Oak Creek. The trail ends near an old road that comes down from the highway above. Although short, the Allens Bend Trail is a pleasant, shady walk along the rushing waters of Oak Creek. It also provides an alternate access to the Casner Canyon Trail, which crosses the creek at the end of this trail.

Geology

In this area, the red rocks near the creek are sandstones, shales, and limestones of the Supai Group. The Supai begins to outcrop here and forms the inner gorge of Oak Creek Canyon below this point. In general, the Supai Group forms the layered pedestals of the red rock formations in the Sedona area; the Schnebly Hill Formation forms the buttes themselves.

Springs

Water is rare and precious in Arizona, as any thirsty hiker can attest. Permanent streams such as Oak Creek are rare in Arizona, partly because of the generally arid climate, but also because of water diversions and groundwater pumping. Oak Creek's water comes from a series of springs along its length, starting with Sterling Spring just above the confluence with Pumphouse Wash, at the head of the canyon. As the creek

Reflections in a quiet pool along Oak Creek near the Allens Bend Trail

descends south through its lush canyon, other springs, such as the ones at Pine Flat and Cave Springs Campgrounds, contribute more water to its flow.

These springs appear deep within the canyon for two hydrological reasons. One is that rain and snowmelt quickly soak into the porous rocks—mostly sandstone, limestone, and volcanic—that make up the surface and upper rock layers of the surrounding Coconino Plateau. Groundwater sinks deeper through these rock layers until it encounters impervious layers of shale and forms an aquifer.

Groundwater takes advantage not only of porous rock to slowly percolate but also of weaknesses in the rock such as faults. Because Oak Creek Canyon formed along a major fault, groundwater moves more readily along the fault and comes to the surface as numerous springs.

Allens Bend Trail

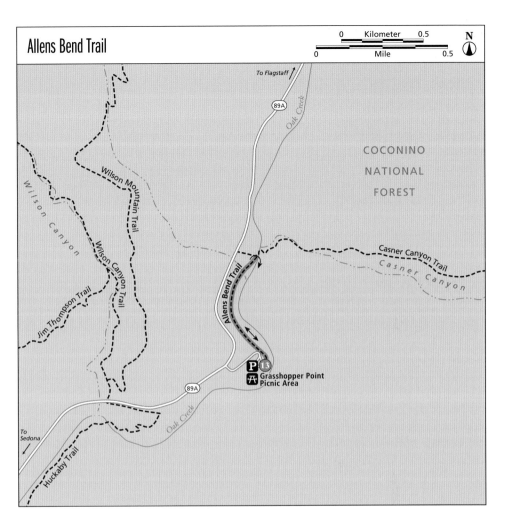

Miles and Directions

0.0 Start at the unsigned trailhead.

0.3 The trail ends; return the way you came.

0.6 Arrive back at the trailhead.

GREEN TIP
Toilet paper should be burned or packed out. To carry it with you, put a small piece of an ammonia-soaked sponge in your bag to help kill bacteria and odor.

14 Casner Canyon Trail

A little-used trail to the east rim of Oak Creek Canyon.

Distance: 3.6 miles out and back
Hiking time: About 3 hours
Difficulty: Moderate
Seasons: Year-round
Trail surface: Dirt and rocks; boulder-hopping in the bed of Oak Creek Canyon
Water: None
Other trail users: None

Canine compatibility: Dogs under control allowed
Land status: Coconino National Forest
Fees and permits: None
Maps: Trails Illustrated Flagstaff and Sedona; USGS Munds Park; Coconino National Forest
Trail contacts: Coconino National Forest, 1824 S. Thompson St., Flagstaff 86001; (928) 527-3600; fs.usda.gov/coconino

Finding the trailhead: From Sedona, drive about 2.4 miles north on AZ 89A; park on the right (east) side of the highway at a closed road. The trailhead is 0.3 mile north of Grasshopper Point Picnic Area. GPS: N34 53.485' / W111 44.035'

The Hike

The trail follows the closed road down to Oak Creek then crosses the creek and heads up the bed of Casner Canyon. There is no trail across the creek because of the damage from the massive flood in 1993. The key is to locate the mouth of Casner Canyon on the east side of the creek, downstream of the point where you first reach the creek; the topographic map may be useful. After following the bed of Casner Canyon for a few hundred yards, the trail climbs out onto the north slope. It turns northwest into an unnamed side canyon below Indian Point then climbs to reach the rim at the head of this side canyon. Most of the trail is on a dry, south-facing slope, and the low chaparral brush allows good views. This is a good trail to hike on weekends and holidays when other trails are crowded.

Pioneer Trails

Many of the trails we modern hikers enjoy were built by early settlers in the area. They in turn often followed routes and trails created by the local Native Americans, who had thousands of years of presence in the Sedona area. But the native trails and routes were mostly worked out by people traveling on foot—native peoples only acquired horses about 500 years ago, from the Spanish explorers and missionaries.

The European settlers who arrived in the mid-nineteenth century needed to move large herds of livestock from pasture to pasture, and eventually to a town or a railroad to get to market. The settlers also needed to move freight and supplies by wagon and people via stagecoach. This led to a progression of trail improvements. Settlers along Oak Creek Canyon in particular needed to get to Flagstaff, the nearest point of supply,

Casner Canyon Trail

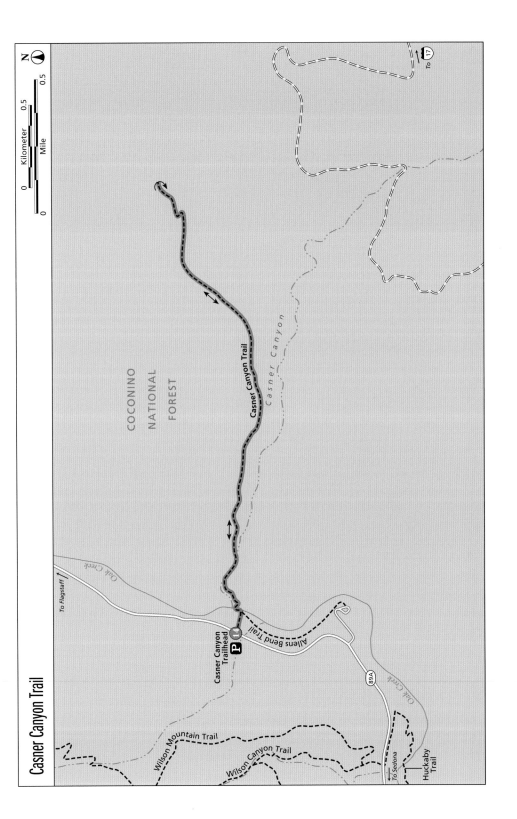

N

Kilometer
0   0.5

Mile
0   0.5

COCONINO
NATIONAL
FOREST

Casner Canyon Trail

Casner Canyon

To Flagstaff

Oak Creek

Casner Canyon
Trailhead

Allens Bend Trail

P

89A

Oak Creek

Wilson Mountain Trail

Wilson Canyon Trail

To Sedona

Huckaby
Trail

To 17

Oak Creek shimmers under a blue sky at the beginning of the Casner Canyon Trail.

because the town was on a transcontinental railroad. That same railroad gave the Oak Creek settlers access to a national market—if they could get their cattle and sheep there.

This resulted in at least half a dozen trails being built from Oak Creek up to the rims of the canyon. Because of movement along the Oak Creek Fault, the east rim of the canyon is 500 feet lower than the west rim and affords significantly better terrain for trail building—fewer cliffs and more slopes. Also, the distance from the east rim to Flagstaff is less. As a result, only one trail climbs the west slopes, the AB Young Trail, and it reaches the rim south of the canyon of the West Fork—a major barrier to travel toward Flagstaff. It's likely that AB Young used his trail primarily to move livestock to summer pastures in the forests and meadows on the plateau.

Aside from the easier construction, another reason there are so many trails on the east rim is that settlers tended to build their own trail from their own homestead. Trails take a lot of time and hard work to build, and pioneers who invested in a trail tended to want to get some money for their effort in the form of tolls. That of course provided an incentive for the next settler down the canyon to build his or her own trail.

Since trails such as the Casner Canyon Trail and the others farther upstream weren't suitable for wagons, some settlers started leaving wagons at the rim of the canyon. They would ride and lead horses from their homestead up to the rim and then hitch the team to their wagon and head to town. When they got their load of supplies, they would probably make several trips back and forth to the rim in order to haul all the supplies down into the canyon.

Of course the next step would be to build an actual wagon road up to the rim. But this didn't happen until the early twentieth century.

Miles and Directions

0.0   Start at the trailhead and follow the closed road.

0.1   Cross Oak Creek and pick up the trail.

1.8   Reach the East Rim of Oak Creek Canyon; return the way you came.

3.6   Arrive back at the trailhead.

15 North Wilson Mountain Trail

This is a good hike on a hot day, as much of the trail is in a north-facing, shady canyon. You'll have excellent views of Oak Creek Canyon, the Dry Creek basin, and the Mogollon Rim.

Distance: 7.6 miles out and back
Hiking time: About 5 hours
Difficulty: Strenuous
Seasons: Spring through fall
Trail surface: Dirt and rocks
Water: None
Other trail users: None
Canine compatibility: Dogs under control allowed

Land status: Red Rock–Secret Mountain Wilderness, Coconino National Forest
Fees and permits: None
Maps: Trails Illustrated Flagstaff and Sedona; USGS Munds Park, Wilson Mountain; Coconino National Forest
Trail contacts: Coconino National Forest, 1824 S. Thompson St., Flagstaff 86001; (928) 527-3600; fs.usda.gov/coconino

Finding the trailhead: From Sedona, drive about 5 miles north on AZ 89A to the Encinoso Picnic Area. Park in the trailhead parking area at the entrance to the picnic area. GPS: N34 55.534' / W111 44.104'

The Hike

The trailhead is signed, although the North Wilson Mountain Trail is not shown on the topographic map. The trail starts climbing immediately through mixed chaparral, ponderosa pine, and oak forest. When the trail reaches the ridge above the picnic area, it turns to the south and follows the ridge a short distance, giving you good views of Oak Creek Canyon. After leaving the ridge, the trail climbs southwest up a heavily wooded drainage. The shade of the large ponderosa pines is a welcome relief on hot days. As the trail nears the base of the massive, buff-colored Coconino Sandstone cliffs, it crosses the drainage and begins to switchback up the slope to the east. There are more fine views when the trail reaches the ridge at the top of this slope. Now the trail turns to the south again and follows the ridge onto the First Bench of Wilson Mountain, a gently sloping volcanic plateau level with the east rim of Oak Creek Canyon.

Near the south end of the bench, the North Wilson Mountain Trail meets the Wilson Mountain Trail at a signed junction. This trail is shown on the topographic map. Turn right (west) here and follow the Wilson Mountain Trail as it climbs Wilson Mountain itself. Several switchbacks lead through the basalt cliffs near the rim. The trail swings left into a drainage, which it follows to reach a gentle saddle on the wooded summit plateau. The actual summit is a small knob just to the north of this saddle.

There is a signed trail junction in the saddle. Continue straight ahead and follow the trail northwest about 1.4 miles to the north end of Wilson Mountain. The

The north side of Wilson Mountain in the distance, as seen from the AB Young Trail

topographic map shows the trail ending just west of the point marked 7,076 on the map, but it actually continues to the rim. Here you are overlooking Sterling Pass, upper Dry Creek, Oak Creek, the Mogollon Rim, and the San Francisco Peaks. The view of the maze of red, buff, and gray cliffs is well worth the long hike.

Chaparral

The lower slopes of Oak Creek are covered with a dense mixture of brush known as chaparral. You'll hike through some patches of chaparral as you ascend the lower part of this trail, and then get a good view of the extensive chaparral covering the east

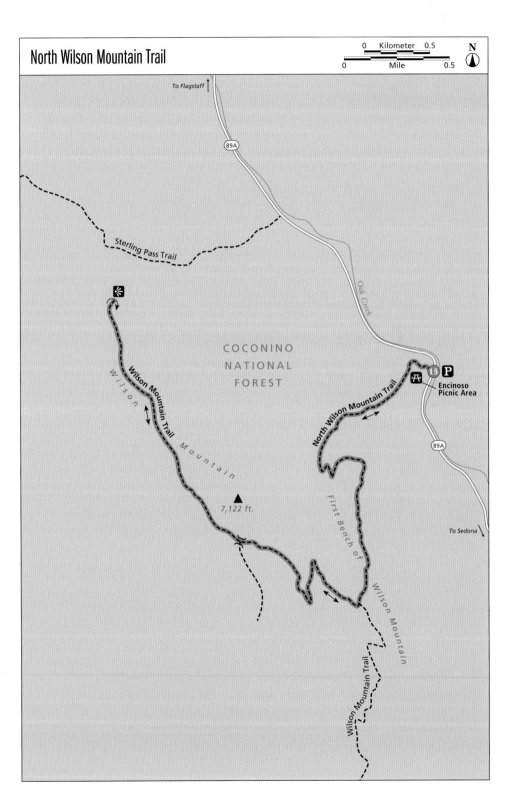

North Wilson Mountain Trail

0 Kilometer 0.5
0 Mile 0.5

N

To Flagstaff

89A

Oak Creek

Sterling Pass Trail

COCONINO
NATIONAL
FOREST

Wilson Mountain Trail

Wilson   Mountain

7,122 ft.

North Wilson Mountain Trail

15 P

Encinoso
Picnic Area

89A

To Sedona

First Bench of

Wilson Mountain

Wilson Mountain Trail

slopes above Oak Creek Canyon from the First Bench of Wilson Mountain. At these elevations, chaparral favors warmer and drier west- and south-facing slopes.

Chaparral is not a plant; it's a term that refers to a common association of shrubs that varies from place to place. In Arizona, and Oak Creek in particular, chaparral is a mix of manzanita, various species of scrub oak, and mountain mahogany, which are all evergreen plants. All are tough plants from a couple of feet to as much as 10 feet in height, and they combine to form almost impenetrable thickets. Impenetrable to humans, anyway. But the shady ground beneath provides essential habitat and cover for wildlife.

Manzanita is Spanish for "little apples," a perfect description of the tiny fruit that appears after the tiny pink flowers. Manzanita has thin reddish bark and small apple-green leaves, and the branches are brittle. Manzanita alone isn't impossible to travel through—you can mostly pick your way through small openings between the clumps of brush, breaking some of the brittle branches if you have to.

Scrub oak and mountain mahogany are a different story. Their branches are tough yet springy, and the combination of all three is not fun to attempt to make your way through.

Chaparral is very well adapted to wildfire. As you might imagine, the dense brush burns furiously during the dry season, leaving nothing behind but charred stumps. But as soon as the next rains come—usually the late summer monsoon thunderstorms—green shoots appear from the root systems that were untouched by the fire that raged overhead. Not only do the chaparral plants regrow, but the flowers and grasses that have survived the fire either as seeds or roots soon start to grow as well. The chaparral plant community grows so fast that after ten years or so it can be difficult to see that a fire ever swept through the area.

Faults

Oak Creek Canyon eroded out along the Oak Creek Fault. Movement along the fault raised the west rim of the canyon about 500 feet higher than the east rim. The canyon follows the fault until the lower end, where the creek veers east. The fault line then continues across the east side of Wilson Mountain, which is why the First Bench of Wilson Mountain is about 500 feet lower than the summit plateau.

Miles and Directions

0.0 Start at the North Wilson Mountain Trailhead.

1.4 Reach the First Bench of Wilson Mountain.

1.8 Turn right on the Wilson Mountain Trail.

2.4 Continue straight at the summit trail junction.

3.8 Reach the north rim of Wilson Mountain; return the way you came.

7.6 Arrive back at the trailhead.

16 Sterling Pass Trail

A less-used trail below the impressive cliffs on the north face of Wilson Mountain.

Distance: 1.8 miles out and back
Hiking time: About 1.5 hours
Difficulty: Moderate
Seasons: Spring through fall
Trail surface: Dirt and rocks
Water: None
Other trail users: None
Canine compatibility: Dogs under control allowed

Land status: Red Rock–Secret Mountain Wilderness, Coconino National Forest
Fees and permits: None
Maps: Trails Illustrated Flagstaff and Sedona; USGS Munds Park, Wilson Mountain; Coconino National Forest
Trail contacts: Coconino National Forest, 1824 S. Thompson St., Flagstaff 86001; (928) 527-3600; fs.usda.gov/coconino

Finding the trailhead: From Sedona, drive about 6 miles north on AZ 89A to the Manzanita Campground. The trail starts from the west side of the highway just north of the campground, but parking is very limited. You may have to park at the pullouts south of the campground then walk through the campground to reach the trailhead. GPS: N34 56.198' / W111 44.832'

The Hike

The Sterling Pass Trail is not shown on the topographic map. It climbs steeply up a drainage after leaving the highway, through a fine stand of ponderosa pines. It skirts a dry waterfall then begins a series of short, steep switchbacks. There are occasional views of the massive cliffs that form the north side of Wilson Mountain. The hike ends at Sterling Pass, the sharp notch between the Mogollon Rim and Wilson Mountain.

Option

From Sterling Pass, you can hike west on the Vultee Arch Trail to the Dry Creek Trailhead. This would require a car shuttle if hiked one way.

Native Trails

The Sterling Pass Trail is a classic example of a modern trail following a Native American route. To the trained eye of a wilderness hiker, which the local natives most certainly were, both sides of Sterling Pass look like an obvious route between Wilson Mountain and the Mogollon Rim.

The natives didn't tend to go in for the kind of serious trail construction that later European settlers would engage in. But they often cut small steps into the rock to get up short cliffs, or put up leaning logs with steps cut into them as a way of getting up cliffs.

Fall color in Oak Creek Canyon

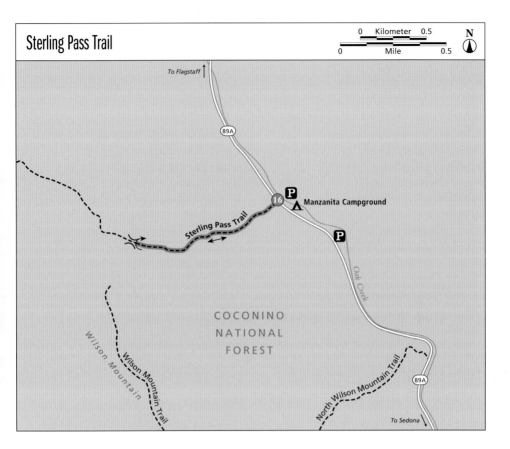

Miles and Directions

0.0 Start at the trailhead north of Manzanita Campground.

0.9 Reach Sterling Pass; return the way you came.

1.8 Arrive back at the trailhead.

GREEN TIP

Stay on the trail. Cutting through from one part of a switchback to another can destroy fragile plant life and causes erosion of the trail and the surrounding slopes. And while cutting switchbacks may seem like a shortcut, it actually takes more energy than staying on the smoothly graded trail.

17 AB Young Trail

This good trail to the west rim of Oak Creek Canyon offers the best views of the canyon of all the rim trails.

Distance: 4.4 miles out and back
Hiking time: About 3 hours
Difficulty: Moderate
Seasons: Spring through fall
Trail surface: Dirt and rocks
Water: None
Other trail users: None
Canine compatibility: Dogs under control allowed

Land status: Red Rock–Secret Mountain Wilderness, Coconino National Forest
Fees and permits: None
Maps: Trails Illustrated Flagstaff and Sedona; USGS Munds Park, Wilson Mountain ; Coconino National Forest
Trail contacts: Coconino National Forest, 1824 S. Thompson St., Flagstaff 86001; (928) 527-3600; fs.usda.gov/coconino

Finding the trailhead: From Sedona, drive about 9 miles north on AZ 89A to the Bootlegger Day Use Area. Do not block the entrance; park in the highway pullout just to the north. GPS: N34 58.214' / W111 45.029'

The Hike

Walk through the day use area and cross Oak Creek. Turn left (south) on the trail, which parallels the creek, and watch for the signed junction with the AB Young Trail. This good, maintained trail turns sharply right and starts climbing to the northwest. The broadleaf trees in the riparian habitat along the creek are soon left behind as the trail climbs through ponderosa pine forest. After a short distance, the trail begins switchbacking directly up the steep slope. The dry southwest exposure supports dense chaparral brush, and the view opens up as you climb. Just below the rim, the trail veers north in a long final switchback. At the rim, the trail enters pine forest again. Turn southwest and follow the cairned trail, which is fainter, along the pine-forested rim to the crest of an east–west ridge. Here the trail turns west and follows the flat-topped ridge to East Pocket Knob and the end of the trail at the USDA Forest Service fire tower. Get permission from the lookout before climbing the tower for a panoramic view of the Mogollon Rim and Oak Creek Canyon.

Civilian Conservation Corps

The AB Young Trail was originally built to move cattle to and from the rim country, then improved by the Civilian Conservation Corps in the 1930s. The CCC, along with several other conservation agencies, built thousands of miles of trails in the national forests and parks from 1933 to 1942. Part of President Franklin D. Roosevelt's New Deal program, the CCC employed unmarried young men on public works projects and was intended to help mitigate the effects of the Great Depression.

Hiking the AB Young Trail on the west side of Oak Creek Canyon

AB Young Trail

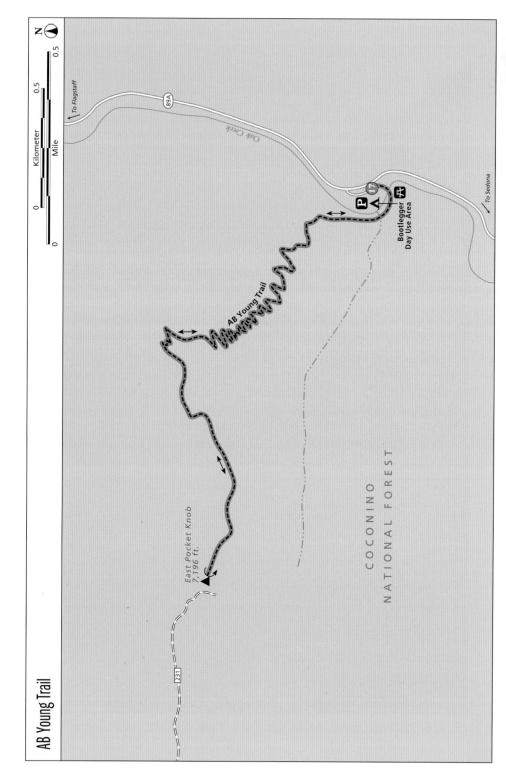

To Flagstaff

89A

Oak Creek

AB Young Trail

East Pocket Knob
7,196 ft.

231

COCONINO
NATIONAL FOREST

Bootlegger
Day Use Area

To Sedona

P

N

Kilometer
0   0.5

Mile
0   0.5

Supervised by experienced park and forest rangers, the CCC workers built to last. Much of their work survives today, not only in well-graded trails such as the AB Young Trail but also in the form of fire lookout towers, fire guard cabins, stone bridges, campgrounds, and many other structures.

Workers were paid a modest amount by today's standards and were required to send part of their wages home to their families. But in a time of uncertainty, these young men were provided guaranteed meals, shelter, and satisfying jobs and were able to acquire skills that enabled them to move on to stable employment.

With the advent of World War II and the draft, the program was no longer needed. Congress terminated the CCC in 1942, but the Corps' legacy lives on in the form of such programs as the Student Conservation Association, American Conservation Experience, and numerous state conservation corps.

Wilderness Courtesy, Take 1

While out on the trail, be courteous of others. Most people visit natural areas for quiet, peace, and solitude, so avoid making loud noises and intruding on others' privacy. Groups should talk quietly among themselves rather than shouting—and keep in mind that the quieter you are, the more likely you are to see wildlife.

Consider buying outerwear, packs, and tents in muted colors such as green, blues, and browns instead of bright colors like yellow, orange, and red. In desert wilderness, many more people can share an area without feeling crowded if their gear and clothing don't "pop."

And when camping in the backcountry, choose a site away from the trail and away from other campers. Except in places where backpackers must camp in designated sites (as of this writing, there are no designated backcountry camps in the Sedona area), camping out of sight of others increases everyone's feeling of solitude.

Avoid the use of outdoor camp lanterns in wilderness camps. Instead use a headlamp, which is much more efficient with its targeted beam and adjustable intensity. Camp lanterns are more useful inside your tent anyway, where they envelope everything in a warm, cozy glow. There are plenty of low-power, LED lanterns to choose from.

Miles and Directions

0.0 Start at the trailhead at Bootlegger Day Use Area.

1.4 Reach the west rim of Oak Creek Canyon. Turn southwest and follow the cairned trail along the rim.

1.8 Trail leaves the rim.

2.2 Reach East Pocket Lookout; return the way you came.

4.4 Arrive back at the trailhead.

18 Thomas Point Trail

This hike is a great alternative to the crowded West Fork Trail, and is right across the highway. There are excellent views of the West Fork of Oak Creek and Oak Creek Canyon itself.

Distance: 2.0 miles out and back
Hiking time: About 1.5 hours
Difficulty: Moderate
Seasons: Spring through fall
Trail surface: Dirt and rocks
Water: None
Other trail users: None
Canine compatibility: Dogs under control allowed

Land status: Coconino National Forest
Fees and permits: Fee for parking at Call of the Canyon parking area
Maps: Trails Illustrated Flagstaff and Sedona; USGS Munds Park; Coconino National Forest
Trail contacts: Coconino National Forest, 1824 S. Thompson St., Flagstaff 86001; (928) 527-3600; fs.usda.gov/coconino

Finding the trailhead: From Sedona, drive about 11 miles north on AZ 89A, then turn left into the Call of the Canyon parking area. GPS: N34 59.431' / W111 44.518'

The Hike

Like most of the old trails in Oak Creek Canyon, this trail is not shown on the topographic map. From the parking area, follow the trail south through the old orchard for about 100 yards, then cross the highway to a trail sign. The trail climbs south through shady ponderosa pine–Gambel oak forest then turns a corner onto a much drier, south-facing slope. Here, because of the increased temperature and evaporation, chaparral plants—scrub oak, mountain mahogany, and manzanita—dominate. There are fine views down the canyon to the flat-topped mesa of Wilson Mountain. A switchback leads to a point overlooking the mouth of the West Fork, then the trail turns east again and climbs into a pine saddle. The trail finishes by following the ridge east 100 yards to the rim, where views are limited because of the thick forest. You'll find a better viewpoint by walking about 100 yards west from the saddle onto a rock outcrop. Here you're looking up the West Fork of Oak Creek.

2014: The Slide Fire

From the viewpoint on the Thomas Point Trail, you can see the effects of the Slide Fire on the west side of Oak Creek Canyon and in the canyon of the West Fork. This wildfire started from an abandoned illegal campfire just north of Slide Rock State Park in summer 2014. A fire on a hot, windy day after a dry winter is the worst nightmare for wildland firefighters and for people living along Oak Creek. The chimney effect in Oak Creek Canyon could easily create a firestorm that would not only

Looking across Oak Creek Canyon from the Thomas Point Trail into the lower end of the West Fork's canyon

consume all the trees and structures in the canyon but also sweep onto the Mogollon Rim above and threaten Flagstaff and its suburbs.

As a former wildland firefighter myself, I am often critical of the way in which fire management handles wildfires. But in this case I have nothing but praise. Since I live in Flagstaff and often fly air tours out of Sedona Airport, I tracked the progress of the fire closely. Since the fire was controlled, I have flown over the burn many times and had a bird's-eye view of the fire's aftermath.

First, a little background on wildfire suppression: Wildland firefighters do not "put out" large fires, as the media would have it. Though small fires—single-tree fires from lightning strikes and the like—can be put out completely (a process known as "mopping up"), this is impossible with large fires. Instead, a wildfire is attacked by "containment." Fire crews, sometimes aided by bulldozers and other bladed equipment, as well as fire engines if terrain permits, build a fire line completely around the fire. Fire lines vary, but a fire line made with hand tools is usually about 5 feet wide. Everything that could burn—small trees, brush, and duff—is removed from the line, which is scraped down to bare mineral soil. Even tree roots, which could carry the fire across the line, are chopped away. Dead trees and brush near the line that could topple across it, are cut down and stacked away from the fire line.

Small, slow-moving fires can be attacked directly by building a fire line from the point of origin, around the flanks of the fire, and across the head. When the fire reaches the fire line, it runs out of fuel and stops. Then the next stages begin—burnout and mop-up. Crews patrol the line, deliberately setting fires inside the burn to remove any unburned fuel that could flare up and carry embers over the line. Once everything has pretty much burned out, crews work through the burn, putting out anything still smoldering. On small fires, the entire burn can be mopped up; but on large fires such as the Slide Fire, the fire is mopped up several hundred feet inside the line and the interior allowed to burn out on its own.

When crews began the initial attack against the Slide Fire, the head of the fire was already too intense and fast-moving for direct attack. Instead, crews built a fire line along the east flank of the fire and, aided by helicopter water drops and retardant drops from air tankers, herded the fire up the west side of the canyon, away from Oak Creek. When the fire reached the west rim of Oak Creek and started burning in the ponderosa pine forest on the plateau, similar techniques were used to keep the fire from spreading west.

It was hoped that the fire could be stopped before reaching the West Fork of Oak Creek, but it could not. Often, fire managers try to attack a fire too closely, and it jumps the fire line before the line can be completed. In this case, when it was clear that the northward progress of the fire could not be stopped before it crossed the West Fork, firefighters fell back to an east–west forest road on the north side of the West Fork. This gave them the time to turn the road into a defensible fire line. In addition, burnout operations were conducted to broaden the fire line. Burnout was

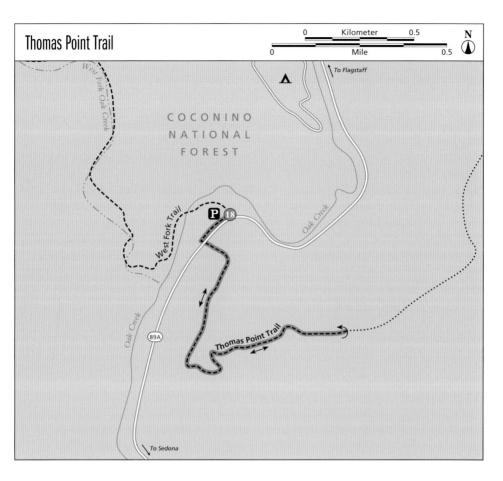

Thomas Point Trail

COCONINO
NATIONAL
FOREST

West Fork Oak Creek

To Flagstaff

West Fork Trail

P 18

Oak Creek

Oak Creek

89A

Thomas Point Trail

To Sedona

done mostly at night, when fire intensity is lower and the deliberately set fire would stay on the ground and not kill the trees.

These techniques were effective not only in stopping the Slide Fire but also in keeping its intensity low. From the air, it appears that less than 20 percent of the fire crowned and killed the trees. Most of the fire burned as a low-intensity ground fire, which is the kind of fire the ponderosa forest is well adapted to. Such fires remove thick stands of small trees and underbrush and keep the forest open and resistant to high-intensity, destructive fires.

Miles and Directions

0.0 Start from the trailhead at the Call of the Canyon parking area.

0.4 The trail emerges onto the south-facing slope.

1.0 Reach the east rim of Oak Creek Canyon; return the way you came.

2.0 Arrive back at the trailhead.

19 West Fork Trail

A very popular hike traverses the spectacular West Fork of Oak Creek.

Distance: 6.0 miles out and back
Hiking time: About 3 hours
Difficulty: Easy
Seasons: Spring through fall
Trail surface: Dirt and rocks, shallow creek crossings
Water: West Fork Oak Creek
Other trail users: None
Canine compatibility: Dogs under control allowed
Land status: Red Rock–Secret Mountain Wilderness, Coconino National Forest

Fees and permits: Fee for parking at Call of the Canyon parking area. The lower 6 miles of the West Fork is closed to camping due to heavy use.
Maps: Trails Illustrated Flagstaff and Sedona; USGS Dutton Hill, Wilson Mountain, Munds Park; Coconino National Forest
Trail contacts: Coconino National Forest, 1824 S. Thompson St., Flagstaff 86001; (928) 527-3600; fs.usda.gov/coconino

Finding the trailhead: From Sedona, drive about 11 miles north on AZ 89A, then turn left into the Call of the Canyon parking area. GPS: N34 59.431' / W111 44.518'

The Hike

The West Fork is an easy but extremely popular hike. It is not the place to go to escape crowds, especially on weekends. For solitude, try the Thomas Point Trail on the opposite side of Oak Creek. Note that the forest service prohibits camping in the lower West Fork due to heavy use. Stay on the trail, and do not pick flowers or otherwise disturb this fragile environment. Watch for poison ivy, which is common along the trail. The trail is not shown on the topographic map.

Cross Oak Creek on a footbridge, and follow the West Fork Trail south to the mouth of the West Fork canyon, where the trail turns right (west) and enters this most impressive gorge. Soon you'll leave the sounds of the busy highway behind and be able to hear the pleasant murmur of the creek and the whisper of the wind in the trees. Buttresses of Coconino Sandstone tower on the left, while the canyon floor is filled with a tall ponderosa pine and Douglas fir forest. The trail crosses the creek several times, ending about 3 miles up the canyon. Walking is very easy to this point, which is the end of the hike.

Options

Experienced canyon hikers can continue up the West Fork to its head near FR 231. This cross-country hike requires canyoneering skills, including wading in the creek and occasional swimming to cross deep pools. There is a serious danger of flash

A quiet pool along the West Fork of Oak Creek

Fall colors along the West Fork Trail

flooding; do not continue unless you have a stable weather forecast and are prepared to handle the deep, often cold, pools.

Another possible hike for the adventurous, experienced canyon hiker is to hike cross-country up the canyon to the nameless canyon just west of West Buzzard Point

West Fork Trail

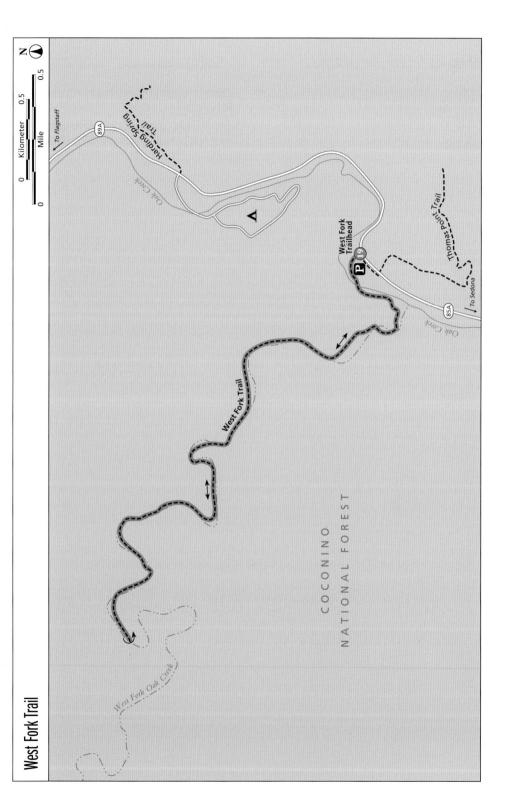

N

Kilometer
0   0.5

Mile
0   0.5

To Flagstaff

89A

Oak Creek

Harding Spring Trail

West Fork Trailhead

P 19

Thomas Point Trail

To Sedona

89A

Oak Creek

West Fork Trail

COCONINO
NATIONAL FOREST

West Fork Oak Creek

and then climb to the south rim of the canyon. From here, hike cross-country to East Pocket Knob and descend the AB Young Trail to Oak Creek Canyon. You would need a shuttle vehicle at the AB Young Trailhead.

Canyoneering

Canyoneering is the sport of traversing deep canyons, often with the aid of technical mountaineering skills such as rappelling. The upper West Fork can provide a gentle introduction to canyoneering. Because of flooding and snow runoff, the obstacles in the upper canyon change from year to year. The first time I planned the hike was during April after a very snowy winter. By April, much of the snow on the plateau had melted, but the ground was saturated and every drainage was running with snowmelt. The West Fork was running high and cold—not a good place to be.

When I finally did the hike, it was a dry, warm May. The water was a bit chilly, but I got past every pool by just wading. One deep pool was pretty interesting. At first it looked as though I'd have to swim, but I was able to walk along an underwater ledge and the water never got more than waist high. One slip though, and I would have been swimming, so I made sure my gear was waterproofed. I also unfastened my hip belt and sternum strap so I could quickly get out of my pack if I took an accidental plunge. I was able to walk and wade the canyon floor to the exit near West Buzzard Point in a few hours. In different years, other parties have had to swim and float their gear across numerous pools and have taken a couple of days to travel the same distance.

On my trip, I carried an air mattress to float my pack across pools and waterproofed my gear with large trash bags. Now there are specially made, lightweight pack rafts that you can use to float your gear and even yourself across deep, cold pools, as well as waterproof canyoneering packs that work just like the dry bags used on river trips. If you really get into canyoneering, this specialized gear is worth every penny. I've used pack rafts to descend canyons in the Mazatzal Wilderness, as well as to cross the turbulent, cold Colorado River in the Grand Canyon.

Miles and Directions

0.0 Start at the West Fork Trailhead; cross the footbridge over Oak Creek and head south on the trail.

0.4 Reach the mouth of the West Fork canyon and enter the gorge.

3.0 The trail ends; return the way you came.

6.0 Arrive back at the trailhead.

20 Harding Spring Trail

A cool shady hike through ponderosa pine and Douglas fir forest to the east rim of Oak Creek canyon.

Distance: 1.4 miles out and back
Hiking time: About 1.5 hours
Difficulty: Moderate
Seasons: Spring through fall
Trail surface: Dirt and rocks
Water: None
Other trail users: None
Canine compatibility: Dogs under control allowed

Land status: Coconino National Forest
Fees and permits: None
Maps: Trails Illustrated Flagstaff and Sedona; USGS Mountainaire; Coconino National Forest
Trail contacts: Coconino National Forest, 1824 S. Thompson St., Flagstaff 86001; (928) 527-3600; fs.usda.gov/coconino

Finding the trailhead: From Sedona, drive about 12 miles north on AZ 89A to the Cave Springs Campground turnoff. (The campground sign may be missing when the campground is closed for the winter.) The turnoff is on the left (west); park in the pullout just to the north. GPS: N35 0.025' / W111 44.239'

Looking down upper Oak Creek Canyon, forested in a mix of ponderosa pine and Douglas fir

The Hike

Although the trail is not shown on the topographic map, the signed trailhead is across the highway to the east. The trail immediately starts to climb. (Ignore the trail that doesn't.) Originally built by early settlers as a route to move their cattle to and from the plateau above, the Harding Springs Trail is still in good shape. The dense, cool forest offers welcome shade, making this is a good hike for a hot day.

Options

You can hike north cross-country along the east rim of Oak Creek Canyon and descend via the Cookstove Trail. Another option is to hike south cross-country along the east rim of Oak Creek Canyon and descend via the Thomas Point Trail. You should have the topographic map and have hiked your planned descent trail at least once so that you will be able to find its upper end.

FALSE FIRS

Douglas fir is common on cooler, north-facing slopes in upper Oak Creek Canyon. This is the Rocky Mountain variety of the coastal Douglas fir that is found on the coastal sides of the mountains in the Pacific Northwest. The Rocky Mountain variety reaches about 3 feet in diameter and a height of around 100 feet. The spire-like evergreen conifer is named for David Douglas, the Scottish botanist who first studied the tree. The coastal Douglas fir reaches more than 300 feet tall and 6 feet in diameter. It is a valuable source of lumber and is heavily logged.

Douglas fir is not a true fir. All true firs have cones that stand upright from the branches, but Douglas fir cones hang down. White fir is a true fir, and though rarer than Douglas firs, it mixes with them in the same habitats. From a distance, white fir is a lighter shade of green than Douglas fir, but the true giveaway is a close-up view of the needles. Douglas fir needles are pure green in color; white fir has two bluish-white stripes on the underside of its needles.

White firs have a more conical crown than Douglas firs, and are widely planted as ornamentals and used as Christmas trees. The largest white firs are found in the central Sierra Nevada of California, where they reach almost 200 feet. In Arizona, white fir rarely grows taller than about 100 feet.

In higher, cooler areas, several varieties of spruce start to mix in with the firs near the top of their ranges and are often confused with the firs. Again, the needles are the clue to tell whether a tree is a spruce or a fir. Fir needles, including Douglas fir, are flat and won't roll between your fingers. Spruce needles, on the other hand, are square and roll easily.

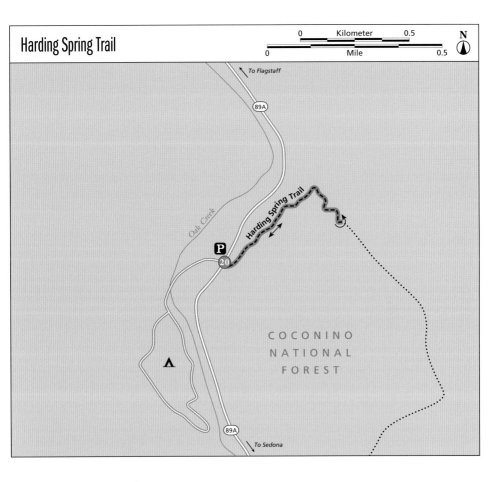

Harding Spring Trail

Trail Courtesy, Take 2

Before you start for home, have you left the wilderness as you'd want to see it? Don't litter—and if you want to feel really good about yourself, pick up some litter left by others. Most litter in the backcountry is accidental, not deliberate, and if we all pick up a bit of litter on each hike, the trails will stay clean for everyone.

Miles and Directions

0.0   Start at the trailhead and immediately start to climb.

0.7   Reach the east rim of Oak Creek Canyon; return the way you came.

1.4   Arrive back at the trailhead.

21 Cookstove Trail

This is the shortest trail from the banks of Oak Creek to the rim of the canyon, and it offers unique views of upper Oak Creek Canyon.

Distance: 1.0 mile out and back
Hiking time: About 1 hour
Difficulty: Easy
Seasons: Spring through fall
Trail surface: Dirt and rocks
Water: None
Other trail users: None
Canine compatibility: Dogs under control allowed

Land status: Coconino National Forest
Fees and permits: None
Maps: Trails Illustrated Flagstaff and Sedona; USGS Mountainaire; Coconino National Forest
Trail contacts: Coconino National Forest, 1824 S. Thompson St., Flagstaff 86001; (928) 527-3600; fs.usda.gov/coconino

Finding the trailhead: From Sedona, drive about 13 miles north on AZ 89A to the north end of Pine Flat Campground; park along the highway. GPS: N35 0.868' / W111 44.263'

The Hike

The trail, which is not shown on the topographic map but is shown on the Trails Illustrated map, starts just north of the campground on the east side of the highway. It

A ponderosa pine snag near the Cookstove Trail

climbs directly up the ridge just south of Cookstove Draw. Although the trail is steep, it has been maintained in recent years and is in good shape. There are good views of upper Oak Creek Canyon, which is heavily forested with ponderosa pine, Gambel oak, and Douglas fir. Alligator junipers are also common and are easily identified by their bark, which is broken into deep squares like an alligator's hide. Some alligator junipers reach massive sizes. The trail, originally built for firefighting access, reaches the rim just south of Cookstove Draw.

Option

It's possible to hike south cross-country along the east rim of Oak Creek Canyon about 1.0 mile and descend back into Oak Creek Canyon via the Harding Spring Trail. The total one-way distance for this hike is 2.4 miles. The point where the Harding Spring Trail leaves the rim is obscure, so you should be familiar with the Harding Spring Trail before doing this option. You would also need to arrange a pickup or a shuttle vehicle at the Harding Spring Trailhead. GPS: N35 0.025' / W111 44.239'

Oak Creek Fault

Oak Creek Canyon cuts into the southern edge of the Colorado Plateau. Compared to the Central Mountains to the south, the Rocky Mountains to the east and north, and the Basin and Range Province to the west, the Colorado Plateau is relatively stable, geologically speaking. While mountains composed of igneous and volcanic rock have been raised up, tilted, and eroded all around it, the Colorado Plateau was raised 1 to 2 miles above sea level in a gentler fashion, preserving its generally sedimentary rocks in their horizontal positions. Mostly.

It's pretty unlikely that the mountain-building tectonic forces that lifted the plateau would act equally on the entire plateau, which covers parts of four states. Inevitably, some parts of the plateau were lifted higher and faster than others. And at time, parts of the plateau have sunk downward.

When large areas of rock move relative to other areas, something has to give. Rocks near the surface break and shatter along the zone of movement, which geologists call a "fault." Rocks on one side of the fault always move in the opposite direction to the rocks on the other side. The plane of movement can be vertical, tilted, or even horizontal.

Rocks that are buried far below the surface become plastic and flow like toothpaste under the influence of heat and pressure. Rather than breaking, the layers bend, often forming a "monocline," where the horizontal layers bend upward for dozens or hundreds of feet then level out at a higher level on the far side of the movement zone.

The Oak Creek Fault is a classic example of a vertical fault. From the Cookstove Trail or any of the creek-to-rim trails along Oak Creek Canyon, you can clearly see that the west rim of the canyon is hundreds of feet higher than the east rim. This is because movement along the Oak Creek Fault raised the rock layers on the west side

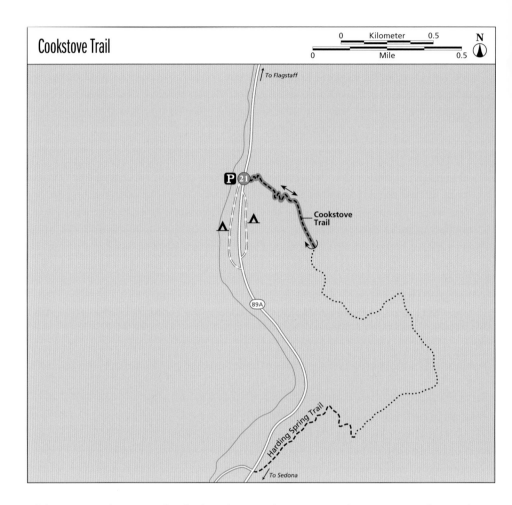

Cookstove Trail

To Flagstaff

P 21

Cookstove
Trail

89A

Harding Spring Trail

To Sedona

0 Kilometer 0.5
0 Mile 0.5
N

of the canyon about 500 feet higher than on the east rim. The movement shattered the rocks along the fault, creating a weak zone that water then exploited to carve out Oak Creek Canyon. That's why the canyon runs more or less straight south from its head to Wilson Mountain. The fault runs from the head of the canyon along the east side of Wilson Mountain.

Miles and Directions

0.0   Start at the trailhead just north of Pine Flat Campground.

0.5   Reach the east rim of Oak Creek Canyon; return the way you came.

1.0   Arrive back at the trailhead.

22 Pumphouse Wash

A cross-country hike through a narrow sandstone canyon near Oak Creek Canyon.

Distance: 6.2 miles out and back
Hiking time: About 4 hours
Difficulty: Moderate
Seasons: Spring through fall
Trail surface: Dirt and rocks
Water: Seasonal in Pumphouse Wash
Other trail users: None
Canine compatibility: Dogs under control allowed

Land status: Coconino National Forest
Fees and permits: None
Maps: Trails Illustrated Flagstaff and Sedona; USGS Mountainaire; Coconino National Forest
Trail contacts: Coconino National Forest, 1824 S. Thompson St., Flagstaff 86001; (928) 527-3600; fs.usda.gov/coconino

Finding the trailhead: From Flagstaff, drive south about 15 miles on AZ 89A. The highway descends into the canyon via a series of switchbacks then crosses the bridge over Pumphouse Wash. Park just south of the bridge at the pullout on the right. GPS: N35 1.470' / W111 44.163'

The Hike

From the highway pullout, drop down the bank into Oak Creek, then turn right and hike upstream cross-country. In just a few yards, Pumphouse Wash joins from the right. Most of the flow in Oak Creek comes from Sterling Spring, which is about 0.3 mile up Oak Creek. During summer and fall, Pumphouse Wash usually has little or no flow, but during spring snowmelt or after a summer thunderstorm, there may be so much water that this hike is impossible. Follow the wash upstream, under the highway bridge. Soon the canyon meanders around a couple of bends, and the sounds of the highway are left behind. The lower canyon walls here are composed of the buff-colored Coconino Sandstone. The rock was deposited as windblown sand dunes in a vast, Sahara-like desert. If you look closely at the rock, you can see the cross-bedded, sloping surfaces of the petrified sand dunes.

After a gentle curve to the right, followed by a straight section of about 0.5 mile, the canyon swings sharply left and heads northwest. Here the canyon is about 500 feet deep. In fall, the dark greens of the firs and pines growing in the canyon are supplemented by the bright yellows, oranges, and reds of the deciduous trees. Potholes carved in the sandstone bed of the canyon sometimes hold water. Now the canyon turns gradually north then sharply left again and becomes noticeably shallower. James Canyon enters from the right. Another 0.7 mile of straight canyon heading northwest ends with another sharp turn, this time to the right. This is the end of our hike.

The walk up Pumphouse Wash is off-trail, but the scenery is worth it.

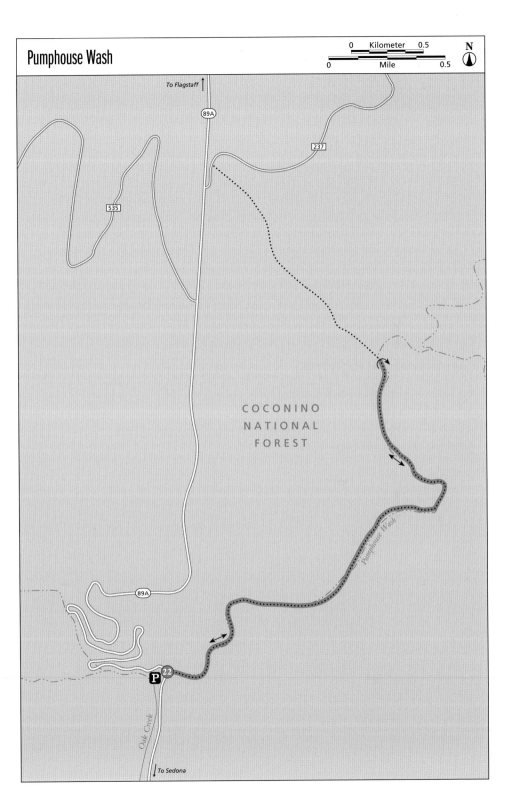

Pumphouse Wash

To Flagstaff

89A

237

535

COCONINO
NATIONAL
FOREST

Pumphouse Wash

89A

P 22

Oak Creek

To Sedona

Options

You can go northwest up a short side canyon from the end of the hike and reach AZ 89A near the FR 237 turnoff in 0.6 mile. Another option is to continue upstream from the end of the hike. Although Pumphouse Wash becomes less spectacular, it is a long canyon that has its headwaters just south of Flagstaff. In fact, Pumphouse Wash is the major drainage feeding Oak Creek Canyon.

Floods in Oak Creek

Pumphouse Wash is actually the true head of Oak Creek, and its headwaters are just south of Flagstaff. The Oak Creek watershed is small compared to Sycamore Canyon to the west along the rim, and the watershed is forested with ponderosa pines. Oak Creek experiences large floods every decade or so, usually when several inches of rain falls on ground already saturated by snowmelt or a previous rainstorm. Such floods have peaked at several thousand cubic feet per second, which is about the same as the historic low flows of the Colorado River in Grand Canyon. This is amazing in view of the relative sizes of their watersheds—the Colorado River has its headwaters in the Rocky Mountains of Wyoming and Colorado and drains much of the Colorado Plateau.

Miles and Directions

0.0 Start at the pullout south of Pumphouse Wash Bridge.

1.7 Come to the first sharp left bend.

3.1 The hike ends at the side canyon near the highway; return the way you came.

6.2 Arrive back at the trailhead.

Canyons

Sycamore Canyon is the next major canyon west of Oak Creek Canyon and is actually about four times longer than Oak Creek Canyon. Because it lies in a wilderness area and the canyon bottom is only accessible by trail, it is not nearly as well known or as crowded as the Sedona–Oak Creek area, but like Oak Creek, Sycamore Canyon has a perennial, spring-fed stream as well as colorful red rock formations and towering cliffs. A trail system provides access to portions of the wilderness, while other areas are only accessible by hiking cross-country.

Numerous smaller canyons cut into the Mogollon Rim between Sycamore and Oak Creek Canyons. Dry Creek and its tributaries form a network of canyons known locally as "Seven Canyons." Each of these canyons has a trail partway up it, though none of the trails climb all the way to the Mogollon Rim.

Two other canyons, Loy and Mooney, do feature trails that traverse their entire length and climb to the rim. The Mooney Trail offers a great view into the midsection of Sycamore Canyon. The Loy Trail provides access to the ponderosa forest on the rim and the network of trails atop Secret Mountain.

23 Devils Bridge

This easy trail ends at a natural arch set amid striking red rock scenery on the north side of Capitol Butte.

Distance: 1.4 miles out and back
Hiking time: About 1 hour
Difficulty: Easy
Seasons: Year round
Trail surface: Dirt and rocks
Water: None
Other trail users: Horses
Canine compatibility: Dogs under control allowed

Land status: Red Rock-Secret Mountain Wilderness, Coconino National Forest
Fees and permits: None
Maps: Trails Illustrated Flagstaff and Sedona; USGS Wilson Mountain; Coconino National Forest
Trail contacts: Coconino National Forest, 1824 S. Thompson St., Flagstaff 86001; (928) 527-3600; fs.usda.gov/coconino

Finding the trailhead: From Sedona, drive to the west end of town on AZ 89A, then turn right at a traffic light onto Dry Creek Road. After 2 miles turn right on dirt FR 152 (also called Dry Creek Road). Although this road is maintained, it receives a lot of traffic, and its condition varies. Drive 1.2 miles then turn right into the Devils Bridge Trailhead. Parking is limited, but there are other parking spots nearby. GPS: N34 54.179' / W111 48.839'

The Hike

On the first section of the walk, you'll parallel a wash as the trail follows a former jeep road. The well-used trail is easy to follow. Then the trail turns right and starts to climb the slope toward the imposing mass of Capitol Butte. It soon reaches a red sandstone ledge and works its way to the top via a series of stone steps. Follow the trail a few hundred feet east to the top of the bridge.

Is It an Arch or a Bridge?

Devils Bridge is technically a natural arch, since it doesn't span a stream course. The arch was formed by weathering of both sides of the narrow fin of sandstone. First, water erosion exploited a joint, or crack, in the rock that was parallel to the rim, separating the fin from the main ledge. Then, weathering of the natural cement holding the sand grains together caused the base of the fin to grow thinner. Finally, the fin was eroded completely though, and the arch was formed.

In contrast, a natural bridge forms where a stream running through a canyon erodes away the outside of a meander and eventually wears a hole through the narrow fin of rock, diverting the stream through the newly created shortcut. The stream doesn't have to be perennial—seasonal streams and normally dry washes are perfectly capable of creating natural bridges.

Devils Bridge is technically a natural arch, not a bridge, because it does not span a watercourse.

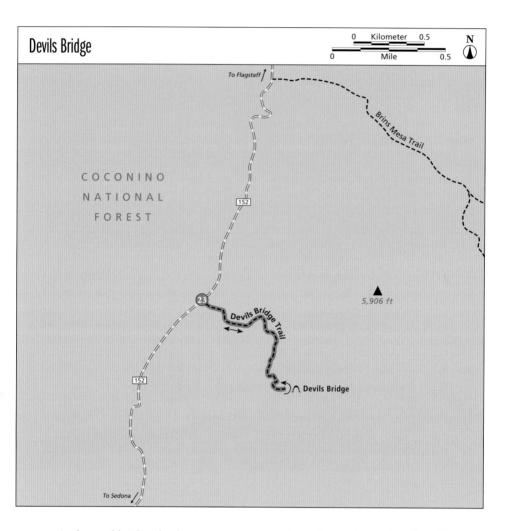

Arches and bridges both are most common in sandstone formations in arid country with few earthquakes, where watercourses are rapidly deepened by floodwaters. After formation, both natural bridges and arches continue to be enlarged by erosion, which causes pieces of rock to fall out of the underside of the span, Eventually, the remaining rock becomes too weak to support the span, and it collapses.

Several natural features in the Sedona area bear names starting with "Devil." The explanation is that before good trails and roads were built, the early cowboys and settlers found the area very difficult to travel in. Because of the roughness of the country and the striking red rocks, the pioneers called the area "Hells Hole" and named several features for the devil, including Devils Bridge, Devils Kitchen, and Devils Dining Room. The last two are natural sinkholes where an underlying limestone cavern collapsed, creating a natural pit.

What's in a Name?

Devils Bridge is on the north side of Capitol Butte, also known as Sugarloaf and Thunder Mountain. Which is correct? Technically, Capitol Butte. Both individual states and the federal government maintain databases of official place names. The US Board on Geographic Names maintains the federal place name database, the Geographic Names Information System (GNIS). Anyone can look up place names in the public database at geonames.usgs.gov/domestic. A search on that site confirms that the correct name is Capitol Butte and its elevation is 6,342 feet. The place names listed in GNIS are the place names used on official maps, including the USGS topo maps and the digital National Map. However, if you look at Capitol Butte on the USGS Wilson Mountain quad, its elevation is shown as 6,355 feet. Why the difference? GNIS is kept up to date with the latest survey data, while USGS topo maps are no longer being updated. So the elevation in GNIS represents the latest survey data.

Most of the red rock formations around Sedona do not have official names. Getting a place name approved takes a bit of time, and certain rules must be followed. For example, a natural feature can't be named for a living person.

Miles and Directions

0.0 Start at the Devils Bridge Trailhead.

0.4 The trail turns uphill.

0.7 Reach Devils Bridge; return the way you came.

1.4 Arrive back at the trailhead.

24 Brins Mesa

This is a mostly on-trail hike, with a short section of easy cross-country, to a very scenic viewpoint overlooking Sedona, Dry Creek, and the high cliffs of Wilson Mountain.

Distance: 5.8 miles out and back
Hiking time: About 3.5 hours
Difficulty: Easy
Seasons: Year-round
Trail surface: Dirt and rocks
Water: None
Other trail users: Horses
Canine compatibility: Dogs under control allowed

Land status: Red Rock–Secret Mountain Wilderness, Coconino National Forest
Fees and permits: None
Maps: Trails Illustrated Flagstaff and Sedona; USGS Wilson Mountain; Coconino National Forest
Trail contacts: Coconino National Forest, 1824 S. Thompson St., Flagstaff 86001; (928) 527-3600; fs.usda.gov/coconino

Finding the trailhead: From Sedona, drive to the west end of town on AZ 89A, then turn right at a traffic light onto Dry Creek Road. After 2 miles turn right on dirt FR 152 (also called Dry Creek Road). Although this road is maintained, it receives a lot of traffic, and its condition varies. Drive 2.2 miles then turn right into the trailhead parking area. Parking is limited, but there are other parking spots nearby. GPS: N34 55.007' / W111 48.511'

The Hike

A small metal sign at the east side of the parking area marks the start of the Brins Mesa Trail. About 1.1 miles from the trailhead, the unsigned Soldier Pass Trail turns right (south). Stay left on the Brins Mesa Trail. For nearly 2.0 miles the trail follows a normally dry wash, crossing the bed as necessary. The forest is mixed pinyon pine, juniper, and Arizona cypress, and views are limited until the trail climbs onto Brins Mesa. After crossing the flat mesa, the trail drops abruptly off the southeast side. Leave the trail here and go left, walking cross-country (there is actually a faint trail) along the southeast edge of the mesa. Brins Mesa tilts up to the northeast, and the view gets better as you continue. At the northeast end of the mesa, about 0.5 mile from the trail, work your way onto a red outcrop. This is the end of the hike, a point that offers close-up views of Wilson Mountain and the sandstone spires at the head of Mormon Canyon.

Return to the trail by walking directly down the center of the mesa, through the open meadow. You'll intercept the Brins Mesa Trail before you reach the end of the meadow; turn right (northwest) to return to the trailhead.

Looking toward Sedona from Brins Mesa

Option

The Brins Mesa Trail continues from the point where you left it, dropping into Mormon Canyon.

Layers upon Layers

At the viewpoint, you're standing on the Schnebly Hill Formation, which is responsible for most of the red sandstone cliffs and rock formations in the Sedona area. The impressive off-white cliffs above the red Schnebly Hill Formation on the west face of Wilson Mountain are formed from Coconino Sandstone. Usually, sedimentary rocks such as these are deposited underwater. But a close look at the Coconino Sandstone shows that it is cross-bedded on a fairly large scale. The Coconino Sandstone was once a dune field, part of a desert that was probably much like the present Sahara, and far from any water. As sand dunes move in the wind, sand blows up the windward face and then is deposited in sloping layers in the lee side. As the wind shifts, dunes are partially excavated by the wind and new sloping layers form in a different direction. The sloping cross-beds of the Coconino Sandstone are, literally, petrified sand dunes.

The clincher is that a microscopic look shows that the particles of sand that make up the Coconino Sandstone are round and fairly uniform in size, and their surfaces are pitted from being tumbled in the wind. In contrast, particles that have been tumbled in water are polished, not pitted.

Brins Mesa

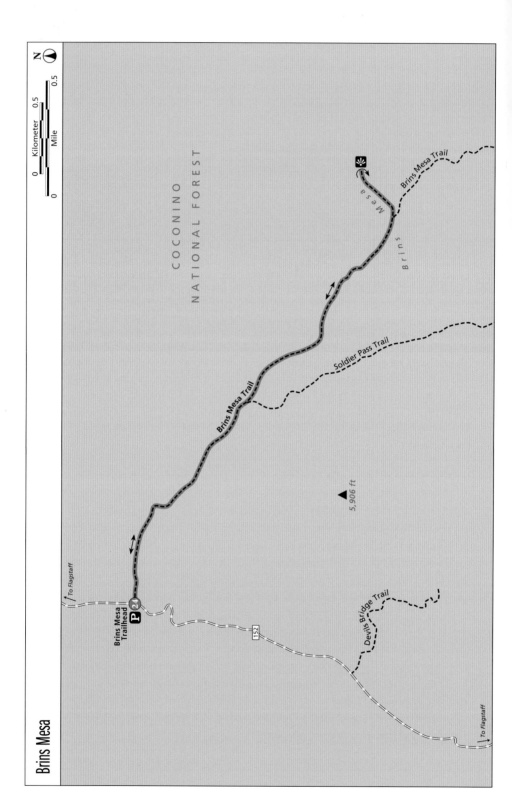

COCONINO

NATIONAL FOREST

Brins Mesa Trail

Soldier Pass Trail

Brins Mesa Trail

Mesa

Brins

5,906 ft

Brins Mesa Trailhead

P 2.4

To Flagstaff

152

Devils Bridge Trail

To Flagstaff

N

0   Kilometer   0.5

0   Mile   0.5

The Toroweap Formation and Kaibab Limestone lie above the Coconino Sand stone and are visible as bands of light-colored limestone. Both formations were deposited about 265 to 255 million years ago and represent a return to an environment of shallow seas and arid coastal plains. Like the rock formations below, the Kaibab and Toroweap Formations are present over much of the southwestern corner of the Colorado Plateau, including the Grand Canyon and the Mogollon Rim southeast of Sedona.

In the Oak Creek Canyon area, both formations are mostly limestone, which was deposited in a shallow sea. But elsewhere there are layers of siltstone, mudstone, shale, cross-bedded sandstone, and dolomite, showing that the shallow seas encroached on the area many times and then retreated. At various times, sediments were laid down in tidal flats then covered with coast sand dunes as the sea retreated.

Finally, if you look up at the rim of Wilson Mountain, you'll see gray layers of basalt rocks, which were the result of volcanic lava flows. The hard basalt protects the softer rocks below so that erosion by water has shaped Wilson Mountain into a flat-topped mesa. In contrast, look southwest at Capitol Butte. It lacks a basalt cap, and the soft Coconino Sandstone has eroded into a dome shape.

The lava flows that cap Wilson Mountain and parts of the Mogollon Rim above Sedona and Oak Creek Canyon came from the San Francisco volcanic field, which surrounds Flagstaff to the north. Some 800 volcanoes erupted starting several million years ago and continued until 1066 AD, when Sunset Crater, the last active volcano, erupted. Layers of basalt and other volcanic rocks lie on top of the sedimentary rocks in much of the country north of the Mogollon Rim.

Miles and Directions

0.0 Start at the trailhead by the small metal sign.

1.1 Intersect Soldiers Pass Trail; stay left.

2.4 Reach Brins Mesa.

2.9 Arrive at the viewpoint; return the way you came.

5.8 Arrive back at the trailhead.

This is an exceptionally fine hike up the longest canyon in the "Seven Canyons" area of the Dry Creek basin. Its length keeps the crowds away.

Distance: 7.8 miles out and back
Hiking time: About 5 hours
Difficulty: Moderate
Seasons: Year-round
Trail surface: Dirt and rocks
Water: Upper Secret Canyon
Other trail users: Horses
Canine compatibility: Dogs under control allowed

Land status: Red Rock–Secret Mountain Wilderness, Coconino National Forest
Fees and permits: None
Maps: Trails Illustrated Flagstaff and Sedona; USGS Wilson Mountain; Coconino National Forest
Trail contacts: Coconino National Forest, 1824 S. Thompson St., Flagstaff 86001; (928) 527-3600; fs.usda.gov/coconino

Finding the trailhead: From Sedona, drive to the west end of town on AZ 89A, then turn right at a traffic light onto Dry Creek Road. After 2 miles turn right on dirt FR 152 (also called Dry Creek Road). Although this road is maintained, it receives a lot of traffic, and its condition varies. Drive 3.2 miles to the Secret Canyon Trailhead on the left side of the road. The parking area is small, but there are other parking spots nearby. GPS: N34 55.803' / W111 48.401'

The Hike

Secret Canyon is the longest and most remote canyon in the Dry Creek Basin, and as nearly as long as its more famous neighbor, Oak Creek. It also has permanent water in the upper section, a rarity in the red rock area.

The Secret Canyon Trail crosses Dry Creek and enters the Red Rock–Secret Mountain Wilderness only a few yards from the road. You'll cross Secret Canyon wash several times; if either it or Dry Creek is flooding, this hike will be impossible. Normally, however, Secret Canyon is dry in the lower section, and the hike is easy through the pinyon-juniper-cypress forest. About 0.5 mile from the trailhead, the HS Canyon Trail branches left. The David Miller Trail comes in from the right at a small clearing with good views into upper Secret Canyon; stay left to continue on the Secret Canyon Trail.

Now the trail contours along the north side of the drainage for a short distance before dropping back into the bed. The canyon walls become narrower here and are formed by the Mogollon Rim on the north and Maroon Mountain on the south. There is normally water in this section. Watch for poison ivy, a low-growing plant with shiny leaves that grow in groups of three. Fall colors in this part of the canyon are a beautiful mix of reds, oranges, and violets, with most of the color provided by Arizona bigtooth maple and poison ivy. About 4.0 miles from the trailhead, our hike

Fall color in Secret Canyon

ends as the trail fades out. Only those willing to do difficult cross-country hiking should continue above this point.

Creating the Red Rock–Secret Mountain Wilderness

You may notice how wide the first portion of the trail is. In fact, it used to be a jeep trail before designation of the wilderness area. The American wilderness movement

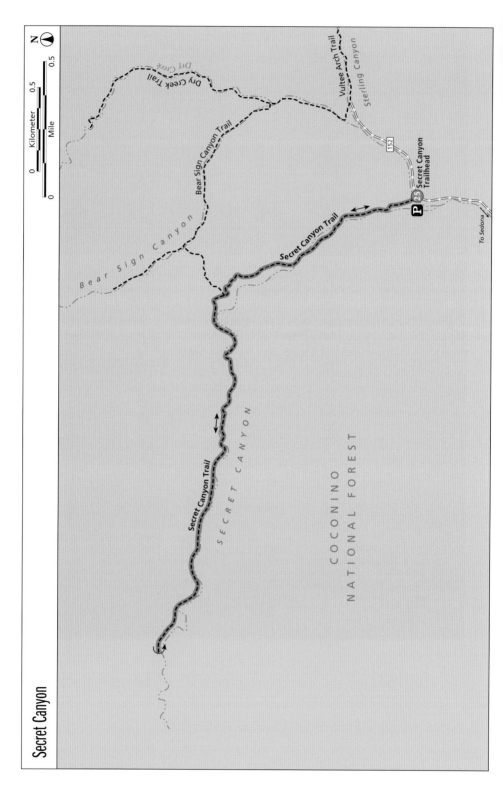

Secret Canyon

began in the 1930s, when Aldo Leopold and others began advocating that much of our nation's remaining pristine, roadless lands should be preserved in a wilderness state, with man-made improvements limited to trails and trail signs. The concept called for the highest level of protection for these lands, higher even than the "crown jewels" of America, the national parks. Development of roads, campgrounds, lodges, restaurants, and other amenities is allowed in national parks, but not in wilderness areas.

The USDA Forest Service responded by administratively designating some national forest land as "Primitive Areas." The first primitive areas in Arizona were Sycamore Canyon and Pine Mountain. Later, the Blue Range Primitive Area was designated in eastern Arizona and western New Mexico, along the far eastern Mogollon Rim.

The problem with primitive areas was that they were protected only administratively—any chief of the forest service could create or rescind them. So wilderness advocates lobbied the US Congress to pass a law protecting these wild areas. The Wilderness Society was created in 1934 specifically to work toward such a law. Along with other conservation groups, including the Sierra Club, wilderness advocates succeeded when Congress passed the Wilderness Act in 1964, creating the National Wilderness Preservation System. Most of the designated primitive areas in the national forests were immediately protected as Wilderness Areas.

Gradually, Congress added all the remaining primitive areas to the Wilderness System, until today only one primitive area remains, the portion of the Blue Range in Arizona. And this area is certainly deserving of wilderness protection.

The Wilderness Act also required that the National Park Service study the national parks and monuments under its jurisdiction, and today many national park and monument areas contain Wilderness Areas. Since the passage of the Wilderness Act, Wilderness Areas have also been created on lands managed by the Bureau of Land Management and the US Fish and Wildlife Service.

Three Wilderness Areas contain most of the hikes in this book—Sycamore Canyon Wilderness, created from the primitive area in 1964, and the Red Rock–Secret Mountain and Munds Mountain Wildernesses, both created in 1984.

From the Wilderness Act: "A wilderness, in contrast with those areas where man and his works dominate the landscape, is hereby recognized as an area where the earth and its community of life are untrammeled by man, where man himself is a visitor who does not remain."

Miles and Directions

0.0 Start at the Secret Canyon Trailhead.

1.8 Junction with David Miller Trail; stay left.

3.9 The trail ends in Secret Canyon; return the way you came.

7.8 Arrive back at the trailhead.

26 Vultee Arch

This is a pleasant and easy walk to a small but graceful natural arch below the ramparts of the Mogollon Rim.

Distance: 3.6 miles out and back
Hiking time: About 2.5 hours
Difficulty: Easy
Seasons: Year-round
Trail surface: Dirt and rocks
Water: None
Other trail users: Horses
Canine compatibility: Dogs under control allowed

Land status: Red Rock–Secret Mountain Wilderness, Coconino National Forest
Fees and permits: None
Maps: Trails Illustrated Flagstaff and Sedona; USGS Wilson Mountain; Coconino National Forest
Trail contacts: Coconino National Forest, 1824 S. Thompson St., Flagstaff 86001; (928) 527-3600; fs.usda.gov/coconino

Finding the trailhead: From Sedona, drive to the west end of town on AZ 89A, then turn right at a traffic light onto Dry Creek Road. After 2 miles turn right on dirt FR 152 (also called Dry Creek Road). Although this road is maintained, it receives a lot of traffic, and its condition varies. Drive 4 miles to the end of the road at the Dry Creek Trailhead. GPS: N34 56.235' / W111 47.662'

The Hike

Hike east on the Vultee Arch Trail, which follows Sterling Canyon. This is an easy walk though pleasant pinyon-juniper-cypress forest, and the canyon is nearly straight. After about 1.6 miles, right where Sterling Canyon takes a turn to the southeast, follow a trail left (north) out of the canyon bed to reach the arch.

Option
The trail up Sterling Canyon continues to its head, a pass overlooking Oak Creek Canyon. With a car shuttle, you can do a one-way hike to Oak Creek.

Sedona and Airplanes
Vultee Arch was named for the president of Vultee Aircraft, who was killed in a plane crash nearby in the 1930s.

At that time, the tiny village of Sedona didn't have an airport, and that was still true going into the 1950s. Pilots who wanted to fly for fun had to keep their aircraft at Cottonwood Airport. Around this time a few Sedona pilots had the idea that Table Mesa, the flat-topped mesa about a mile southwest of town, might be a site for a potential airport. Some of the pilots hiked up to the top of the mesa and paced out its length (there were no detailed maps of the area then) and reported that the top was nearly flat and just under a mile southwest to northeast.

By 1955, a dirt road had been built to the top of the mesa and a dirt strip constructed. But even a shower, let alone snow-melt, was enough to turn the dirt strip into a quagmire, so the runway was paved. Since then, the airport facilities have continued to grow to match the growth in air traffic. From about 1985 to 1995, Sedona Airport offered scheduled flights to Phoenix's Sky Harbor Airport, peaking at five round-trips daily in the 1990s.

Several helicopter and airplane tour companies operate out of Sedona, taking people on scenic flights around the red rocks and to other scenic destinations, including Grand Canyon and Monument Valley.

Sedona Airport is a popular destination for pilots based in the greater Phoenix area. Looking for any excuse to fly their planes, they come in droves almost every weekend and holiday to eat at the airport restaurant or head into Sedona to shop or hike.

Fall color in a hidden canyon under the Mogollon Rim

In parallel with the airport's growth, the city of Sedona has grown to surround Airport Mesa, as Table Mesa is now called, on all sides. Some residents have complained about the airport noise, but they need to consider two things: The airport was there before the town expanded around the mesa, and the airport is a major economic contributor to Sedona.

The USDA Forest Service, which administers the three wilderness areas that include most of the red rock country around Sedona, does not have jurisdiction over the airspace. However, aeronautical charts do show the wilderness boundaries, and the Forest Service asks that pilots voluntarily avoid flying lower than 2,000 feet above the highest parts of the wilderness.

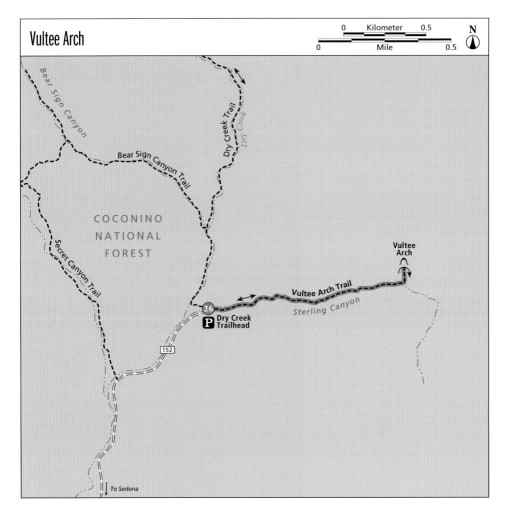

Miles and Directions

0.0 Start at the Dry Creek Trailhead

1.6 Turn left on the trail to Vultee Arch.

1.8 Reach Vultee Arch; return the way you came.

3.6 Arrive back at the trailhead.

27 Dry Creek

This is a demanding cross-country hike to the Mogollon Rim at the headwaters of Dry Creek.

Distance: 7.0 miles out and back
Hiking time: About 6 hours
Difficulty: Strenuous
Seasons: Year-round
Trail surface: Dirt and rocks
Water: Seasonal in Dry Creek
Other trail users: Horses
Canine compatibility: Dogs under control allowed

Land status: Red Rock–Secret Mountain Wilderness, Coconino National Forest
Fees and permits: None
Maps: Trails Illustrated Flagstaff and Sedona; USGS Wilson Mountain; Coconino National Forest
Trail contacts: Coconino National Forest, 1824 S. Thompson St., Flagstaff 86001; (928) 527-3600; fs.usda.gov/coconino

Finding the trailhead: From Sedona, drive to the west end of town on AZ 89A, then turn right at a traffic light onto Dry Creek Road. After 2 miles, turn right on dirt FR 152 (also called Dry Creek Road). Although this road is maintained, it receives a lot of traffic, and its condition varies. Drive 4 miles to the end of the road at the Dry Creek Trailhead. GPS: N34 56.235' / W111 47.662'

The Hike

Follow the Dry Creek Trail north out of the parking area. After 0.6 mile Bear Sign Canyon branches left; continue north on the trail along Dry Creek. The informal trail fades out after a while, and this makes a good destination for an easy day hike.

Hiking in a golden glow along upper Dry Creek

You'll need the topographic map for the remainder of this hike. Continue cross-country up the bed of Dry Creek. As the canyon heads against the impressive cliffs and ramparts of the Mogollon Rim, the canyon itself opens up a bit. Looking east, you'll see glimpses of brushy ridges descending from the rim, which offer the possibility of a route. Turn right (east) up the side canyon that enters Dry Creek just below the 5,600-foot contour on the topographic map. Follow this side canyon until it becomes difficult to continue, then turn right (southeast) and continue up the brushy ridge to reach the Mogollon Rim. This is the destination for our hike.

Option

An option that requires a car shuttle links this hike with the AB Young Trail into Oak Creek Canyon. To do this, walk cross-country north through the rim forest to FR 231, then turn right to reach East Pocket Knob. There is a forest fire lookout tower on the top of this hill. From here you can follow the AB Young Trail east to the rim and down to Oak Creek.

Mogollon Rim

The Mogollon Rim runs from west to east across Arizona, marking the southern edge of the Colorado Plateau and the northern extent of the Central Mountains. The western Mogollon Rim and the Sedona area are arguably the most spectacular piece of the rim, combining red rock buttes, towering white cliffs, and deep canyons with permanent streams into a really special mix. The central and eastern Mogollon Rim are certainly impressive, but nowhere else do all of the Sedona features appear together.

So why here? The answer lies in the drainage pattern. From Sycamore Canyon west of Sedona to Fossil Creek to the southeast, the Colorado Plateau north of the rim drains toward the rim—that is, south and southeast—into the Verde River. East of Fossil Creek, toward Payson and beyond, the plateau north of the rim slopes northward, draining northward into the Little Colorado River and ultimately into the Colorado River in the depths of the eastern Grand Canyon. The rim itself is the watershed divide, and although drainage south of the rim is into the Verde and Salt Rivers, it does not cut canyons deep into the plateau north of the rim.

The key factor lies in how water erodes the landscape. Since water flows downhill under the influence of gravity, always seeking the lowest level, the sea, it erodes the land by carrying away soil, silt, and sand. These in turn act as a watery rasp, chewing away at solid rock. Water also chemically dissolves rock, especially limestone.

Water flows more quickly the steeper the slope, and water's ability to carry debris goes up with the cube of its velocity. This means that water rushing down the steep slopes found in canyon heads has many times the carrying capacity of streams meandering down a gently sloping valley. In fact, floods that start in the headwaters of a canyon system often contain more debris—in the form and sand, rocks, and even boulders—than water. This means that the heads of canyons erode far faster than the lower portions.

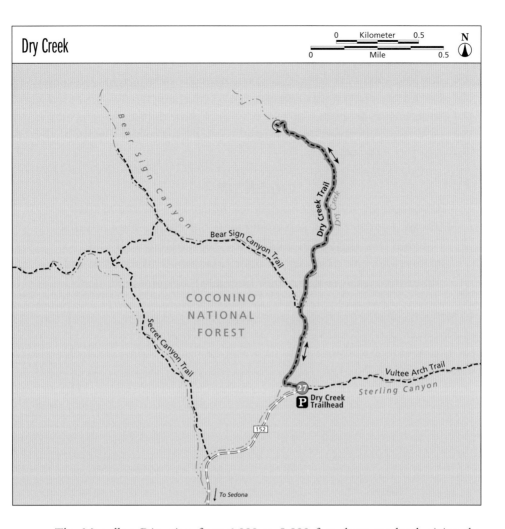

The Mogollon Rim rises from 6,000 to 9,000 feet above sea level, giving the rain that falls on it, as well as snowmelt, immense power to erode out canyons. East of Fossil Creek, several major canyon systems are cut into the northern slopes of the Mogollon Rim, but since the headwaters are gently sloped, the canyons and their tributaries are just a few hundred feet deep.

In the Sedona area, the canyons run more than 1,000 feet deep, and their headwaters are steep. These canyons and their tributaries have cut the rim into sharp relief. In fact, the pinnacles, buttes, and mesas around Sedona are the remnants of the Mogollon Rim after canyon-cutting sliced and diced, leaving only isolated pieces.

Another factor is that some of the sedimentary rock layers found in the Sedona area either don't occur elsewhere along the rim or aren't as thick elsewhere. The Coconino Sandstone becomes much thinner to the east, and the Schnebly Hill Formation is unique to the Sedona area.

Miles and Directions

0.0   Start at the Dry Creek Trailhead.

0.6   Bear Sign Canyon Trail branches left; continue north along Dry Creek.

1.1   Start the cross-country portion of the hike.

2.7   Turn right, up a side canyon.

3.5   Reach Mogollon Rim; return the way you came.

7.0   Arrive back at the trailhead.

GREEN TIP

Rechargeable (reusable) batteries reduce one source of toxic garbage. For day hikes, just make sure you charge the batteries in your flashlight or headlamp the night before your hike. Backpackers can use a lightweight solar panel attached to the lid of their pack to keep their headlamp batteries charged.

28 Bear Sign Canyon

A very easy hike into a red rock canyon below the ramparts of the Mogollon Rim.

Distance: 7.6 miles out and back
Hiking time: About 2 hours
Difficulty: Moderate
Seasons: Year-round
Trail surface: Dirt and rocks
Water: Seasonal in Bear Sign Canyon
Other trail users: Horses
Canine compatibility: Dogs under control allowed

Land status: Red Rock–Secret Mountain Wilderness, Coconino National Forest
Fees and permits: None
Maps: Trails Illustrated Flagstaff and Sedona; USGS Wilson Mountain; Coconino National Forest
Trail contacts: Coconino National Forest, 1824 S. Thompson St., Flagstaff 86001; (928) 527-3600; fs.usda.gov/coconino

Finding the trailhead: From Sedona, drive to the west end of town on AZ 89A, then turn right at a traffic light onto Dry Creek Road. After 2 miles turn right on dirt FR 152 (also called Dry Creek Road). Although this road is maintained, it receives a lot of traffic, and its condition varies. Drive 4 miles to the end of the road at the Dry Creek Trailhead. GPS: N34 56.235' / W111 47.662'

The Hike

Start out on the Dry Creek Trail. (Two trails begin at this trailhead. The Dry Creek Trail goes north; the Vultee Arch Trail goes east.) Hike 0.6 mile north, then turn left (northwest) at Bear Sign Canyon, the first side canyon on the left. There are some fine stands of Arizona cypress, especially along the first section of the trail.

The David Miller Trail joins from the left; our hike continues straight ahead, up the canyon. The trail continues about 1.0 mile up Bear Sign Canyon before fading out. It is possible to go farther, but the canyon becomes much rougher. There are great views of the cliffs of the Mogollon Rim, and after wet periods, the creek will be running. The vegetation is the usual, but still delightful, mix of Arizona cypress, pinyon pine, juniper trees, and chaparral brush.

Notice how Arizona cypress tends to favor places with more moisture, such as the canyon bottom and north-facing slopes. Chaparral brush, on the other hand, likes drier areas, such as south-facing slopes.

It's a Bear of a Problem

Black bears used to be more common than they are now. They are generally shy of people and are found primarily in wooded areas in Arizona, both pinyon-juniper woodland and ponderosa pine forest. In areas such as the Santa Catalina, Rincon, and Chiricahua Mountains of southeast Arizona, black bears have become accustomed to people and their food, and thus have become a nuisance. If you are lucky enough to see a black bear, don't even think about giving it a treat. You'd be doing the bear and yourself no favor.

Grizzly bears used to roam most of Arizona, including Sycamore Canyon, Oak Creek Canyon, and the Mogollon Rim but were hunted to extinction in the state by about 1935. As ranchers and sheepmen moved into Arizona in the second half of the nineteenth century, predators were perceived as a threat to the developing industry. Coyotes, Mexican gray wolves, and mountain lions were hunted relentlessly. As the top predator, grizzlies were probably blamed for more than their share of livestock losses. But it didn't take proof to find predators guilty. Any dead domesticated animal was usually blamed on a wild animal attack. Predators were regarded as troublesome "varmints," and killing as many as possible was considered a good thing. By the 1930s, even the federal government was killing as many predators as possible, under the guise of "wildlife control."

As a result, grizzlies and Mexican gray wolves (the native Southwestern wolf) were hunted to extinction within Arizona, and foxes and mountain lion numbers were greatly reduced. Only the coyote, whom the Navajo call the "trickster," was canny enough to not only survive but actually increase its range and numbers. Even today, coyotes can be seen trotting cautiously down streets in the middle of Phoenix.

The result of all this aggressive predator control was a disaster. Without their natural predators, so-called "game animals" multiplied and literally ate themselves out of house and home. The North Kaibab deer herd is the infamous example. President Theodore Roosevelt established the Grand Canyon Game Preserve in 1905, primarily to protect and increase the Kaibab deer herd. Hunting was stopped and aggressive predator control began. It's estimated that between 1907 and 1939, 816 mountain lions, 20 wolves, 7,388 coyotes, and more than 500 bobcats were killed. Without predators to cull the herd, the deer population exploded—from an estimated 4,000 deer to as many as 100,000. The exact numbers are uncertain because systematic counting was not done, but the results were obvious. The deer population outran the amount of forage available, and deer began to starve. By the late 1920s, the health of the Kaibab deer population was declining. You can still see the results today. The Kaibab deer are stunted compared to mule deer herds elsewhere, and even from AZ 67, which traverses the plateau to the North Rim of Grand Canyon, you can see the browse line in aspen groves where the deer have eaten everything they can reach.

Now that the role of predators in the ecology is better understood, steps are being taken. Arizona no longer places a bounty on predators—instead managing them as game animals—and the Mexican gray wolf has been reintroduced successfully along the eastern Mogollon Rim in Arizona and New Mexico. Recently the wolf recovery area was expanded to include the central Mogollon Rim, and advocates are pushing for wolves to be reintroduced to the western rim and the Kaibab Plateau.

Lunch break on the red rocks above Bear Sign Canyon

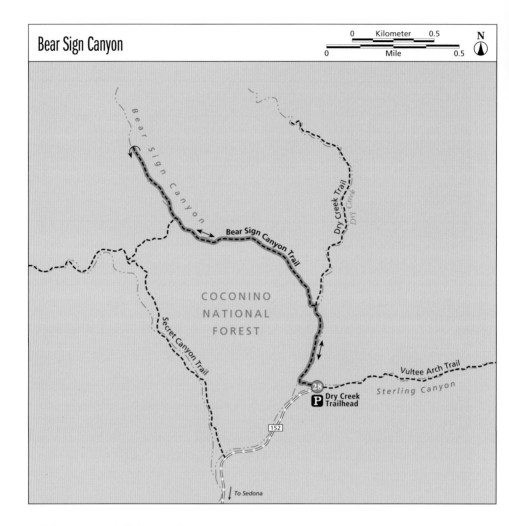

Bear Sign Canyon

Miles and Directions

0.0 Start at the Dry Creek Trailhead.

0.6 Turn left on the Bear Sign Canyon Trail.

2.8 Intersect the David Miller Trail on the left; continue straight on Bear Sign Canyon Trail.

3.8 The hike ends as the trail fades out; return the way you came.

7.6 Arrive back at the trailhead.

29 Long Canyon

A easy walk up a less-visited canyon in the Dry Creek basin below the Mogollon Rim.

Distance: 4.8 miles out and back
Hiking time: About 3 hours
Difficulty: Easy
Seasons: Year-round
Trail surface: Dirt and rocks
Water: None
Fees and permits: None
Other trail users: Horses
Canine compatibility: Dogs under control allowed

Land status: Red Rock-Secret Mountain Wilderness, Coconino National Forest
Fees and permits: None
Maps: Trails Illustrated Flagstaff and Sedona; USGS Wilson Mountain; Coconino National Forest
Trail contacts: Coconino National Forest, 1824 S. Thompson St., Flagstaff 86001; (928) 527-3600; fs.usda.gov/coconino

Finding the trailhead: From Sedona, drive to the west end of town on AZ 89A, then turn right at the traffic light onto Dry Creek Road. Continue 2.8 miles, then turn right onto Long Canyon Road. Drive 0.6 mile to the trailhead parking, on the left. (The road continues to a private subdivision.) GPS: N34 54.399' / W111 49.453'

The Hike

Like several other hikes in the Dry Creek area, this trail starts out as an old jeep trail. The mouth of Long Canyon is more than a mile from the trailhead, so the first section of the hike is through open pinyon-juniper flats, with tantalizing views of the canyon walls ahead, as well as Mescal Mountain to the south. As you pass the north tip of Mescal Mountain, you'll reach the wilderness boundary and the junction with the Deadman Pass Trail.

The canyon walls gradually close in as you continue, and the trail starts to fade out. It's possible to continue the hike cross-country, and also to explore several side canyons. If you end the hike when the trail fades out, you'll be turning back about 2.4 miles from the trailhead.

Whose Joint Is This?

Erosion along faults and joints is largely responsible for the pattern of erosion in the red rock country. A fault is a break in the rock caused by movement on one or both sides of the fault relative to the other. The movement weakens and shatters the rocks, providing a ready path for erosion.

Joints, on the other hand, are stress fractures that mainly occur as rock layers are exposed by the erosion and removal of overlying layers of rock. Deeply buried rock layers are under extreme pressure, and as the rocks above are worn away, the release of pressure causes the rock to fracture along even planes, resulting in joints. The

Gray foxes are not nearly as common as coyotes.

giveaway that you're dealing with a joint rather than a fault is the lack of movement of the rocks on either side of the joint.

Joints are far more common than faults and tend to run at right angles to each other. As erosion in the form of water, ice, and even plant roots exploits the weakness of a joint, massive rock layers are carved into isolated mesas, buttes, and pinnacles.

Next time you walk over a fairly level slab of exposed rock, watch for plants growing in straight lines across the bare rock. These plants are taking advantage of the joint as a place to put down roots. As water erodes joints, soil forms and takes advantage of the water that tends to collect in joints to encourage plants.

Plateaus, Mesas, Buttes, and Pinnacles

These four terms are often used interchangeably, but they are defined differently in the science of geomorphology—the study of landforms and how they evolve.

A plateau is a flat-topped, elevated landform that is many times wider than it is high. The Colorado Plateau is actually a poor example, because it is one of the largest plateaus in the world.

A mesa is always wider than it is high, and a butte is taller than it is wide. If you remember that "mesa" is the Spanish word for "table," you'll be able to remember the difference.

Finally, a pinnacle or spire is much taller than it is wide. There are several unnamed pinnacles on either side of the trail as you enter Long Canyon. At the end of the hike, you're looking up at the flat-topped summit of Secret Mountain, which, because it is much wider than it is high, is a mesa.

To the north, Maroon Mountain is definitely a butte, although not a very flat-topped one. East of Sedona, Munds and Lee Mountains are definitely mesas.

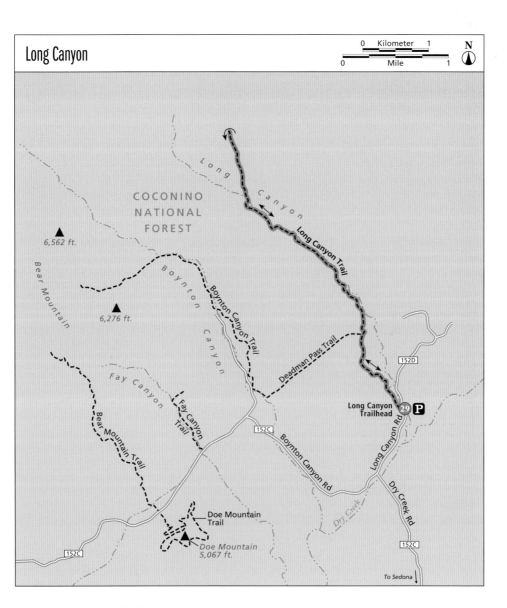

0   Kilometer   1

0   Mile   1

N

COCONINO
NATIONAL
FOREST

6,562 ft.

Long Canyon

Long Canyon Trail

Bear Mountain

Boynton Canyon Trail

6,276 ft.

Boynton Canyon

Deadman Pass Trail

152D

Fay Canyon

Long Canyon
Trailhead   29   P

Bear Mountain Trail

Fay Canyon Trail

152C

Boynton Canyon Rd

Long Canyon Rd

Doe Mountain
Trail

Dry Creek

Dry Creek Rd

152C

Doe Mountain
5,067 ft.

152C

To Sedona

Miles and Directions

0.0 Start at the Long Canyon Trailhead.

1.0 Pass junction with Deadman Pass Trail.

2.4 The trail fades out; return the way you came.

4.8 Arrive back at the trailhead.

30 Boynton Canyon

This very popular hike into a spectacular red rock canyon heads below the towering cliffs of Bear Mountain.

Distance: 5.0 miles out and back
Hiking time: About 3 hours
Difficulty: Moderate
Seasons: Year-round
Trail surface: Dirt and rocks
Water: None
Other trail users: None
Canine compatibility: Dogs under control allowed

Land status: Red Rock-Secret Mountain Wilderness, Coconino National Forest
Fees and permits: None
Maps: Trails Illustrated Flagstaff and Sedona; USGS Wilson Mountain; Coconino National Forest
Trail contacts: Coconino National Forest, 1824 S. Thompson St., Flagstaff 86001; (928) 527-3600; fs.usda.gov/coconino

Finding the trailhead: From Sedona, drive to the west end of town on AZ 89A, then turn right at the traffic light onto Dry Creek Road. Continue 2.8 miles and turn left onto Boynton Canyon Road. Drive 1.6 miles; turn right, remaining on Boynton Canyon Road. Go 0.3 mile and park at the Boynton Canyon Trailhead, on the right. If you reach the entrance to a private resort, you've gone too far. GPS: N34 54.441' / W111 50.905'

The Hike

This popular hike skirts a large resort for its first mile, so don't expect a wilderness experience.

The Boynton Canyon Trail climbs along the north side of the canyon to avoid the resort, then drops into the canyon. Here a spur trail to the resort joins from the left. Now the Boynton Canyon Trail follows the drainage to the northwest. In another 0.5 mile or so, both the canyon and the trail turn toward the southwest, and the noises of the resort are left behind. The head of the canyon is formed by massive walls of Coconino Sandstone on the east face of Bear Mountain. The trail becomes fainter near the end as it winds through cool pine-fir forest. A final short climb leads out of the dense forest to a viewpoint on the brushy slope above. Allow some time to linger here—this is a fine spot.

Ranches and Resorts

The resort that the first part of the trail skirts was originally a private ranch that dated back to the homestead days. Up until the start of the twentieth century, the federal government, which by default owns all land not deeded to states or Native American tribes, allowed settlers to claim various amounts of land in return for living on it and making certain improvements.

Cactus blooms in late spring.

Originally homesteaded by John Boeington, the ranch passed through several owners until it was finally bought by tennis player John Gardiner in 1987. The previous owners had all allowed hikers access on the original trail through the ranch property, but when Gardiner started developing Enchantment Resort, access was closed off. The USDA Forest Service eventually built the present bypass trail, which starts from a new trailhead and skirts the private property on the north side.

Land and Water Conservation Fund

Loss of access to public land because of the development of private land is an ongoing problem throughout the West. Several historic trails have been lost in the Sedona area because there is no public access. For example, the Purtymun Trail used to climb the east slopes of Oak Creek Canyon above Junipine Resort, but now there is no access for trail workers and hikers because of the resort.

Most federal land management agencies are allowed to buy private inholdings within national forests, parks, and monuments, but agencies rarely have the budget to do so. Sometimes an agency can trade a piece of federal land that is outside designated unit boundaries for an inholding.

Enter the Land and Water Conservation Fund. This landmark law, passed in 1965, uses fees collected from offshore oil and gas drilling to fund land purchases and recreation projects in national forests, national monuments, national parks, and wildlife refuges. In addition, grants are made to states, counties, and cities for recreation projects such as national scenic trails and urban trails and parks.

Since its inception, the LWCF has had a built-in expiration date, and Congress has allowed the law to expire several times—most recently in October 2018. But as I write this, Congress has passed a bill that permanently reauthorizes the LWCF, a huge victory for conservationists.

Cliffs and Terraces

At the end of the trail, the head of Boynton Canyon is surrounded by towering cliffs formed from the Coconino Sandstone, the Toroweap Formation, and the Kaibab Limestone. Why is the head of this canyon so sheer, while along Oak Creek Canyon and other places around the red rock country, the canyon walls consist of alternating cliffs and terraces?

It's mostly because of the different kinds of rock that make up the layers. Hard rocks such as sandstone and limestone form cliffs, while soft rocks such as shale, siltstone, and mudstone erode into slopes. As they erode, the soft rocks undermine the cliffs above, causing large pieces to break off—a process called "spalling." As the cliffs retreat, that in turn exposes more of the soft rocks to the effects of erosion.

The Coconino Sandstone tends to form cliffs because it is a monolithic, nearly pure sandstone formation more than 400 feet thick in the Sedona area. The Toroweap Formation and the Kaibab Limestone, in comparison, tend to have some soft layers of shale in between the hard limestone and sandstone layers. At the head of Boynton Canyon, both the Toroweap and Kaibab appear to have less in the way of shale and greater thicknesses of hard limestone and sandstone. The result is that these two formations form nearly sheer cliffs above the Coconino, making for an impressive effect.

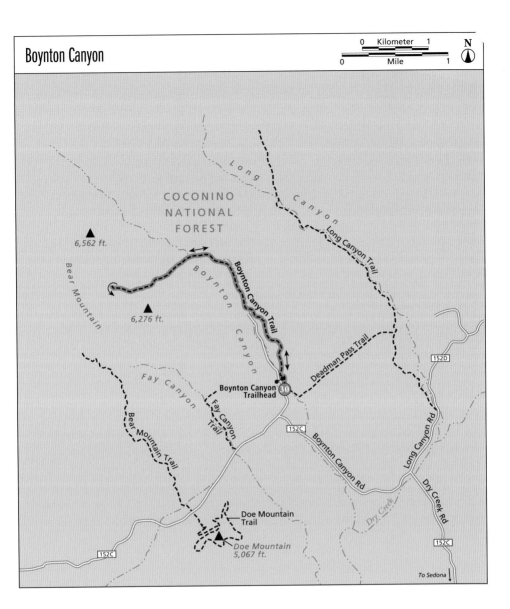

Miles and Directions

0.0   Start at the Boynton Canyon Trailhead.

1.0   Pass a spur trail to the resort.

2.5   The trail ends below Bear Mountain; return the way you came.

5.0   Arrive back at the trailhead.

This is a very easy hike to a hidden natural arch, tucked up high on the north canyon wall.

Distance: 1.6 miles out and back
Hiking time: About 1 hour
Difficulty: Easy
Seasons: Year-round
Trail surface: Dirt and rocks
Water: None
Other trail users: Horses
Canine compatibility: Dogs under control allowed

Land status: Red Rock–Secret Mountain Wilderness, Coconino National Forest
Fees and permits: None
Maps: Trails Illustrated Flagstaff and Sedona; USGS Wilson Mountain; Coconino National Forest
Trail contacts: Coconino National Forest, 1824 S. Thompson St., Flagstaff 86001; (928) 527-3600; fs.usda.gov/coconino

Finding the trailhead: From Sedona, drive to the west end of town on AZ 89A, then turn right at a traffic light onto Dry Creek Road. Drive 2.8 miles and turn left onto Boynton Canyon Road. Continue 1.6 miles, then turn left onto FR 152C. Go 0.5 mile to the Fay Canyon Trailhead, on the right. GPS: N34 54.113' / W111 51.434'

The Hike

The Fay Canyon Trail starts out as an easy walk through pinyon-juniper forest along a former jeep road. The only difficulty is a few false trails near the beginning. About 0.6 mile from the trailhead, watch for an unmarked trail going right (northeast) toward the canyon wall. This trail climbs steeply about 0.2 mile to Fay Canyon Arch, which is difficult to see until you are very close. Formed from a massive fin in the Schnebly Hill Formation, the arch stands close to the cliff behind it so that little skylight shines through.

Option

It is also worthwhile to continue on the main trail up Fay Canyon. It fades out about 1.0 miles from the trailhead, at a fork in the canyon, so this side trip would add 2.0 miles to the hike.

Talus

From Fay Canyon Arch looking toward the mouth of the canyon, you'll notice that the lower slopes below the cliffs lie at a fairly steep angle. These slopes are known as talus and are made up mostly of rock fragments that have broken off the cliffs above and tumbled down the slope until coming to rest. The talus slope tends to form at its "angle of repose," the steepest angle that the rocks can rest and be stable. Any steeper and the talus would slide into the canyon bottom as a rockslide.

Looking at Bear Mountain through Fay Canyon Arch

Talus tends to form in high mountains and in arid climates like Arizona. In moist climates, talus weathers rapidly into soil, which then supports dense plant life, which in turn anchors the slope. In high mountains above timberline, often the only plant that grows on talus is lichen, so alpine talus tends to be unstable. In Arizona's desert climate, talus can be either bare or anchored with some plant life, as it is in lower Fay

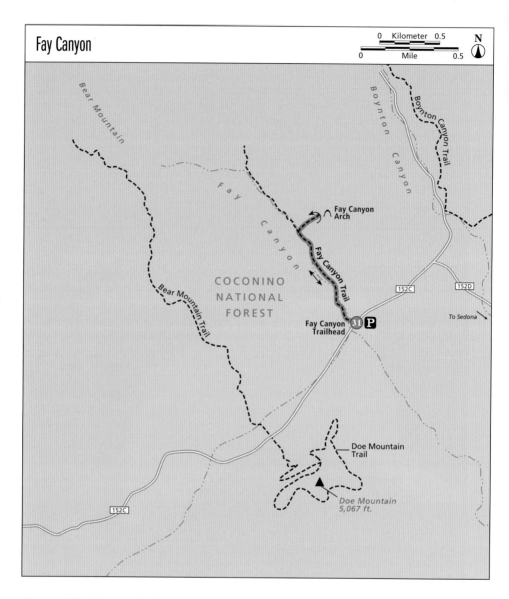

Canyon. The slopes of Oak Creek Canyon are composed of typical Arizona talus and are mostly covered with chaparral. In a few places, there are bare talus slopes.

Miles and Directions

0.0 Start at the Fay Canyon Trailhead.

0.6 Come to the arch turnoff.

0.8 Reach Fay Canyon Arch; return the way you came.

1.6 Arrive back at the trailhead.

32 Doe Mountain

The top of Doe Mountain is easy to reach and features fine views of Bear Mountain and the Dry Creek basin.

Distance: 2.8 miles on-trail and cross-country lollipop
Hiking time: About 2 hours
Difficulty: Easy
Seasons: Year-round
Trail surface: Dirt and rocks
Water: None
Other trail users: Mountain bikes and horses
Canine compatibility: Dogs under control allowed

Land status: Coconino National Forest
Fees and permits: None
Maps: Trails Illustrated Flagstaff and Sedona; USGS Wilson Mountain; Coconino National Forest
Trail contacts: Coconino National Forest, 1824 S. Thompson St., Flagstaff 86001; (928) 527-3600; fs.usda.gov/coconino

Finding the trailhead: From Sedona, drive to the west end of town on AZ 89A, then turn right at a traffic light onto Dry Creek Road. Drive 2.8 miles and turn left onto Boynton Canyon Road. Continue 1.6 miles, then turn left onto FR 152C. Go 1.3 miles to the Bear Mountain Trailhead. GPS: N34 53.595' / W111 51.903'

The Hike

Doe Mountain is the flat red mesa to the southwest. Cross the road and walk up the Doe Mountain Trail, which starts as an old jeep road heading directly toward a large ravine splitting the northwest side of the mesa. After a few hundred yards the trail becomes a foot trail and turns right as the slope becomes steeper. A single long switchback takes the trail back into the ravine, which it climbs to reach the rim of Doe Mountain. The trail ends; now turn right and follow the rim cross-country. The walk is easy and nearly level along mostly bare sandstone ledges, and the reward is a series of views in all directions. Rejoin the trail to return to the trailhead.

Seven Canyons

Most of the hikes in this book are in canyons, but a few lead to high points with scenic views. Doe Mountain only rises a few hundred feet above the surrounding terrain, but its position as an isolated small mesa provides great views of the Dry Creek Basin. Also known locally as "Seven Canyons," the Dry Creek Basin got its nickname from the fact that there are seven major canyons cutting back into the Mogollon Rim, all drained by Dry Creek. Dry Creek ultimately runs past the west end of Airport Mesa then joins Oak Creek just upstream of Red Rock State Park.

From east to west, the seven canyons are Sterling Canyon, Dry Creek, Bear Sign Canyon, Secret Canyon, Long Canyon, Boynton Canyon, and Fay Canyon. There are no constructed trails from the Dry Creek Basin to the Mogollon Rim at present, although there certainly could have been trails built by the first settlers. The Native Americans who lived in the area before the European settlers arrive almost certainly had routes to the rim.

When the Doe Mountain Trail reaches the rim of Doe Mountain, look back the way you came. Bear Mountain dominates the view to the northwest. The last outlier of a rugged ridge that connects north to the Mogollon Rim, Bear Mountain is separated by a deep, cliff-bound notch from Lost Mountain, which is in turn separated by a deep notch from Secret Mountain. In turn, Secret Mountain is separated from the Mogollon Rim by the saddle between Loy and Secret Canyons. A good trail runs up Loy Canyon to this saddle and joins the Secret Mountain Trail, which climbs a short distance north to the rim and the Secret Mountain Trailhead.

Still looking northwest and just to the right of Bear Mountain, you're looking almost into Fay Canyon, but the arch is very difficult to pick out unless the light is just right.

As you start the walk south along the rim of Doe Mountain, you'll get some great views of the Verde Valley.

As you round the south tip of Doe Mountain, you can see a small isolated red rock butte to the south, the Cockscomb. From Doe Mountain, it's hard to see how the Cockscomb got it name, but it's obvious from the east or west. The area around the Cockscomb and Doe Mountain is very popular with mountain bikers, since it's not in the Red Rock–Secret Mountain Wilderness and bicycles are legal.

Along the rim of Doe Mountain—an easy cross-country hike with superb views

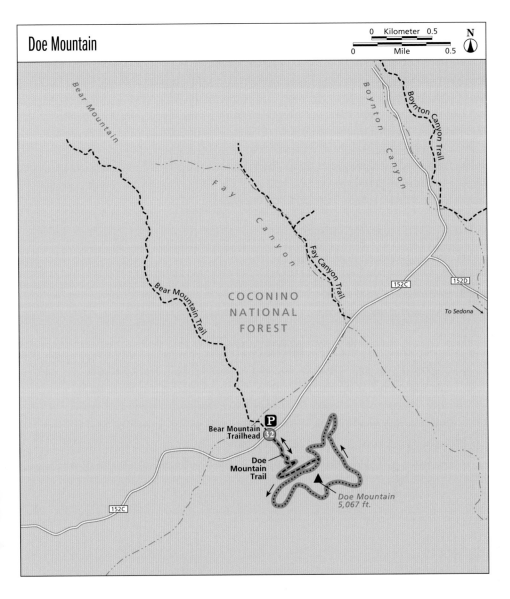

As you round the eastern side of Doe Mountain, Capitol Butte dominates the view to the east. From this angle, it's easy to see why some locals call it Sugarloaf. Capitol Butte's other nickname is Thunder Mountain—hopefully because someone saw lightning hitting the mountain and not because of some hiker's bad experience.

Above and just to the left of Capitol Butte, Wilson Mountain forms the skyline. Even from this distance, you can see the scorched trees from the wildfires that have burned the slopes and summit plateau of the mesa-like mountain. Lost Wilson Mountain, a small isolated outlier on the northwest side of Wilson Mountain, is hard to pick out unless the light is right. The local settlers seemed to like the name "Lost" for isolated buttes that were difficult to see or reach.

To the right of Capitol Butte, you can see Chimney Rock, a small spire just at its base. Airport Mesa is visible, and to the right lie blocky Courthouse Butte, Bell Rock, and Cathedral Butte.

Left of Wilson Mountain, the Mogollon Rim forms the skyline. The peninsula that projects south from the rim toward Wilson Mountain is called East Pocket. Locally, a "pocket" is an isolated section of rim. A small forested hill just north of East Pocket, East Pocket Knob, has a wood fire lookout tower. You'll need binoculars to see the tower from this distance. Still farther to the left is Maroon Mountain, an outlier of Secret Mountain just beyond Long Canyon.

Miles and Directions

0.0 Start at the Bear Mountain Trailhead.

0.5 Reach the Doe Mountain rim. Turn right and follow the rim cross-country.

2.3 Rejoin the Doe Mountain Trail.

2.8 Arrive back at the trailhead.

GREEN TIP
When you just have to go, use a facility at a trailhead or campground, if one is available. Otherwise, dig a hole 6 to 8 inches deep and at least 200 feet from water, camps, and trails. Carry a zippered plastic bag to carry out toilet paper, or use a natural substitute such as leaves instead (but not poison ivy!). Fill in the hole with soil and other natural materials when you're done.

33 Bear Mountain

Because it is steep and rugged, this trail is less-used than most others in the Red Rock–Secret Mountain Wilderness. As a reward, it features some of the best views in the area.

Distance: 4.2 miles out and back
Hiking time: About 3 hours
Difficulty: Moderate
Seasons: Fall through spring
Trail surface: Dirt and rocks
Water: None
Other trail users: None—not suitable for horses
Canine compatibility: Dogs under control allowed

Land status: Red Rock–Secret Mountain Wilderness, Coconino National Forest
Fees and permits: None
Maps: Trails Illustrated Sycamore Canyon, Verde Valley; USGS Loy Butte, Wilson Mountain; Coconino National Forest
Trail contacts: Coconino National Forest, 1824 S. Thompson St., Flagstaff 86001; (928) 527-3600; fs.usda.gov/coconino

Finding the trailhead: From Sedona, drive to the west end of town on AZ 89A, then turn right at a traffic light onto Dry Creek Road. Drive 2.8 miles and turn left onto Boynton Canyon Road. Continue 1.6 miles, then turn left onto FR 152C. Go 1.3 miles to the Bear Mountain Trailhead. GPS: N34 53.595' / W111 51.903'

The Hike

This trail is dry and exposed to the south for its entire length, and is hot in summer. Be sure to carry plenty of water. As you start up the trail, you are looking at massive Bear Mountain directly ahead. The trail crosses several small gulches and is confused by false trails. Keep in mind that you are heading directly to the base of Bear Mountain (the trail is visible as it starts the climb) and you won't have any problems. After a pleasant stroll across the flat, the trail climbs steeply up the talus slopes and surmounts the lowest cliff band via a break to the right. It then starts a gentle climb along the terrace to the left. Already the views are excellent—looking to the southeast, you are now level with the top of Doe Mountain. As the trail swings into a bay, you should be able to pick out the break the trail will use to climb the imposing cliffs above.

The trail climbs very steeply up the gully then swings right to gain the top of the second terrace. The south summit of Bear Mountain, the end of the hike, is now visible about 1 mile ahead. Fainter now but marked by a few cairns, the trail crosses the mesa to its west rim then stays along the ridge crest as it crosses through several shallow notches. The trail climbs steeply again on the final slopes. About halfway up this climb, it ascends a beautiful section of cross-bedded Coconino Sandstone, with the route marked by a few cairns. Along the top of this outcrop, a few windblown

Agave grows on the dry south slopes of Bear Mountain. It blooms only once, then dies.

ponderosa pines grace the stark rock slabs. The eye can sweep over an immense view, from Mingus Mountain to the west to the Mogollon Rim and the Dry Creek basin to the northeast. This section of the trail climbs along the brushy ridge to the northwest. The trail ends at the southernmost summit of Bear Mountain in a thick pinyon-juniper forest. The views are restricted except for a glimpse of Red Canyon to the northwest. Although our hike ends here, you can walk cross-country about 1.5 miles north through the forest to the highest point on Bear Mountain, which is about 120 feet higher than the end of the trail.

The View from the Top

Well, not quite the top, as the trail doesn't go to the highest point of Bear Mountain, but the viewpoint is only a few feet lower. Still, this hike offers a magnificent panoramic view.

Looking north, you can see the three distinct peaks of the San Francisco Peaks north of Flagstaff. The highest mountain in Arizona, the "Peaks" are often visible from more than 100 miles away. To the northeast, the forested mesa of Mormon Mountain can be seen, topped with radio towers. The dome-shaped white summit of Capitol Butte is in the foreground to the east, and just to the right and barely on the skyline is Apache Maid Mountain, the site of a fire lookout tower. Closer and to the right are the red rock buttes near the village of Oak Creek—Courthouse Butte, Bell Rock, and Cathedral Butte. These are easily spotted because of their distinctive shapes.

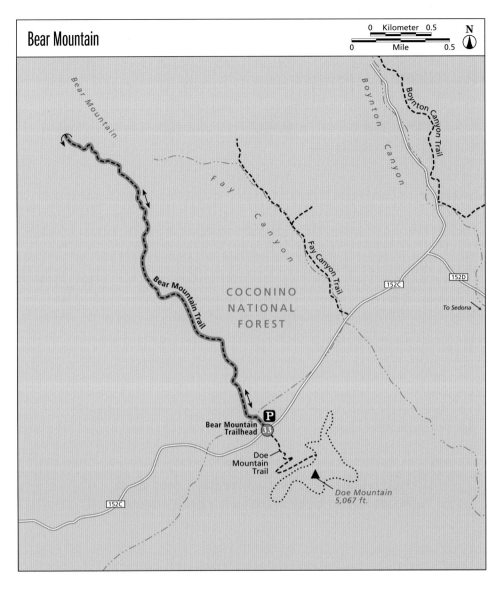

In the distance to the far southeast, beyond the Verde Valley, the northern Mazatzal Mountains form the rugged skyline. This area is one of the largest wilderness areas in Arizona and offers many miles of remote, seldom-used trails that can be used for some fine backpack trips. Just to the right and to the west of the Verde River Canyon, flat-topped Pine Mountain is the highest point on the Verde Rim. This is the centerpiece of a small wilderness area with many trails that are popular with day hikers.

To the southwest across the Verde Valley, the mesa-like mass of Mingus Mountain is the highest point of the Black Hills, the northern extension of the Verde Rim. Mingus Mountain is actually three separate flat-topped mountains: Mingus, Bickey, and Woodchute. To the right of the north end of Mingus Mountain, you may be able see a small knob far beyond Mingus. This is Mount Hope, which lies in the center of the Baca Float, 144 square miles of privately owned ranchland that was granted to the original ranchers by the king of Spain in the seventeenth century, when Arizona was still part of the Spanish Empire.

Much closer at hand and about due west, is Black Mountain, so named because of the black lava flows that cover its flat summit. Flat-topped Casner Mountain is just to the right, and Sycamore Canyon lies just to the west of both mountains.

Miles and Directions

0.0 Start at the Bear Mountain Trailhead.

0.9 Reach the top of the second terrace.

2.1 The trail ends at Bear Mountain's southernmost summit; return the way you came.

4.2 Arrive back at the trailhead.

GREEN TIP

Pass it down—the best way to instill good green habits in your children is to set a good example.

34 Loy Canyon Trail

A scenic hike up a red rock canyon to the edge of the Mogollon Rim. This is one of the few hikes that climbs through the red rock country to the rim.

Distance: 9.6 miles out and back
Hiking time: About 6 hours
Difficulty: Moderate
Seasons: Year-round
Trail surface: Dirt and rocks
Water: None
Other trail users: Horses
Canine compatibility: Dogs under control allowed

Land status: Red Rock–Secret Mountain Wilderness, Coconino National Forest
Fees and permits: None
Maps: Trails Illustrated Sycamore Canyon, Verde Valley; USGS Loy Butte; Coconino National Forest
Trail contacts: Coconino National Forest, 1824 S. Thompson St., Flagstaff 86001; (928) 527-3600; fs.usda.gov/coconino

Finding the trailhead: From Sedona, drive to the west end of town on AZ 89A, then turn right at a traffic light onto Dry Creek Road. Drive 2.8 miles and turn left onto Boynton Canyon Road. Continue 1.6 miles, then turn left onto FR 152C, a maintained dirt road. After 3 miles turn right onto FR 525. Continue 3.7 miles to the Loy Canyon Trailhead. (If you go too far, you will see the Hancock Ranch to the right.) GPS: N34 55.943' / W111 55.481'

The Hike

Initially the trail skirts the Hancock Ranch along its east boundary, then joins the dry creek bed, which it follows northward through the open pinyon pine, juniper, and Arizona cypress forest. Conical Loy Butte looms to the west, and the cliffs of Secret Mountain tower over Loy Canyon on the east. After 2.1 miles the canyon becomes narrower, and the trail turns slightly toward the northeast. In another 0.9 mile the trail turns toward the east as the canyon opens up a bit. The buff-colored Coconino Sandstone cliffs of the Mogollon Rim tower above the trail to the north, and matching cliffs form the north end of Secret Mountain. Watch carefully for the point where the trail leaves the canyon bottom and begins climbing the north side of the canyon in a series of switchbacks. Though it is a steep climb, the reward is an expanding view of Loy Canyon. Notice the contrast between the brushy vegetation on this dry south-facing slope and the cool, moist pine and fir forest across the canyon to the south.

The Loy Canyon Trail ends where it joins the Secret Mountain Trail in the saddle between Secret Mountain and the Mogollon Rim. Turn left here and climb the short distance to the rim and the Secret Mountain Trailhead. Views are limited here, but if you walk a few hundred yards along the road, there is a great view down Loy Canyon.

Option

From the junction with the Secret Mountain Trail, you can turn right and hike the Secret Mountain Trail 4.5 miles to a very scenic overlook at the southwest side of Secret Mountain. This would add 9.0 miles to the hike from the Loy Canyon Trail, for a total out-and-back distance of 17.8 miles. You can do this as a very long day hike or an overnight backpack. There are plenty of places to camp on Secret Mountain, though you would have to carry water for a dry camp.

Prehistoric Americans

The earliest evidence of human occupation of the Verde Valley was a Clovis projectile point found in nearby Honanki Ruins. The Clovis culture is the earliest known group of Native Americans known to have inhabited the Southwest. Several other Clovis points have been found in the Verde Valley, proving that Paleo-Indians inhabited the area as early as 11,500 BC. The Clovis were primarily hunters, stalking and killing large game such as giant sloths, saber-toothed tigers, mammoths, horses, bison, and camels, as well as small game.

The end for the Clovis people seems to have come abruptly with the end of big game hunting, around 9000 BC. Archaeologists aren't certain of the cause, but overhunting combined with climate change may have killed off the large animals. There is surviving evidence of overkills in the form of bison falls, where large herds of bison were driven over cliffs. Only a few of the animals were harvested—the majority were left to rot.

Looking down Loy Canyon

The next occupation of the Verde Valley was by the Western Archaic culture, from 9000 BC to 300 AD—by far the longest settlement by any group. These people were nomadic hunter-gatherers, and the rich variety of resources in the Verde Valley contributed to their long occupation of the area—longer than in any other area in which they lived. Several trails distinguish the Western Archaic from other ancient cultures, including the widespread use of plant fibers for clothing, cordage, and basketmaking. They also used grinding stones, manos and metates, which are commonly found, durable artifacts.

Around 650 AD, the Sinagua people moved in from the east. There were two main groups: the northern Sinagua, who lived around Flagstaff, and the southern Sinagua, who lived in the Verde Valley, along the middle reaches of the Verde River. The Sinagua rapidly learned about the plants, animals, climate, and mineral resources of the area, and they developed active trade and an exchange of ideas with the Puebloan people to the north and the Hohokam to the south, which enriched everyone's lives. "Sinagua" is Spanish for "without water," and a more fitting name for these vanished people can't be imagined. Although the Verde River and its tributaries, such as Oak and Sycamore Creeks, provided relative riches in water for the Sinagua in the Verde Valley, elsewhere they exercised amazing ingenuity in living where water was scarce.

Around 1125 AD the Sinagua began to build cliff dwellings in the Sedona and Red Rock area, which was probably made possible by a wetter cycle in the climate at the time. Up in the canyons, there was enough moisture to raise crops by dry land farming, a technique still practiced by modern Hopi Indians on their high mesas in the Painted Desert, northeast of Flagstaff.

Between 1150 and 1300, the southern Sinagua reached their highest population in the Verde Valley, with villages of three to ten families occupying every environment in the Verde Valley—from cliff dwellings in the red rock canyons to hilltop pueblos. Many of these villages still remain as ruins today. Trouble started to appear between 1300 and 1400. The climate fluctuated wildly between drought and wet cycles, and the northern Sinagua were forced to abandon the Flagstaff area. There were also major disruptions in the Hohokam culture to the south and the Pueblo people to the north. These factors, among others, caused the Sinagua to congregate into about fifty large villages, each occupied by around fifty to one hundred families. Most of these masonry villages were built along the Verde River and its perennial tributaries, which enabled the Sinagua to enjoy the fertile, well-watered bottom lands while still harvesting the abundant wild plants and game along the high country of the Mogollon Rim.

By 1400 most people appear to have fled northern Arizona, probably due to extended drought, and the Sinagua abandoned the Verde Valley. There is some evidence linking the Sinagua with the modern Hopi who live in northeastern Arizona; and the Yavapai Apache later claimed there were still a few Sinagua families living in the Verde Valley who had intermarried with the newcomers.

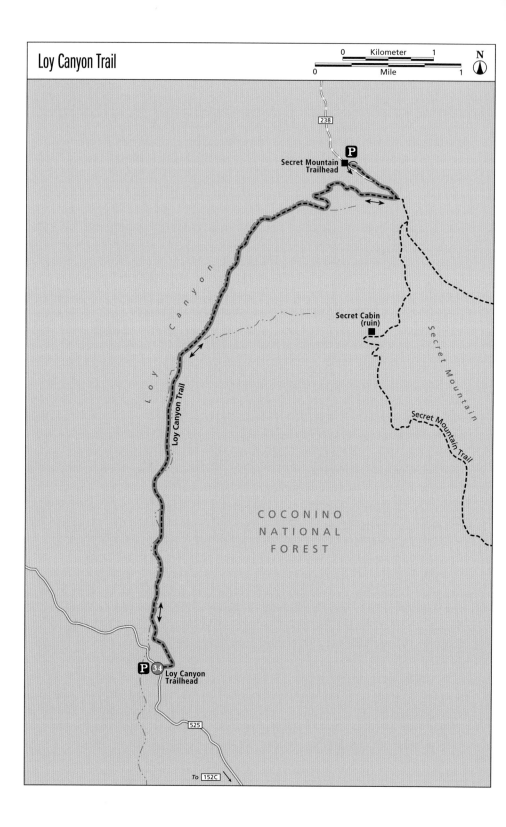

Loy Canyon Trail

0 Kilometer 1

0 Mile 1

N

238

Secret Mountain
Trailhead

P

Secret Cabin
(ruin)

Secret Mountain

Loy Canyon

Loy Canyon Trail

Secret Mountain Trail

COCONINO
NATIONAL
FOREST

P 34 Loy Canyon
Trailhead

525

To 152C

DRY CAMPING

When camping, you can avoid heavily used sites, which are usually too close to water sources anyway, by planning on a dry camp. Carry collapsible water bottles and fill them at the last water source you pass, then camp on a durable surface such as pine needles, sand, gravel, or a rock slab. In Arizona, it is actually illegal to camp within 0.25 mile of an isolated spring, because wildlife will not have access to a vital water source if campers are present.

If you wish to visit Honanki Ruins before or after your hike, continue northwest on FR 525 for 0.7 mile past the Loy Canyon Trailhead to the parking for Honanki Ruins, on the left. Then follow the trail 0.2 mile to the ruins, a small cliff dwelling.

Among the best-preserved Sinagua ruins in the Verde Valley area are Palatki Heritage Site, just off FR 525 in Red Canyon, and two protected as national monuments—Tuzigoot, near Clarkdale, and Montezuma Castle, off I-17 just north of Camp Verde.

Miles and Directions

0.0 Start at the Loy Canyon Trailhead.

2.1 The canyon narrows.

3.0 End of narrows.

4.4 Junction with Secret Mountain Trail; turn left.

4.8 Reach the Secret Mountain Trailhead; return the way you came.

9.6 Arrive back at the trailhead.

35 Robbers Roost

This is a very easy walk to a scenic red rock overlook and a small cave in the Coconino National Forest. According to local lore, the cave was once an outlaw hideout.

Distance: 0.6 mile out and back
Hiking time: About 1 hour
Difficulty: Easy
Seasons: Year-round
Trail surface: Dirt and rocks
Water: None
Other trail users: None
Canine compatibility: Dogs under control allowed

Land status: Coconino National Forest
Fees and permits: None
Maps: Trails Illustrated Sycamore Canyon, Verde Valley; USGS Loy Butte; Coconino National Forest
Trail contacts: Coconino National Forest, 1824 S. Thompson St., Flagstaff 86001; (928) 527-3600; fs.usda.gov/coconino

Finding the trailhead: From Sedona, drive west about 8 miles on AZ 89A, then turn right (northwest) on FR 525, a maintained dirt road. Go 2.2 miles, turning left (west) at a sign for FR 525C. Continue 7.5 miles, then turn right (north) on an unmaintained road that climbs up a ridge toward the east side of Casner Mountain. (Casner Mountain can be identified by the power line that runs down its south slopes.) Go 1.1 miles up this road until you are directly west of Robber's Roost, a low red-rock mesa across the gully to the east. The trailhead and trail are unmarked. GPS: N34 55.858' / W111 58.327'

The Hike

Follow an unmarked trail (it's not shown on the topographic map either) across the shallow gully and up to the north side of Robber's Roost. Then traverse a red sandstone ledge around to a cave on the east side of the rock, just below the rim. Inside the cave, a small wall was supposedly built by the robbers for defense. The main attraction, however, is the picture-window view of Secret Mountain, Bear Mountain, and the Sedona area from within the cave. A hole though a small fin provides a smaller window. It is also interesting to explore the top of this small mesa. After a rain, there will be temporary water pockets that reflect the sky and the red rocks.

Hiking with the Little Ones

Note: See the "Trail Finder" for hikes recommended for children.

Most children love the outdoors. I have personal knowledge of this, as I was once a child myself. I can say with authority that the outdoors is a wonderland for kids. The key is to keep them warm, dry, and fed—and in the summer, cool and hydrated. This should be easy because you're already taking the same care of yourself, right?

Make absolutely certain you have the essentials—it's even more important when you have kids who are dependent on you.

Bobcats are seen far more often than their bigger cousin, the mountain lion.

Watch the weather like a hawk. If the forecast is for wind and rain, you should postpone your hike for a better day, especially with very young kids. During summer, thunderstorms can develop quickly, so plan your hike for the cool morning hours. If it's going to be a really hot day, choose a higher elevation hike and start early; better yet, head to the high country less than an hour way near Flagstaff (see my Falcon-Guides *Best Easy Day Hikes Flagstaff* and *Hiking Northern Arizona*).

Work with your inner child. For a kid, nature is full of wonders within a few feet of the trailhead or camp. You don't have to walk far to help children have a great adventure. Consider bringing a few field guides to natural things such as flowers, trees, birds, and wildlife. If you are car-camping or backpacking, bring a pair of binoculars and a star guide. If possible, get the e-book edition of the field guides so you can carry several on your phone or small tablet. Electronic bird guides such as the Sibley Birds app can be a huge amount of fun for kids. They can listen to birdsong and then try to hear the same bird in the app.

Kids of any age can enjoy the outdoors. In Scandinavia, babies are taken cross-country skiing—swaddled in warm clothes and blankets on a sled. You can do the same with a good-quality baby carrier. Just make sure you have the carrier fitted to you, and test it at home before hitting the trail. Make sure you have all the supplies you need; good carriers have compartments to organize everything; and make sure you apply a sunscreen designed for infants and cover your baby with a sunhat broad enough to protect his or her neck. You don't have to hike far; the hiking motion will probably put your child to sleep anyway.

Toddlers love having their own pack—just make sure you get one that fits. Don't overload it. The essentials are a few favorite snacks and a brightly colored kids water bottle that will encourage them to drink. Toddlers don't need boots; sneakers are fine. Make sure you have extra socks and clothing, because little feet are strongly attracted to water and mud, and don't venture too far from the trailhead—you may suddenly have a tired toddler you have to carry. It's better to pick safe areas free of hazards such as cactus and poison ivy and let your child explore. A change of clothes in the car is a good idea too, unless your camp, hotel, or home is very near the trailhead.

Grade-school children can hike on their own two feet, and they are chock-full of energy, so you need to lay down some ground rules for their safety. Children should always have a safety whistle attached to their pack. Teach your kids to "hug a tree" if lost and to blow their whistle in bursts of three. They should be taught to always stay within sight of a parent on the trail. Plan your destination for kid fun—a pool where they can swim or skip rocks, or a place where they scramble around on rocks (check for rattlesnakes before turning them loose). Adult destinations such as scenic views hold little interest for children. Kids will get bored just walking along, so plan activities like leaf races in creeks, spotting squirrels, and geocaching. Encourage your kids to bring a friend and share the fun. At this age you should teach your kids to "Leave No Trace" in the backcountry, and encourage them to catch you messing up. Most kids love maps; bring a trail or topo map for them, and teach them to read it. As they get older, designate them the expedition navigator—they'll love the responsibility.

Teenagers and Backpacking

This could be the subject of a whole book! But if you've exposed your kids to the trail, they'll probably carry right on loving the outdoors. Your responsibility is to tailor the trip for the kids. Don't pick a really hard trail or cross-country hike unless and until they develop some interest and skill in such hiking. Pick a destination with interesting things to do—a creek or a historic site, for example.

Learning outdoor skills such as navigation, selecting a campsite to avoid prolonged shade on a cold morning, pitching the tent, and storing food safely help hold older kids' attention. As noted above, e-book field guides can be a great way to get kids interested in their surroundings.

And always operate in kid mode. To kids, something interesting they've spotted along the trail is always more important than some adult destination that's miles away. If you do it right, your child will grow into an adult with a great respect for wild country and an interest in helping protect and preserve it.

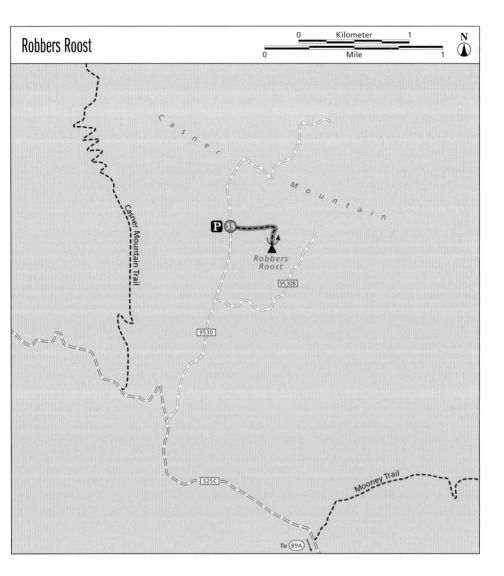

Miles and Directions

0.0 Start at the unmarked trailhead.

0.3 Reach Robber's Roost; return the way you came.

0.6 Arrive back at the trailhead.

36 Mooney-Casner Loop

This hike loops through a little-traveled red rock canyon to the scenic top of Casner Mountain.

Distance: 14.1-mile loop
Hiking time: About 9 hours
Difficulty: Strenuous
Seasons: Spring through fall
Trail surface: Dirt and rocks
Water: None
Other trail users: Horses
Canine compatibility: Dogs under control allowed

Land status: Red Rock–Secret Mountain Wilderness, Coconino National Forest
Fees and permits: None
Maps: Trails Illustrated Sycamore Canyon, Verde Valley; USGS Loy Butte; Coconino National Forest
Trail contacts: Coconino National Forest, 1824 S. Thompson St., Flagstaff 86001; (928) 527-3600; fs.usda.gov/coconino

Finding the trailhead: From Sedona, drive about 8 miles south on AZ 89A, then turn right (northwest) on FR 525, a maintained dirt road. Go 2.2 miles and turn left (west) onto FR 525C. Continue 7.2 miles to the Mooney Trailhead at Black Tank. GPS: N111 54.419' / W111 57.857'
    The Casner Mountain Trail, the return trail for the loop, meets FR 525C 1.6 miles west. GPS: N33 54.939' / W111 58.699'

The Hike

This scenic loop can be done as a long day hike or as an overnight backpack if you carry water for a dry camp. The Mooney Trail follows an old road northeast toward a long, low ridge. It climbs east onto the ridge then follows it north. Where the ridge butts up against the steep slopes of Casner Mountain, the Mooney Trail contours into Mooney Canyon. It follows the normally dry bed of Spring Creek, which drains Mooney Canyon, past some red rock outcrops, then climbs the brushy northwest side of the canyon. At the top of the ridge, turn left on the Casner Mountain Trail and follow this scenic old road south over the top of Casner Mountain and down to FR 525C. Turn left and walk 1.6 miles southeast to your vehicle.

Machines in the Wilderness

Many people don't understand the meaning of wilderness and think anything outside the city is wilderness. In Arizona, where there are vast amounts of open space in the form of public land—national forests, national parks and monuments, other federal land, state parks and other state land, and county parks, as well as large areas of private land used for ranching—people often think it's all wilderness, but if it's accessible by road, it's not wilderness.

    The American concept of protected wilderness as developed in the 1920s calls for an area to be preserved in a wild state, where there is little or no evidence of humans.

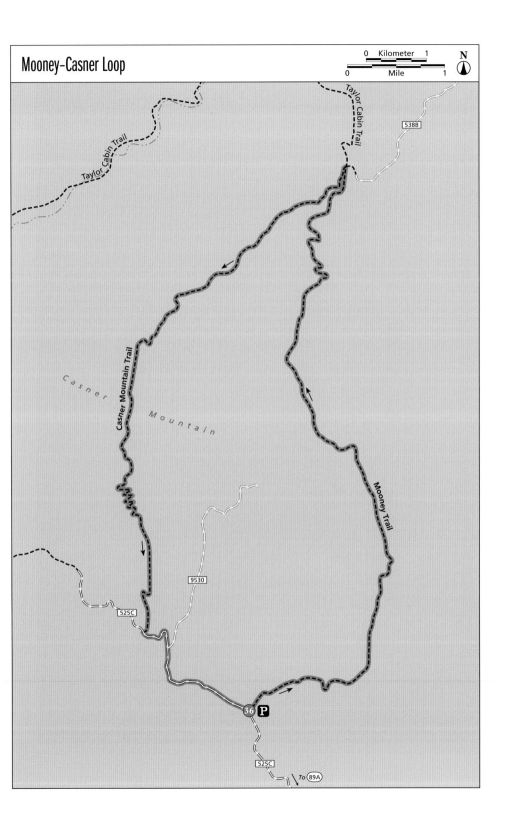

Mooney-Casner Loop

Taylor Cabin Trail

Taylor Cabin Trail

538B

Casner Mountain Trail

C a s n e r

M o u n t a i n

Mooney Trail

9530

525C

36 P

525C   To 89A

More remote trails such as the Mooney-Casner loop can be enjoyed as long day hikes, but it's a great pleasure to camp under the stars.

Under the Wilderness Act of 1964, only trails, trail signs, and structures such as fire lookout towers that are administratively necessary are allowed in units of the National Wilderness Preservation System. Mechanized devices, including bicycles and motorized vehicles, are specifically excluded under the act, and the USDA Forest Service has interpreted the law to exclude hang gliders and drones. Travel must be by foot or on horseback (pack animals, including horses, donkeys, mules, and llamas are also allowed). Airdrops and landings by aircraft are also prohibited, except in an emergency. Even wildland firefighting is now carried out with a light touch, as fire managers have realized that the use of bulldozers, engines, and other heavy equipment in wilderness causes more damage than the fire itself. Most wild country is adapted to or even dependent on wildfire, so lightning-caused wildfires usually are allowed to burn in wilderness areas. Suppression is only carried out if a fire might escape the wilderness and threaten man-made infrastructure.

The key idea is to preserve the primitive and allow modern humans to experience the environment we evolved for, away from the clatter of civilization—cars, cell phones, television, etc. Wilderness advocates are looking for a balance. In the United States, the amount of roadless, protected and unprotected wilderness remaining is just about equal to the amount of land that is urbanized. (The remainder of the country is rural—crisscrossed with roads, power lines, and human infrastructure, and used for ranching, farming, mining, and other extractive activities.)

You'll sometimes hear motorized recreation advocates decry wilderness protection as "locking up the land" and violating their "rights" to operate their off-road or four-wheel-drive vehicles anywhere they want. No one has this right. We don't allow motor vehicles in museums and churches, and we have the responsibility to treat our American landscapes with the same care. Only about 10 percent of America is wilderness. The rest is open to motor vehicles.

Miles and Directions

0.0 Start at the Mooney Trailhead and bear right.

1.7 Reach the ridgetop; follow the ridge north.

2.9 The trail contours into Mooney Canyon.

5.0 Leave Spring Creek.

6.5 Turn left on the Casner Mountain Trail.

10.1 Reach the Casner Mountain summit.

12.5 Turn left on FR 525C.

14.1 Arrive back at the trailhead.

37 Taylor Cabin Loop

This is a fine hike through the remote red rock canyons of Sycamore Canyon and along the top of Casner Mountain, which gives you outstanding views of Sycamore Canyon below to the west.

Distance: 18.8-mile loop
Hiking time: 1 long day or 2-day backpack
Difficulty: Strenuous
Seasons: Spring through fall
Trail surface: Dirt and rocks
Water: Seasonal in Sycamore Creek
Other trail users: Horses on trails
Canine compatibility: Dogs under control allowed
Land status: Sycamore Canyon Wilderness, Coconino National Forest

Fees and permits: None
Maps: Trails Illustrated Sycamore Canyon, Verde Valley; USGS Sycamore Point, Sycamore Basin, Loy Butte; Coconino National Forest; Prescott National Forest
Trail contacts: Coconino National Forest, 1824 S. Thompson St., Flagstaff 86001; (928) 527-3600; fs.usda.gov/coconino. Prescott National Forest, 344 S. Cortez St., Prescott 86303; (928) 443-8000; fs.usda.gov/prescott.

Finding the trailhead: From Sedona, drive about 8 miles south on AZ 89A, then turn right (northwest) on FR 525, a maintained dirt road. Go 2.2 miles and turn left (west) onto FR 525C. Continue 8.8 miles to the end of the road at the Sycamore Pass Trailhead. *Note:* The last mile or two frequently washes out and may be very rough, but the rest is passable to ordinary cars. GPS: N34 55.391' / W111 59.638'

The Casner Mountain Trail, the return trail for the loop, meets FR 525C 0.8 mile east of the Sycamore Pass Trailhead. GPS: N34 55.106' / W111 58.972'

The Hike

There is usually water in Sycamore Creek during the spring, but it is dry later in the year. Enough water should be carried for a dry camp if the creek is dry. On the other hand, Sycamore Creek may be flooding and be impassible during snowmelt or after a major storm. In this case you'll have to make the hike an out-and-back, which you can do in a day.

The start of the Dogie Trail is shown on the USGS Loy Butte quad, but not on the Sycamore Basin quad. You'll climb a short distance to cross Sycamore Pass then descend gradually to the west. The trail turns north and works its way along a sloping terrace through pinyon–juniper forest. The inner gorge of Sycamore Canyon is visible to the west, and the cliffs of Casner Mountain rise on the east. Finally the trail descends to Sycamore Creek and crosses it to join the Cow Flat and Taylor Cabin Trails on the west bank. There are several campsites for small groups on the bluff just to the south. (In an emergency, you may be able to find water in Cedar Creek.)

Turn right (northeast) on the Taylor Cabin Trail, which stays on the bench to the west of Sycamore Creek. After about 2 miles the trail descends to the creek and becomes harder to find. Watch for Taylor Cabin on the west bank; the trail passes right by this old rancher's line cabin. The trail stays on the west side of the creek after Taylor Cabin. If you lose the trail, boulder-hop directly up the creek bed.

About 1.8 miles from Taylor Cabin, the trail turns right (east) and climbs out of Sycamore Canyon. Watch carefully for the turnoff, which is usually marked by cairns. The topographic maps are essential for finding this trail. Most of the trail follows the major drainage south of Buck Ridge, often staying right in the bed of this very pretty canyon. Near the top, the trail turns more to the south and climbs steeply through a fine stand of ponderosa pine and Douglas fir. A single switchback leads to the top of the ridge, where there are excellent views of Sycamore Canyon and the Taylor Basin. The trail reaches a pass and ends at the junction with the Casner Mountain and Mooney Trails.

Turn right (southwest) on the Casner Mountain Trail, an old road built during power line construction. The road is now closed to vehicles and makes a scenic finish to this loop hike. Follow the trail southwest along the narrow ridge leading to Casner Mountain. There are views of Sycamore Canyon on the west and Mooney Canyon on the east. The trail climbs onto Casner Mountain, a broad plateau capped with dark volcanic rocks. A gradual descent leads to the south edge of the plateau, where the trail descends rapidly in a series of switchbacks. Near the bottom of the descent, the topographic map shows the trail ending; if you lose it, just follow the power line down to FR 525C. Now turn right and walk 0.8 mile up the road to the Sycamore Pass Trailhead.

Line Cabins

Taylor Cabin is well constructed of stone—an unusually fine example of a rancher's line cabin. In the early days of ranching in Arizona, travel was by horse and wagon, and the vast size of ranches made it impractical to travel from headquarters to a worksite and back again in one day. If cowboys planned to get any work done, they had to camp near the worksite. It was a lot more pleasant to have permanent shelter at worksites that were used repeatedly, so small cabins were built from logs or stone—whatever was handy. Line cabins varied considerably in their amenities, but most had bunks and a wood stove. Some had basic kitchens; a few even had running water, piped down from a spring on the hillside above. Toward the end of the line cabin era, a few were actually small houses, with all the amenities modern suburbanites expect, including a well for running water and electric power from a generator.

Most line cabins are more basic, like Taylor Cabin, and most have fallen into ruin, been burned in wildfires, or been removed (in the case of wilderness areas), so don't count on a line cabin as shelter from a storm, but for the rancher, having a cabin waiting after a long day of rounding up or branding cattle, repairing fences, or maintaining water sources was a little bit of heaven.

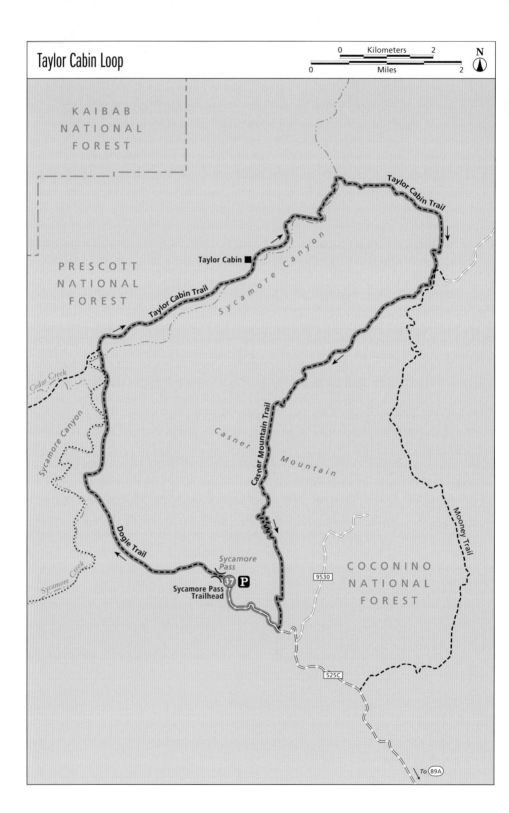

Taylor Cabin Loop

KAIBAB
NATIONAL
FOREST

PRESCOTT
NATIONAL
FOREST

Taylor Cabin Trail

Taylor Cabin

Sycamore Canyon

Taylor Cabin Trail

Cedar Creek

Sycamore Canyon

Casner Mountain Trail

Casner   Mountain

Dogie Trail

Sycamore Creek

Sycamore
Pass

37   P

Sycamore Pass
Trailhead

9530

COCONINO
NATIONAL
FOREST

Mooney Trail

525C

To 89A

Historic Taylor Cabin was built as a rancher's line cabin.

Miles and Directions

0.0   Start at the Sycamore Pass Trailhead and bear left on the Dogie Trail.

0.4   Reach Sycamore Pass.

4.9   Cross Sycamore Creek.

5.0   Taylor Cabin Trail; turn right.

7.9   Reach Taylor Cabin.

9.7   Taylor Cabin Trail turns right, up an unnamed side canyon.

12.0   Turn right on the Casner Mountain Trail.

15.6   The trail climbs onto Casner Mountain.

18.0   Intersect FR 525C; turn right.

18.8   Arrive back at the trailhead.

38 Parsons Trail

This is a challenging day hike or backpack trip through the remote red rock canyon of Sycamore Canyon. It features one of the most beautiful perennial streams in Arizona, red rock formations, and sweeping views.

Distance: 21.4-mile cross-country and on-trail loop

Hiking time: About 10 hours or 2 days

Difficulty: Strenuous

Seasons: Spring and fall

Trail surface: Dirt and rocks; boulder hopping on the cross-country section

Water: Sycamore Creek downstream from Parsons Spring; seasonal pools upstream

Other trail users: Horses on trails

Canine compatibility: Dogs under control allowed

Land status: Sycamore Canyon Wilderness, Coconino and Prescott National Forests

Fees and permits: None

Maps: Trails Illustrated Sycamore Canyon, Verde Valley; USGS Clarkdale, Sycamore Basin; Coconino National Forest; Prescott National Forest

Trail contacts: Coconino National Forest, 1824 S. Thompson St., Flagstaff 86001; (928) 527-3600; fs.usda.gov/coconino. Prescott National Forest, 344 S. Cortez St., Prescott 86303; (928) 443-8000; fs.usda.gov/prescott.

Note: Camping is not allowed in Sycamore Canyon from Parsons Spring downstream to the Verde River.

Finding the trailhead: From Cottonwood, drive to the north end of town on AZ 89A and into the town of Clarkdale, then turn right (east) on the road to Tuzigoot National Monument. After 0.2 mile, just after crossing the Verde River bridge, turn left (north) on CR 139 (it becomes FR 131), a maintained dirt road. Drive 10 miles to the end of the road at the Sycamore Canyon Trailhead. GPS: N34 51.848' / W112 4.162'

The Hike

Sycamore Creek is normally dry above Parsons Spring. In spring, seasonal pools above this point make it possible to do this loop without carrying water. During summer and fall, however, you'll have to pick up enough water at Parsons Spring for your camp farther up the canyon. The catch is that during early spring, Sycamore Creek may be flooding from snowmelt in the high country, making this loop trip impossible. If the creek is running muddy at the trailhead, content yourself with a short day hike to Summers or Parsons Spring. Do not attempt to cross the creek when it is flooding. In summer, this loop is recommended only for hikers experienced at dry camping in hot weather.

From the trailhead follow the good trail 0.2 mile north into Sycamore Creek. On the left, the Packard Trail crosses the creek; this is our return trail. Please note that Sycamore Canyon is closed to camping between the trailhead and Parsons Spring due to overuse. Continue following Sycamore Creek on the broad, easy trail along the east bank. Sycamore Creek flows year-round and supports a rich variety of riparian trees, including the Arizona sycamore for which the canyon is named. About 1.5 miles from the trailhead, the canyon swings sharply left, then right. During the winters of 1993 and 1994, massive flooding completely rearranged the creek bed. Evidence of the flooding is everywhere—saplings leaning downstream, piles of driftwood and even huge logs far above normal stream level, and collapsed streambanks.

Above Parsons Spring, the source of Sycamore Creek, the creek bed dries up. Continue up Sycamore Creek by boulder-hopping along the broad, dry wash. You may see seasonal pools of water in the bends of the creek. Also, watch for petroglyphs along the rock walls of the canyon. Although strenuous, progress up the creek bed is relatively fast because the periodic floods keep the bed clear of brush. The gorge becomes shallower after about 6.0 miles. The Dogie Trail crosses Sycamore Creek 7.6 miles above Parson Spring. Turn left (west) on the Dogie Trail, which quickly ends at the Taylor Cabin and Cow

Hiking upper Sycamore Canyon is an exercise in boulder hopping.

Flat Trails above the west bank. Now turn left (south) on the Cow Flat Trail. There are several good campsites for small groups on the bluffs overlooking the creek to the east. There is no water except for possible seasonal pools in Sycamore Creek.

After the confines of Sycamore Creek and the rugged boulder-hopping, it is a pleasure to walk the easy Cow Flat Trail southwest through the open pinyon–juniper forest. Shortly, the trail crosses Cedar Creek. (This creek is usually dry at the crossing, but water can sometimes be found about 1 mile upstream.) The trail climbs gradually for another 1.0 mile and passes through a broad saddle to enter Sycamore Basin. The walking is very easy through this open basin, with fine views of the surrounding red rock formations. Camping is unlimited—if you carry water for a dry camp. The trail crosses Cow Flat then skirts the head of a side canyon. It then climbs gradually to another pass. On the far side of the pass, the trail ends at a trailhead at the end of FR 181.

Now go south on the Packard Trail. Packard Mesa forms the west rim of lower Sycamore Canyon, and the trail generally stays near the crest as it works its way south

Taking a break along Sycamore Creek, a rare permanent stream

through open pinyon pine and juniper stands. About 4.0 miles from FR 181, the trail turns east and descends into Sycamore Canyon. It crosses the creek and meets the Parsons Trail; turn right to return to the trailhead.

Campfires

Minimize the use and impact of fires. Use designated fire spots or existing fire rings (if permitted). When building fires, use small sticks (less than 1.5 inches in diameter) that you find on the ground. Keep your fire small, burn it to ash, put it out completely, and scatter the cool ashes. Restore the fire pit to natural conditions by filling it with dirt and scattering ground litter over the site.

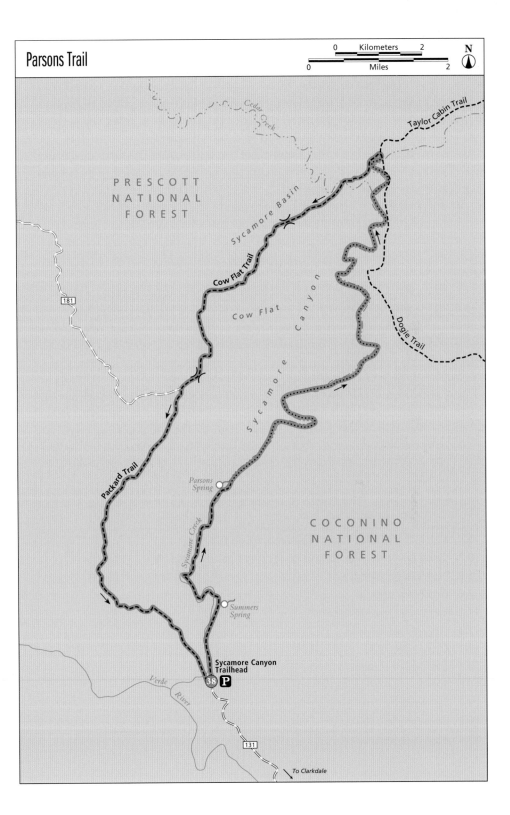

Parsons Trail

Cedar Creek

Taylor Cabin Trail

PRESCOTT
NATIONAL
FOREST

Sycamore Basin

Cow Flat Trail

Cow Flat

Sycamore Canyon

Dogie Trail

181

Packard Trail

Parsons Spring

Sycamore Creek

COCONINO
NATIONAL
FOREST

Summers Spring

Sycamore Canyon Trailhead

38 P

Verde River

131

To Clarkdale

If you can, it's best to avoid making a fire at all. As a lifetime backpacker, I stopped building campfires before I was out of my teens. After just a few backpack trips, I found it much easier to cook on a lightweight backpacking stove than to deal with a fire. In the desert, wood is often scarce. Even in the forest where wood is plentiful, to me a fire is more hassle than it's worth. I'd rather get my meal going on my stove while I set up my snug camp with its cozy sleeping bag than bother to clear an area, dig a fire pit, drag wood into the campsite, break it into small pieces, find suitable dry tinder, light the fire—and then worry about whether sparks are going to burn holes in my expensive tent and sleeping bag.

It's not over yet. In the morning I have to put the fire out with water (if there's any to spare), sending a cloud of ash and smoke into that same expensive equipment—or worse, put the fire out with dirt, which, as you can imagine, takes a lot longer than water does. By the time I've restored the fire pit to look as natural as I can, I'm even filthier than I was when I got to camp. No thanks.

There's only a couple of reasons I'd build a fire now: in an emergency, when I needed the warmth because I'd lost my gear, or as a signal fire to alert rescuers.

People often say they need a fire to stay warm, but if that's the case, you're going to freeze when you get into your inadequate sleeping bag and tent. It's much better to spend a little more money on good gear, which keeps you much warmer than a fire and works all the time, day and night.

The other reason cited for building a fire is that it's part of the wilderness experience—nothing beats staring into the hypnotic flames. That is enjoyable, but I'd rather be part of the night. Without a fire, my eyes adapt to the dark and I can enjoy the glories of the universe overhead and the mysterious silhouettes of the desert skyline. If there's a bright moon, the desert becomes a place of magical light, and without the crackle of a fire, I can hear the owl calling to luring his prey.

Miles and Directions

0.0 Start at the Sycamore Canyon Trailhead and bear right.

0.2 Reach Sycamore Creek; continue along the east bank.

1.2 Pass Summers Spring.

3.6 Pass Parsons Spring.

11.2 Intersect the Dogie Trail; turn left.

11.3 Cow Flat Trail; turn left.

11.7 Cross Cedar Creek.

12.7 Enter Sycamore Basin.

15.8 Traverse a pass where the trail ends at FR 181. Go south on the Packard Trail.

19.8 Walk along the rim of Sycamore Canyon.

21.2 Cross Sycamore Creek.

21.4 Arrive back at the trailhead.

Verde Rim

The western boundary of the Verde Valley is formed by the Black Hills and the Verde Rim. The rim was formed by faulting, which caused it to rise high above the Verde Valley. The highest section of the Verde Rim is formed by flat-topped Mingus and Woodchute Mountains, which both rise to nearly 8,000 feet. A number of trails—remnants of the pre-road transportation system—ascend the pine-covered slopes of these mountains. All afford superb views of the surrounding mountains and valleys. South of I-17, the Black Hills give way to the Verde Rim, which faces the Mogollon Rim across the rugged canyon of the Verde River.

39 Woodchute Trail

This easy trail goes to the north end of Woodchute Mountain. You'll have some panoramic views of the western Mogollon Rim and Sycamore Canyon.

Distance: 7.4 miles out and back
Hiking time: About 4 hours
Difficulty: Easy
Seasons: Summer through fall
Trail surface: Dirt and rocks
Water: None
Other trail users: Horses
Canine compatibility: Dogs under control allowed

Land status: Woodchute Wilderness, Prescott National Forest
Fees and permits: None
Maps: Trails Illustrated Sycamore Canyon, Verde Valley; USGS Hickey Mountain, Munds Draw; Prescott National Forest
Trail contacts: Prescott National Forest, 344 S. Cortez St., Prescott 86303; (928) 443-8000; fs.usda.gov/prescott

Finding the trailhead: From Jerome, drive about 7 miles west on AZ 89A. At the highway pass on Mingus Mountain, turn right at Potato Patch Campground. Go about 0.4 mile and turn left into the Woodchute Trailhead. GPS: N34 42.400' / W112 9.397'

The Hike

Hike north on an old road for 0.4 mile through ponderosa pine woodland. Notice the large alligator junipers—the trees with, appropriately enough, bark that looks like alligator hide. The Woodchute Trail forks right then climbs onto the main crest of the mountain. After crossing several dips in the ridge, it contours into the head of Mescal Gulch then climbs to the south rim of Woodchute Mountain. The trail continues north across the flat summit area and finally reaches the north rim of Woodchute, our destination. (From here, the trail descends the north slopes of Woodchute Mountain and ends at FR 318A. This section of the trail is little used.) From here you have a panoramic view of the headwaters of the Verde River, the western Mogollon Rim, and Sycamore Canyon Wilderness.

Ocean Deeps

As you drive up the slopes of Mingus Mountain along Arizona 89A, you pass through outcrops of a massive layer of rock called the Redwall Limestone.

The Redwall Limestone is a persistent layer of nearly pure, gray limestone that underlies much of the Colorado Plateau, extending from the Mogollon Rim north to the Grand Canyon, where it is the great canyon's most prominent cliff, and to exposures in the plateau and canyon country of Utah, Colorado, and New Mexico. Outcrops of Redwall Limestone occur in Arizona's Central Mountains south of Sedona, notably on Mingus Mountain. In fact, related limestones of similar age occur throughout the Rocky Mountain cordillera, from Mexico to Canada.

Detail of a scorched alligator juniper and a three-needle cluster from a ponderosa pine. Both trees are common along the Woodchute Trail

The Redwall Limestone takes its name from the vast cliffs that run the entire length of the Grand Canyon, below both the north and south rims. These massive cliffs are almost uniformly 550 feet high throughout the Grand Canyon. On fresh exposures, the Redwall is a pearly, almost translucent gray; but in the Grand Canyon and Sedona areas it is overlain by the reddish rocks of the Supai Formation. Runoff

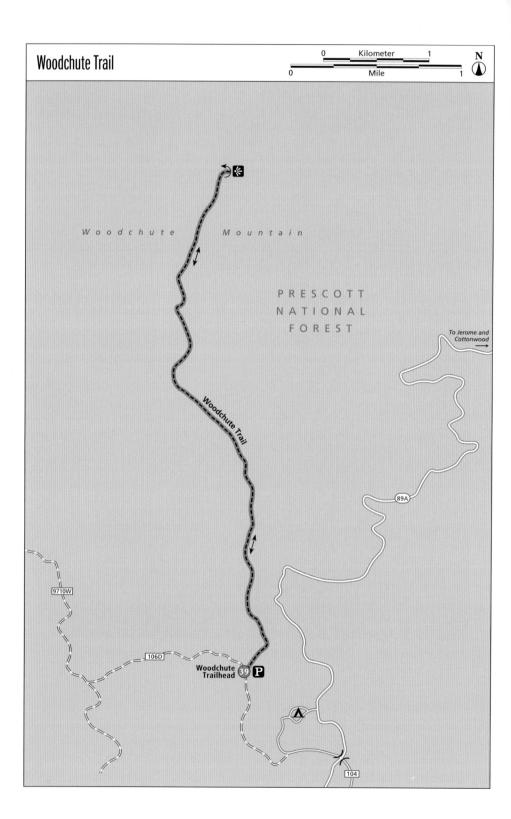

from these red rocks coats the surface of the massive Redwall cliffs below, staining them red.

Geologically, the Redwall Limestone is of Mississippian period, about 300 to 360 million years ago. This is well before the age of dinosaurs and was a time when much of what is now North America was submerged in deep oceans. Land areas that were exposed were often low-lying and tropical, so it was also a time of prolific and wide-spread plant growth. Because the organic remains of the lush plant life was eventually compressed and transformed into vast coal beds worldwide, this period was part of the broader Carboniferous period.

There are four recognized subunits in the Redwall Limestone, representing changes in the deep sea environment over time.

The mostly fine-grained limestone of the Redwall is composed of microscopic fossils—seashells of creatures that swam in the deep oceans. Imagine how many countless trillions of such creatures had to die, and their tiny shells survive to sink to the seafloor, to form layers of sediment that eventually would be compressed into such a massive, widespread rock layer.

Both the top and the bottom of the Redwall Limestone form "unconformities." In geologic-speak, this means there are missing rock layers, representing a period of erosion when the land was above sea level and sediments were removed rather than deposited. At the top of the Redwall Limestone, this period of prolonged erosion is clearly expressed in the uneven surface of the limestone, where runoff created hills, valleys, and stream channels, now filled with the sedimentary layers of the overlying Supai Formation.

Miles and Directions

0.0 Start at the Woodchute Trailhead.

0.4 Turn right on the Woodchute Trail.

1.7 Reach the ridgetop.

2.2 Mescal Gulch.

2.7 South rim of Woodchute Mountain.

3.7 North rim of Woodchute Mountain; return the way you came.

7.4 Arrive back at the trailhead.

40 North Mingus Trail

This is a scenic hike through a historic mining district on Mingus Mountain, with views of Verde Valley and Mogollon Rim.

Distance: 6.0 miles out and back
Hiking time: About 4 hours
Difficulty: Moderate
Seasons: Spring through fall
Trail surface: Dirt and rocks
Water: Mescal Spring
Other trail users: Mountain bikes and horses
Canine compatibility: Dogs under control allowed

Land status: Prescott National Forest
Fees and permits: None
Maps: Trails Illustrated Sycamore Canyon, Verde Valley; USGS Hickey Mountain, Cottonwood; Prescott National Forest
Trail contacts: Prescott National Forest, 344 S. Cortez St., Prescott 86303; (928) 443-8000; fs.usda.gov/prescott

Finding the trailhead: From Jerome, drive about 4 miles west on AZ 89A. Watch for a "Prescott National Forest" sign, then turn left on an unsigned, unmaintained dirt road (FR 338) just before this sign. Low-clearance vehicles should park at the highway. Go through the gate, continue 0.5 mile to Mescal Spring, and park. Mescal Spring is marked by a large cement tank that catches water piped down a few feet from the actual spring. GPS: N34 43.694' / W112 7.990'

The Hike

Walk up the jeep road, which forks right and climbs steeply (it is shown as a foot trail on the topographic map). The little-used jeep road does a switchback then contours around a basin. This section of the road is very easy, pleasant walking. It crosses a ridge just as it enters another basin. Watch carefully for the cairned but unsigned foot trail that goes up this ridge. This junction is 1.2 miles from Mescal Spring. Although it is possible to reach this point in a high-clearance vehicle, there is no parking. The rocky but well-maintained trail climbs through a fine stand of ponderosa pine then starts switchbacking up the north ridge of Mingus Mountain. The view starts to open up as the trail gains elevation. About 1.4 miles from the jeep road, the trail reaches a shallow saddle and the signed junction with Trail 105A. Continue south, directly up the steep ridge, on Trail 105. The trail soon resumes switchbacking and passes through a small aspen grove near the rim. The trail reaches the rim, our destination, about 0.4 mile from the trail junction. The forest is thick here, but good views can be found by walking around. A large section of the Mogollon Rim, the Verde Valley, and the red rock country of Sedona and Sycamore Canyon is visible. A trailhead is located 0.5 mile south.

Strike!

The directions for the hikes on Mingus Mountain take you along AZ 89A through the historic mining town of Jerome, perched precariously on Cleopatra Hill on the steep eastern slopes of the mountain. The little town, once the site of one of the richest copper mines on the planet, is now a tourist destination and artists' colony.

Eruption of a massive volcanic caldera in Precambrian times, 1.75 billion years ago, resulted in the deposition of two rich ore bodies. Cracks in the volcanic rocks allowed seawater to enter and be heated to hundreds of degrees. As this superheated water was forced upward, it chemically altered the rocks and dissolved minerals. When water emerged onto the seafloor through a ring fault in the caldera, the dissolved minerals precipitated out and accumulated on the seafloor. The deposits from the two main vents would later become the United Verde and United Verde Extension Mines. Although much of the later geologic history is missing from the area due to a prolonged period of erosion, eventually the Tapeats Sandstone was deposited in a shallow sea and covered the two ore bodies. Other layers of sedimentary rock, many of which are found in the Sedona area on the far side of the Verde Valley, as well as in the walls of the Grand Canyon, were laid down on top of the Tapeats Sandstone.

During the period of mountain-building known as the Laramide orogeny, about 70 million years ago, the Rocky Mountains were uplifted and the Southwest was subjected to rock movement and faulting. One of these faults, the Verde Fault, runs

Oak brush creates fall color on the north slopes of Mingus Mountain.

directly through Jerome. About 15 million years ago, stretching of the Earth's crust caused more faulting and created the Basin and Range Province that covers most of Nevada, southeastern California, and southwestern Arizona below the Mogollon Rim. This activity renewed movement along the Verde Fault and eventually exposed the United Verde ore body on the surface.

Since this rich copper deposit was visible on the surface, Native Americans very likely picked up pieces of colorful copper ore such as azurite and malachite for use as pigments and as jewelry. Spanish explorers noted the deposit in 1585, but didn't explore it further because they had been instructed to look for silver and gold, not copper.

In 1876 two Anglos filed the first mining claims on Cleopatra Hill, on the exposed ore body that would become the United Verde Mine. This set off a massive mining boom, and prospectors soon swarmed the mountainside, filing claims on everything in sight. Nearly all these claims proved to be worthless. In 1883 Frederick Tritle, Governor of Arizona Territory, and Frederick Thomas, a mining engineer from San Francisco, bought the claims and formed the United Verde Copper Company. The small mining camp that grew up near the mine was named Jerome, for the company's secretary.

Despite the richness of the ore, transportation to the nearest railhead was expensive, and the mine shut down in 1884. William Clark bought the properties in 1888 and started making improvements, including a larger smelter, and, critically, built a narrow-gauge railroad 27 miles to Jerome Junction to connect with the mainline. As mining expanded, Jerome grew from 250 in 1890 to more than 2,500 people in 1900. By then the United Verde had become the largest copper producer in Arizona and one of the largest in the world and employed about 800 men. Over its seventy-seven-year life, 1876 to 1953, the mine produced almost 33 million tons of copper, silver, and gold.

Jerome's boom continued. It had a post office by 1883, a schoolhouse in 1884, and added a public library in 1889. A series of four devastating fires destroyed much of the business district and about half the town's homes between 1894 and 1898, prompting incorporation of the town in 1899. This made it possible to enact building codes to reduce the flammability of structures and to collect money to fund a fire department. By 1900, Jerome had churches, fraternal organizations, telephone service, brick buildings, and electric lights. It also had a population that was 77 percent male, with bars and houses of ill repute being major businesses, giving Jerome a reputation as the "wickedest town in the West."

The second ore body was not exposed on the surface and wasn't discovered until 1914. Legend has it that James Douglas arrived in Jerome to file a claim somewhere but was told by the claims office that everything had already been claimed. Nevertheless, the prospector asked to look at the plats of existing claims and discovered an overlooked triangle of land that had not been claimed. He filed a claim, sank a shaft, and hit the second ore body. Douglas formed a company, the United Verde Extension

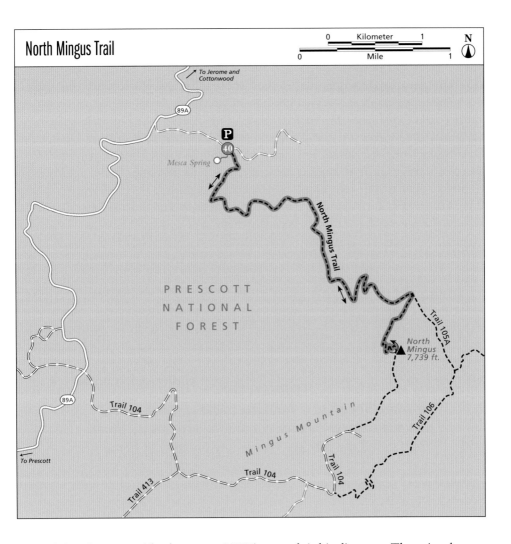

Mining Company (also known as UVX) to exploit his discovery. The mine, known as Little Daisy or UVX, was much smaller than the United Verde Mine, but the ore body was one of the richest ever discovered, averaging more than 10 percent copper and, in places, 45 percent copper. Together, both mines produced more than $1 billion worth of precious metal.

Much of the town of Jerome and the surrounding area lies above mine shafts. This, coupled with the steep slopes and unstable nature of the fault-shattered rock, has made the town unstable since its founding. Structures have cracked and slid downhill, including the famous Sliding Jail, which now lies 200 feet downhill from its original site.

By 1916, problems with fires and flooding in the mine shafts (some of which extend below sea level) prompted the decision to begin open-pit mining at the

United Verde. Both World Wars I and II created a high demand for copper, but by 1953 the price of copper was so low that the mines shut down. From a high of nearly 5,000 residents in 1930, the population sank to fewer than 100 after the last mines closed. To encourage tourism, the Jerome Historical Society was founded, and the town leaders sought designation as a National Historic Landmark for Jerome, which was granted in 1967. The town has successfully rebranded itself as a tourist destination and artists' colony, with a population above 400. In 1962 the heirs of James Douglas donated the Douglas Mansion, just above the site of the UVX Mine, to the State of Arizona, which created Jerome State Historic Park in the building.

Before or after your hike, a visit to Jerome State Historic Park is well worth your time. The exhibits include mining artifacts, photographs, and minerals, as well as a video and a 3-D model of the mines under Jerome.

Miles and Directions

0.0 Start at the trailhead and go through the gate.

1.2 Turn right on the unsigned foot trail.

2.6 Junction with Trail 105A; turn right on Trail 105.

3.0 Reach the rim; return the way you came.

6.0 Arrive back at the trailhead.

GREEN TIP

If you're driving to or from the trailhead, don't let any passenger throw garbage out the window. Keep a small bag in the car that you can empty properly at home.

41 Mingus Rim Loop

This is a very scenic hike along and below the rim of Mingus Mo[...]
views of the Verde Valley and the distant Mogollon Rim.

Distance: 3.6-mile loop
Hiking time: About 2.5 hours
Difficulty: Moderate
Seasons: Summer through fall
Trail surface: Dirt and rocks
Water: None
Other trail users: Mountain bikes and horses
Canine compatibility: Dogs under control allowed

Land status: Prescott National Forest
Fees and permits: None
Maps: Trails Illustrated Sycamore Canyon, Verde Valley; USGS Cottonwood; Prescott National Forest
Trail contacts: Prescott National Forest, 344 S. Cortez St., Prescott 86303; (928) 443-8000; fs.usda.gov/prescott

Finding the trailhead: From Jerome, drive about 7 miles west on AZ 89A to the highway pass on Mingus Mountain, then turn left on the maintained Mingus Mountain Road (FR 104). Go 2.4 miles to the east end of the Mingus Mountain Campground, and park at the viewpoint. This trailhead is also signed for Trail 106. GPS: N34 41.740' / W112 7.259'

The Hike

After checking out the view, descend east on Trail 106. The steep trail leaves the cool pine forest behind as it rapidly descends in a series of switchbacks. Soon the trail starts a gentler descent to the north as it traverses a chaparral slope. The chaparral country is difficult to penetrate without a trail, but the dense brush provides vital wildlife cover.

The trail enters a shadier section of pine forest and meets Trail 105A, which is not shown on the topographic map. This junction is signed; turn left on Trail 105A and follow it as it gradually climbs to another saddle, where it meets Trail 105. Turn left and follow this trail as it climbs to the north rim of Mingus in a series of switchbacks. Walk south to the trailhead at the end of FR 104, then follow the main road to the Mingus Mountain Campground and the start of the hike.

Ponderosa Pine and Fire

The summit plateau of Mingus Mountain lies just under 8,000 feet in elevation; much of it is forested in ponderosa pines, as is the Mogollon Rim country across the Verde Valley. In fact, Arizona contains the largest ponderosa pine forest in the world, stretching from the Kaibab Plateau north of the Grand Canyon, to the Coconino Plateau at the south rim of the canyon, and along the Mogollon Rim from Williams east to the New Mexico line. Ponderosa pine is common throughout the West, from New Mexico to British Columbia. To the north, ponderosa pines tend to grow in

d forests with other evergreens, but in Arizona and New Mexico they are found
nearly pure stands.

When the first settlers arrived in Mogollon Rim country, they reported that the ponderosa forest consisted of open stands of mostly older trees, with a variety of understory plants, including young pines, grasses, flowering plants, and shrubs. Ponderosa pine, also known as western yellow pine, is a valuable timber tree, and logging quickly became a mainstay of the economy in towns within the forest, including Flagstaff. Larger trees are more valuable, so loggers naturally harvested those trees and left the smaller ones. The early settlers also brought herds of cattle and sheep, which quickly grazed off the understory in the pine forests. The third inadvertent blow to the health of the ponderosa forest was active suppression of fires, which rose out of the desire to protect ranches and other property.

What the settlers didn't know is that the ponderosa forest is well-adapted to wildfire—in fact, its health is dependent on frequent wildfires. Before the settlers arrived, lightning started fires that burned through ponderosa stands as frequently as every five years. These fires tended to burn through the understory at low temperatures and short flame lengths, killing young pine seedlings before they could become established but not damaging the mature pines. Ponderosa pine has thick bark with overlapping jigsaw puzzle–like pieces, which insulate the living cambium from fire running up the trunk. Ponderosa pines shed their lower branches as they grow taller, keeping the fire out of the crowns of the trees. Tree-killing crown fires were very rare before settlement. The ground fires released nutrients back into the soil, which helped support a large diversity of plants. This in turn provided cover for wildlife.

Intensive logging removed the mature, fire-resistant trees, leaving the small trees. Fire suppression reduced the number of low-intensity ground fires, which encouraged the growth of thick stands of young trees, but heavy grazing had the worst effect. By removing the ground cover, especially grasses, that grew between the trees, grazing effectively eliminated low-intensity fires. Study plots in heavily grazed areas show that the fire frequency dropped from one fire every five years or so to more than sixty years between fires. Tall grass also shaded out ponderosa seedlings; overgrazing destroyed the grass, allowing many more trees to survive. Ponderosa stands went from as few as 10 or 12 mature trees per acre to 200 or more small, young trees per acre, growing in dense stands with the crowns touching, and the forest floor went from a mosaic of grasses, shrubs, and flowering plants to a dense, thick carpet of pine needles.

When these "doghair thickets" of ponderosa pine catch fire, the thick pine duff burns very hot and retains fire for days after the main flame front has passed through. The increased intensity also increases the chances of the fire climbing the dense, ladder fuels of the crowns, especially during high wind, and becoming a devastating crown fire that kills all the trees and the understory.

The consequences of this inadvertent hundred-year mismanagement of Arizona's ponderosa forest have become very evident. In just the few decades that I've been hiking and exploring the Southwest, fires have greatly increased in intensity and size.

Looking across the Verde Valley to the Sedona red rocks from Mingus Mountain

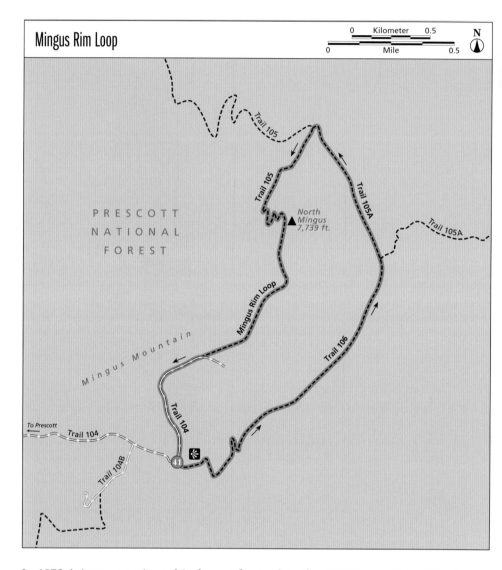

0   Kilometer   0.5

0   Mile   0.5

N

PRESCOTT

NATIONAL

FOREST

Trail 105

Trail 105

North
Mingus
7,739 ft.

Trail 105A

Trail 105A

Mingus Rim Loop

Mingus Mountain

Trail 106

Trail 104

To Prescott
Trail 104

Trail 104B

41

In 1972 Arizona experienced its largest fire to date, the 30,000-acre Battle Fire. As a green new firefighter, I was part of the initial attack on the Battle Fire, but by the time we arrived, the fire was already at 2,000 acres and being pushed by 50-mile-per-hour winds. All we could do was stay out of the way. For years afterward, this fire was studied as an example of an extremely intense, unusually large fire. In 1977 the Radio Fire, started by a teenager playing with matches, roared up the south face of Mount Elden in full view of the residents of Flagstaff. Although it was controlled at only 4,600 acres, the Radio Fire burned the mature forest on the east slopes of Mount Elden with such intensity that it killed nearly every tree and sterilized the soil. Even today, there are only a few stands of quaking aspen, the normal fire succession tree, in the Radio Burn.

In 1990 the Dude Fire burned 28,000 acres in the Mogollon Rim country north of Payson, generating its own pyrotechnic cloud (a thunderstorm-like cloud that forms over extremely intense fires that may even generate its own lightning) and killing six firefighters. Other large fires have burned in ponderosa forests and brush, including the Carr Canyon and Rattlesnake Fires in southern Arizona; then, in 1996 the Lone Fire burned 61,300 acres in the Tonto National Forest.

The worst was to come. After more than five years of exceptional drought in the Southwest, during June 2002, two fires burned together to incinerate 468,000 acres of mostly ponderosa forest on the central Mogollon Rim—Arizona's first mega-fire. The Rodeo Fire was started by an out-of-work firefighter, and the Chediski Fire was started the next day by a person who was stranded on a back road and lit a fire to signal for help. The signal fire got a little bit larger than intended. Together the fires forced the evacuation of several towns and communities in the forest.

Tellingly, the fire burned the hottest where logging activity had been the most intense, on the forested portions of the San Carlos Apache Reservation just south of the central Mogollon Rim. More than 90 percent of the ponderosa pines were killed, completely eliminating the tribe's logging industry in just a few days. However, when the fire reached the Mogollon Rim and the Apache-Sitgreaves National Forest, which had been managed for a lower level of logging, the fire burned in a mosaic pattern, killing large swathes of pines in crown fires, but also dropping to the ground and burning at lower intensity about half the time.

The next year the Aspen Fire burned 84,750 acres on top of Mount Lemmon above Tucson, burning the town of Summerhaven and much of the mixed ponderosa forest. In 2004 a fire did the same thing to 10,000-foot Mount Graham in southeast Arizona. In 2010 the Schultz Fire, started by an abandoned illegal campfire, started on the southeast base of the San Francisco Peaks and burned the entire east slopes of the mountain in a few hours, totaling 15,000 acres.

The Wallow Fire, once again started by an abandoned illegal campfire, burned much of the eastern Mogollon Rim and the White Mountains during the summer of 2011, finally being contained at an incredible 538,000 acres.

We humans have been taught a very harsh lesson. If we want to survive, let alone thrive, in the Southwest's ponderosa pine forests, we urgently have to restore the forest's health and its natural resistance to catastrophic wildfires. Led by the USDA Forest Service, the National Park Service, and other federal and state agencies, several tools are being used to address the problem. As much as possible, lightning-caused fires are allowed to burn at low intensity while conditions are monitored to minimize the threat to communities in the forest. Prescribed fires are deliberately set in carefully planned areas. Near cities and towns, where it is too dangerous to use fire as a management tool, mechanical thinning is being done. This differs from previous logging practices in that only the smaller trees are taken, leaving the fire-resistant large trees. And grazing of domestic animals is being cut back to more sustainable levels.

The effects of these efforts can be seen in the Tusayan District of the Kaibab National Forest, which manages a large stand of ponderosa pines just south of Grand Canyon National Park. Once heavily logged, this unit was one of the earliest in the country to embrace fire as both a natural event and a management tool, and the results are plain to see. The forest is open and beautiful, with a large diversity of plants in the understory, and has never experienced a large, destructive fire.

Miles and Directions

0.0   Start at the Trail 106 trailhead and bear right.
1.4   Turn left on Trail 105A.
2.0   Turn left on Trail 105.
2.4   Reach the north rim of Mingus Mountain.
2.9   Come to the xtrailhead at the end of Forest Road 104.
3.6   Arrive back at the Trail 106 trailhead.

42 Yaeger Canyon Loop

This is an enjoyable loop hike on Mingus Mountain, with views of Prescott Valley.

Distance: 6.0-mile loop
Hiking time: About 4 hours
Difficulty: Moderate
Seasons: Spring through fall
Trail surface: Dirt and rocks
Water: None
Other trail users: Mountain bikes and horses
Canine compatibility: Dogs under control allowed

Land status: Prescott National Forest
Fees and permits: None
Maps: Trails Illustrated Sycamore Canyon, Verde Valley; Apache Creek, Juniper Mesa; USGS Hickey Mountain, Munds Draw; Prescott National Forest
Trail contacts: Prescott National Forest, 344 S. Cortez St., Prescott 86303; (928) 443-8000; fs.usda.gov/prescott

Finding the trailhead: From Prescott, drive 10 miles west on AZ 89A to the unmarked trailhead. The trailhead is 3.2 miles west of the Potato Patch Campground turnoff. Turn left onto the dirt road, and park on either side of the normally dry creek. GPS: N34 40.67' / W112 10.423'

The Hike

The hike starts on the Little Yaeger Canyon Trail, which is signed and begins from the southeast side of the parking area. Several switchbacks through pinyon-juniper forest lead to the top of a gentle ridge, where ponderosa pines begin to take over. The trail climbs more gradually through a small saddle, then meets a dirt road. Turn left and walk down the road 0.2 mile to the Yaeger Cabin Trail (Forest Trail 111), then turn left.

Still in pine-oak forest, the Yaeger Cabin Trail drops slightly as it traverses a side canyon of Little Yaeger Canyon then begins to work its way up the head of the canyon. There is sometimes water in the bed of the canyon near its head. The trail comes out onto a pine flat on the southwest ridge of Mingus Mountain. Turn left on a signed trail. (This side trail also goes right to Allen Spring Road.) Continue 0.1 mile to the end of the Yaeger Cabin Trail at a junction with three other trails. Forest Trail 530 continues straight ahead, while the Yaeger Canyon Trail (Forest Trail 28) crosses from right to left.

Turn left (west), and follow the Yaeger Canyon Trail to the rim, where there is a good view of Little Yaeger Canyon and the rim of Mingus Mountain. The trail descends to the southwest in a series of switchbacks, and the trailhead is visible next to the highway. When the trail reaches the bottom of Yaeger Canyon it turns left on the old highway road bed. It stays on the left (east) side of the creek and doesn't cross on the old highway bridge. Continue down the canyon to your vehicle.

Firecracker penstemon blooms during spring in the high country.

Mountain Lions, Wolves, and Humans

What's the most dangerous animal in Arizona, aside from drunk drivers? If you guessed mountain lions, you're way off. There's never been a documented attack on a human in Arizona. That's not to say it's not going to happen. There have been attacks on people in California and Colorado. The victims are usually trail runners or mountain bikers—it's possible the speed of travel reminds the mountain lion of its natural prey, deer. Usually, though, mountain lions are very shy of people, having been hunted relentlessly until recently. Lions normally hunt from ambush and don't start an attack they can't win. If you see a lion stalking you, experts advise standing your ground and making yourself as large as possible by opening and spreading your jacket, if possible. Keep others in your group, especially children and dogs, close. If attacked, fight back with any means available—knife, rocks, etc.

The native Mexican gray wolf was extinct in Arizona until recently, and now it is found only in low numbers in its recovery area, the central and eastern Mogollon Rim. This wolf is only slightly larger than the far more common coyote, and is often mistaken for one. Like the coyote, Mexican gray wolves are very shy of people, and you can count yourself lucky if you even see one.

Keep in mind that any wild animal may attack if provoked or defending a food source, or especially when defending its young. I was once charged by a common striped skunk with her kits. I was blasting down a steep mountain trail after sunset, thinking about camp and dinner, when I surprised the skunk in the dim light. I stopped as quickly as I could, but the skunk turned and ran at me. I backpedaled as fast as I could, and fortunately the skunk stopped and just gave me the evil eye—no spray. I gave her a wide berth and continued down the trail below her.

The same thing happened with a black bear in broad daylight. In heavy forest, I came upon a couple of black bear cubs next to the trail. They squealed in panic and scampered up a tree. I backed up, looking for momma bear. Then I heard her farther down the trail, chuffing at me. She didn't move, so I backed up farther, then made a wide detour around the bears and rejoined the trail well beyond them.

So if none of the large animals in Arizona are unusually dangerous, what's left? Rattlesnakes? That's the animal novice hikers are the most afraid of in the Southwest. Rattlesnakes certainly deserve your respect, but it's rare for anyone to die from a rattlesnake bite. Their venom is very dangerous though. It's the first stage in the digestion of the small rodents that are a rattlesnake's main prey. When the snake strikes its intended meal, the venom instantly paralyzes the victim so it can't escape. Then the venom starts to digest the prey's tissues. In humans the bite is painful but rarely disabling. But the hemotoxic effects can cause a lot of tissue damage around the bite, and there is a serious danger of infection from the deep puncture wounds. Always seek medical help as soon as possible if bitten by any snake.

Rattlesnakes usually warn you with their unmistakable rattle long before you're within striking range, which is just about half their body length. The rest is common sense. Watch the ground ahead of you as you walk, and stay several feet away from

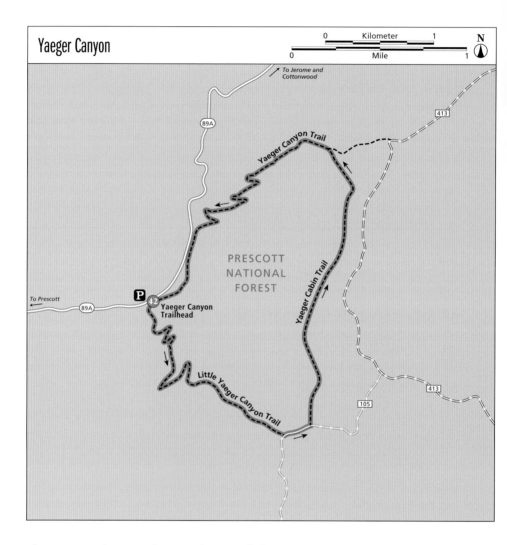

places you can't see, such as overhanging ledges. Keep in mind that rattlesnakes are cold blooded and seek places with temperatures about 80°F. This means that in hot weather, they'll seek shade; in cool weather, you'll find them on open ground sunning themselves, and they den up underground during winter.

The wild animal that has historically killed the most people in Arizona is the desert bark scorpion. Found only in the lower Sonoran Desert of central and southern Arizona, this straw-colored nocturnal scorpion is about 1 inch long. It comes out at night to hunt small insects and hangs out during the day by clinging to the underside of rocks, sticks, and the like—hence the name. Its neurotoxic venom is mainly dangerous to babies, the elderly, and other people with weak immune systems. A healthy adult is going to feel pretty sick, including difficulty breathing, but the sting isn't usually life-threatening. Of course, you should seek medical care as soon as possible.

The larger, brown scorpions found in the pinyon-juniper country look scary, but their sting is no worse than a bee sting, unless you are allergic.

Again, avoiding scorpions is mostly common sense. Since they are active during mild and warm nights, sleep in a net tent rather than under the stars. Under these conditions, the desert is most active at night, with lots of creatures you don't want as bedmates, like cone-nosed kissing bugs. When picking up rocks to anchor your tent or gathering dead wood for a fire, kick the objects before picking them up. Never walk around camp barefoot, and always use a headlamp at night.

In several decades of hiking, backpacking, and climbing in the Southwest backcountry, I've never had a scary encounter with a wild animal—not to say that a few sudden rattlesnake rattles haven't spiked my adrenaline. I wish I could say that about the highways leading to the trailhead. Once I shoulder my pack and start to walk into the wilderness, I start to relax. The hazards are known and relatively simple compared to those of civilization.

Miles and Directions

0.0 Start at the Yaeger Canyon Trailhead and bear right on the Little Yaeger Canyon Trail.

1.6 Turn left on a dirt road.

1.8 Intersect Trail 111; turn left.

3.6 Turn left at an unsigned trail junction.

3.7 Turn left onto Trail 28.

5.5 Reach an old highway; turn left.

6.0 Arrive back at the trailhead.

43 Gaddes Canyon Trail

This enjoyable hike through ponderosa pine and Gambel oak forest on Mingus Mountain offers some good views.

Distance: 5.2 miles out and back
Hiking time: About 3 hours
Difficulty: Moderate
Seasons: Spring through fall
Trail surface: Dirt and rocks
Water: Gaddes Spring
Other trail users: Mountain bikes and horses
Canine compatibility: Dogs under control allowed

Land status: Prescott National Forest
Fees and permits: None
Maps: Trails Illustrated Sycamore Canyon, Verde Valley; USGS Hickey Mountain, Munds Draw; Prescott National Forest
Trail contacts: Prescott National Forest, 344 S. Cortez St., Prescott 86303; (928) 443-8000; fs.usda.gov/prescott

Finding the trailhead: From Jerome, drive about 7 miles east on AZ 89A to the highway pass on Mingus Mountain. Turn left on the maintained Mingus Mountain road (FR 104) and continue 1.4 miles. Turn right on FR 413 (Allen Spring Road). There is a signed junction 2.2 miles down this road; stay left and continue 0.7 mile farther to the trailhead. GPS: N34 40.154' / W112 8.403'

The Hike

The well-graded trail climbs gently north through an open stand of ponderosa pine. After about 0.5 mile the slope becomes steeper and the trail switchbacks past several large rock outcrops to reach the rim of Mingus Mountain. There are glimpses of Prescott Valley to the west and Hickey Mountain to the northwest during this ascent. The trail joins a jeep road as it continues north along the top of the broad, flat ridge. After about 0.6 mile it turns right to leave the jeep road. This junction is signed with the USDA Forest Service trail number, 110. Shortly after, the trail veers north-northeast and descends into Gaddes Canyon. At the bottom of the drainage, our trail passes a junction with Trail 535, a faint trail that heads down the canyon. The Gaddes Canyon Trail ascends the east side of the canyon past Gaddes Spring, which appears to be reliable. There was water here in February 1996, one of the driest winters ever recorded in northern Arizona. The trail reaches the east rim of the canyon then crosses a flat to end at Mingus Lookout Road (FR 104B).

Blazing Trees

Blazing trees to mark wilderness routes is probably as old as tool-using humans. In forested areas, it is easy to leaving a lasting mark on a tree by cutting a vertical slash through the bark with a single swing of an ax, even from horseback. The tree heals itself by growing new bark inward from the edges of the cut, but, at least in the Southwest, it takes decades for a tree to heal a blaze. Even blazes that are healed over

Single-leaf pinyon pine produces a very tasty nut, which was a staple food of Native Americans and is still relished by Arizonans today.

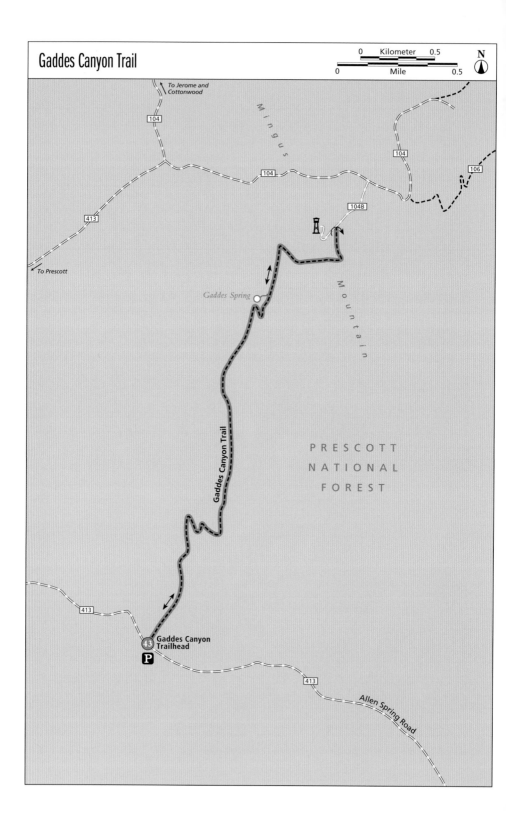

Gaddes Canyon Trail

0 Kilometer 0.5
0 Mile 0.5

N

To Jerome and
Cottonwood

104

Mingus

104

104

104B

104

106

413

To Prescott

Gaddes Spring

Mountain

Gaddes Canyon Trail

PRESCOTT

NATIONAL

FOREST

413

Gaddes Canyon
Trailhead

43

P

413

Allen Spring Road

are often still discernible one hundred years later as a thin vertical scar, especially on the ponderosa pines that are the dominant tree in the Mogollon Rim country and on the highest portions of the Central Mountains, including Woodchute and Mingus Mountains. The only problem with a hasty single-slash tree blaze is that natural events such as a falling rock or a tree scraping another as it falls can create a mark that looks just like a human-made blaze. In the Southwest the forest service uses a short blaze on top of a long blaze to mark official trails. Making such a blaze is slightly more work than a single slash, but a proficient ax wielder can still make one almost without stopping. To make the short blaze, the blade is swung into the trunk horizontally, then a downward swing bites into the bark just above the horizontal cut, sending a short chip of bark flying. This process is repeated just below the short blaze to make a long one.

I find following a line of blazes along a route or very faint trail comforting, especially because of my familiarity with Morse code, which in turn comes from my lifelong amateur radio hobby. What's the connection? Well, in Morse code, sound or light in the form of a short followed by a long represents the letter "A," which I take to mean "All right, I'm on the trail."

Miles and Directions

0.0 Start at the Gaddes Canyon Trailhead.

0.9 Reach the rim of Mingus Mountain.

1.9 Descend into Gaddes Canyon.

2.6 Reach Mingus Lookout Road; return the way you came.

5.2 Arrive back at the trailhead.

44 Coleman Trail

A hike with excellent views of the east side of Mingus Mountain and the Verde Valley.

Distance: 4.0 miles out and back
Hiking time: About 3 hours
Difficulty: Moderate
Seasons: Spring through fall
Trail surface: Dirt and rocks
Water: None
Other trail users: Mountain bikes and horses
Canine compatibility: Dogs under control allowed

Land status: Prescott National Forest
Fees and permits: None
Maps: Trails Illustrated Sycamore Canyon, Verde Valley; USGS Hickey Mountain, Munds Draw; Prescott National Forest
Trail contacts: Prescott National Forest, 344 S. Cortez St., Prescott 86303; (928) 443-8000; fs.usda.gov/prescott

Finding the trailhead: From Jerome, drive about 7 miles west on AZ 89A to the highway pass at the top of Mingus Mountain. Turn left on FR 104, which is maintained dirt. Continue 1.4 miles then turn right on FR 413 (Allen Spring Road). There is a signed junction 2.2 miles down this road; stay left and continue 4.1 miles farther to the signed trailhead. Park about 100 yards east of the trailhead. GPS: N34 40.133' / W112 6.189'

The Hike

The first 0.8 mile of the trail climbs steeply up a brushy slope to the rim of Mingus Mountain. There are good views of upper Black Canyon in the foreground and, beyond, the Black Hills. After the trail reaches the rim, it crosses to the north side of the flat-topped ridge, where the view is superb. The red rock country around Sedona is visible, as are the San Francisco Peaks and most of the western Mogollon Rim. The steep east slopes of Mingus Mountain are in the foreground. The Coleman Trail turns to the northwest along the ridge. After a rocky but short section of trail, the going becomes easier. The last 1.2 miles is a pleasant walk though pinyon-juniper forest, which gradually becomes ponderosa pine forest. The trail ends at FR 104A near a cluster of radio towers.

Extending into Winter

The top of Mingus Mountain lies at nearly 8,000 feet and is often covered with snow during the winter, as is the high country on top of the Mogollon Rim to the north. Since hiking through deep snow (called "postholing" for good reason) is not really much fun, many people don't hike in snow country in the winter. In the Sedona area, you can almost always find lower elevation, snow-free areas for a hike, even in the snowiest Arizona winters. But snow has its own rewards.

Snowshoeing and cross-country skiing are great carbon-free winter activities and, just like hiking, you can make them as easy or as hard as you want—and they extend

The serrated leaves of Gambel oak, which is common along the Gaddes Canyon Trail

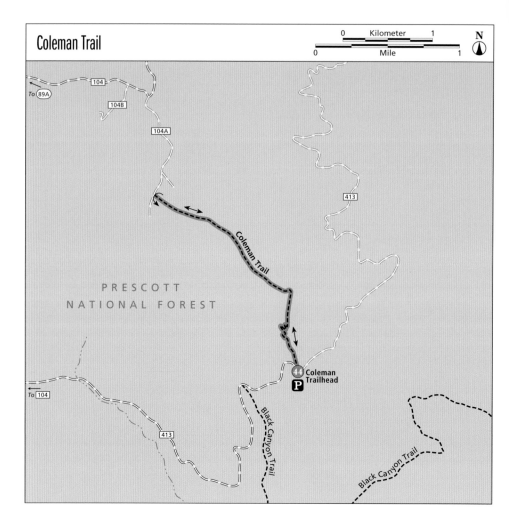

Coleman Trail

0   Kilometer   1

0   Mile   1

N

PRESCOTT
NATIONAL FOREST

Coleman Trail

44 Coleman
Trailhead
P

Black Canyon Trail

Black Canyon Trail

your outdoor seasons into four. Snowshoeing appeals to many because you can just strap 'em on and go . . . well, sort of.

Cross-country, also known as Nordic, skiing is the oldest form of skiing. It started about 4,000 years before the invention of ski lifts and skis (and now snowboards) that are one-dimensional, limited to sliding down hills only. Skis were invented by prehistoric humans, probably in the Scandinavian region, as a way to travel efficiently across deep snow. As a hiker, you like to go places, don't you? You don't ride a lift up a hill, walk down the hill, and repeat all day. Don't get me wrong—sliding down snowy hills is a blast, but so is being able to see tracks where a squirrel emerged from its snug little den, scampered across the snow in a seemingly aimless, sinuous path, then disappeared at the base of a convenient tree. Or seeing the coyote tracks on top of the squirrel tracks and realizing why the squirrel tracks stopped at the base of that tree. Then there are the tracks that start in the middle of a snowy meadow—in the middle of nowhere—and end just as suddenly. Crow tracks!

It's true that using skis does require a bit more technique than snowshoes, especially for the downhill part. So take a lesson. As an experienced ski instructor, I can assure you that you can learn the basics in a couple of hours, which is about two years less time than it took me to figure it out without an instructor!

Miles and Directions

0.0 Start at the signed trailhead.

0.8 Reach the rim of Mingus Mountain.

2.0 The trail ends at FR 104A; return the way you came.

4.0 Arrive back at the trailhead.

45 Black Canyon Trail

This hike starts on the lower slopes of Mingus Mountain and takes you into a rugged canyon and a pine-forested valley. It can also be done one way with a car shuttle.

Distance: 12.0 miles out and back
Hiking time: About 7 hours
Difficulty: Strenuous (moderate with a shuttle)
Seasons: Year-round
Trail surface: Dirt and rocks
Water: None
Other trail users: Mountain bikes and horses
Canine compatibility: Dogs under control allowed

Land status: Prescott National Forest
Fees and permits: None
Maps: Trails Illustrated Sycamore Canyon, Verde Valley; USGS Hickey Mountain, Munds Draw; Prescott National Forest
Trail contacts: Prescott National Forest, 344 S. Cortez St,, Prescott 86303; (928) 443-8000; fs.usda.gov/prescott

Finding the trailhead: From Cottonwood, drive 4 miles south on AZ 260, then turn right on FR 359. Continue 4.5 miles to the end of the road at Quail Springs. GPS: N34 40.308' / W112 2.845'

The Hike

Above Quail Spring, the trail climbs steadily along the brushy slopes above Black Canyon. This chaparral brush becomes thicker as you climb. Although the dense brush is favored wildlife habitat, it's not fun stuff to bash through on a cross-country hike. After nearly 4.0 miles of steady climbing, the trail swings south, crosses a minor saddle, and drops into Black Canyon.

You can leave the trail temporarily and walk 0.4 mile cross-country down the streambed to the point where the stream plunges over the first of many falls and cascades. There is a good flow of water here in spring.

The trail continues up the bed of Black Canyon through a pleasant ponderosa pine forest, then turns right up an unnamed side canyon to end at Allen Spring Road.

Option

From Allen Spring Road you can walk 0.6 mile east on the road then climb to the top of Mingus Mountain via the Coleman Trail. This adds another 4.0 miles round-trip distance and 1,000 feet of elevation gain.

Yavapai-Apache

When the Sinagua began to abandon the Verde Valley, the Yavapai moved in, at least by AD 1300 and possibly earlier. The Yavapai occupied an area extending from the Verde Valley on the west to the Colorado River on the west. They are part of the

Yuman group, which includes the Havasupai and Hualapai peoples of northern Arizona and the Paipai of northern Baja California.

The Tonto Apache also moved into the Verde Valley, which was the western limit of their territory. Totally unrelated to the Yavapai, the Apache are Athabaskan-speaking people who moved into the Southwest sometime after the Sinagua and Hohokam disappeared. The Tonto Apache occupied the area from the Verde Valley eastward along the Mogollon Rim toward the White Mountains. The Apache were nomadic hunters and raiders (the tribe's name for itself means "the hunters"), often traveling through other tribes' lands. They lived lightly on the land and left little lasting evidence of their presence, so it is unclear exactly when they arrived in the Southwest. Some archaeologists place the Apache arrival in the Verde Valley as early as AD 1250; others think they arrived in the late 1500s, only a few decades before the Spanish.

Although culturally different, the two groups appear to have coexisted more or less peacefully in the Verde Valley. Because they were similar in appearance and culture, many Anglo settlers regarded both groups as members of one tribe, which is where the common term "Yavapai-Apache" comes from.

The Yavapai were seminomadic hunter-gathers who traveled in small groups and stuck to the same home territories. The group that occupied the Verde Valley was known as the Wipukupaya.

The first Europeans to see the Verde Valley and Sedona area were Spanish conquistadors led by Coronado in 1540, who came north thousands of miles from Mexico City in search of the fabled Seven Cities of Cibola. These cities were supposed to be so rich that the very walls were built of gold. Coronado never found any riches, but his expedition carried out a remarkable exploration of what is now the American Southwest and literally put it on the map. His expedition traveled as far east as present-day Wichita, Kansas, and west to the Colorado River. Some of his men were the first Europeans to see the Grand Canyon, in 1542.

The Spanish named the Verde River and Verde Valley because the permanent river created a relatively lush oasis in the desert ("verde" is Spanish for "green"). Before the Spaniards' arrival, the valley was home to Native Americans for at least 13,000 years.

After the Coronado expedition, Spain claimed the American Southwest as part of its vast colonial empire. But Spain had little to do with Arizona north of Tucson, the regional capital. Spanish missionaries did build a mission at the Hopi villages in northeast Arizona in an attempt to convert the Hopi to Christianity, but the Hopi eventually became fed up and drove the Spaniards out.

Spanish missionaries had better luck among the pueblo Indians of New Mexico, where they established their regional capital at Santa Fe. Arizona and New Mexico became part of Mexico when that country declared independence from Spain in 1810. By the 1820s, increasing numbers of Anglo settlers were arriving from the east. Tension grew between the Mexican authorities and the Americans, culminating in the Mexican-American War of 1846–1848. The resulting peace treaty ceded much of the Southwest to the United States, with the exception of Arizona south of the Gila

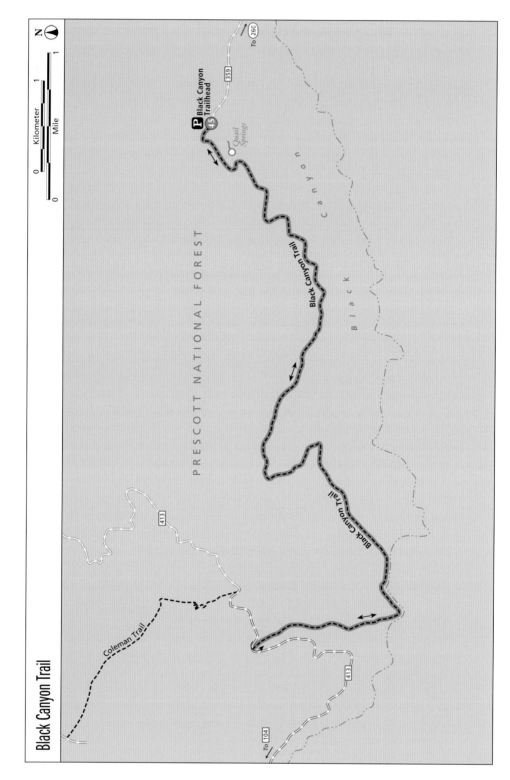

Black Canyon Trail

Never park or camp in a dry wash—heavy rains can send raging floods down canyons.

River and a bit of southern New Mexico. Tensions continued in the borderlands, and in 1854 the United States negotiated the Gadsden Purchase with Mexico, buying the southern lands and creating the modern-day border with Mexico.

American settlement in the Southwest increased rapidly until the American Civil War caused the Union Army and troops of the newly created Confederacy to be withdrawn east to join the fighting. This was perceived by the raiding Apache tribes and others as a sign they were winning the fight to keep the intruders out of their lands, and the Indians increased their attacks. As a result, many settlers and ranchers fled Arizona and New Mexico. After the Civil War ended and the US Army returned to the Southwest, settlement resumed at an increasing pace.

American trappers and explorers reached the Verde Valley after the acquisition from Mexico in 1848, but no one started to settle in the area until 1860. Ranchers and miners established homesteads and mining camps without regard to the existing inhabitants, and friction soon developed.

Miles and Directions

0.0 Start at Quail Springs.

4.4 Reach Black Canyon.

6.0 The trail ends at Allen Spring Road; return the way you came.

12.0 Arrive back at the trailhead.

46 Chasm Creek Trail

This seldom-used trail climbs from Chasm Creek to the Verde Rim. If yo̶̶ ̶̶̶̶ ̶̶ solitude, you'll find it here—and the views are awesome.

Distance: 6.8 miles out and back
Hiking time: About 5 hours
Difficulty: Strenuous
Seasons: Spring and fall
Trail surface: Dirt and rocks
Water: Unnamed spring in Chasm Creek
Other trail users: Horses
Canine compatibility: Dogs under control allowed

Land status: Cedar Bench Wilderness, Prescott National Forest
Fees and permits: None
Maps: Trails Illustrated Sycamore Canyon, Verde Valley; USGS Horner Mountain; Prescott National Forest
Trail contacts: Prescott National Forest, 344 S. Cortez St., Prescott 86303; (928) 443-8000; fs.usda.gov/prescott

Finding the trailhead: From Camp Verde, drive south on the General Crook Trail (FH 9), then turn right on paved CR 163. This turnoff is just before the Verde River bridge. The paved road becomes maintained dirt. Continue generally south and east 11.8 miles, and park on the right just before crossing Chasm Creek. This turnoff is marked with a small hiking trail symbol. GPS: N34 26.985' / W111 49.370'

The Hike

Although most of the trail is easy to follow, there are faint sections as it receives little use. It's a good idea to have the topographic map, which shows the trail correctly. The trail is marked by rock cairns and tree blazes. From the trailhead, go through the wire gate and follow the trail as it descends into Chasm Creek. The section of trail along the creek bed was destroyed in a huge flood in February 1994. Stay generally on the left side of the creek for about 200 yards. The trail climbs out on the left just before a series of rockbound pools and small cascades. There is no more water on the trail after this point. Climbing steeply, the trail heads south away from Chasm Creek itself but stays in the Chasm Creek drainage all the way to the Verde Rim. After the steep climb the grade moderates somewhat as the trail turns more to the west, traversing pleasant pinyon-juniper forest. More steep sections lead to the west slopes of Table Mountain, the prominent flat mesa visible from the approach road. The Verde Rim is visible to the west, across the Chasm Creek basin. About 2.0 miles from the trailhead, the trail reaches a saddle on the ridge west of Table Mountain, and the view to the south opens up. The Verde River canyon is visible, as well as the rugged Mazatzal Mountains and the Mogollon Rim. Finally, the trail follows the ridge southwest and skirts a hill to reach a broad grassy saddle on the Verde Rim, with views of the distant radshaw Mountains to the west. Although the trail continues to FR 528 in another 3.0 miles, this point on the Verde Rim makes a good turnaround point.

Secrets of Water

Hikers who live in wet climates are usually amazed at how obsessed desert hikers are with water. (I'm excluding non-outdoor people here, because desert city dwellers think water somehow appears magically when they turn a tap.) Well, you learn to be when the very air wants to suck your body dry. During June, when the humidity drops to less than 10 percent, and even as low as 5 percent in the low deserts, and temperatures blast past 110°F in the shade, water is life. A human will die in a few hours without water in such extreme conditions.

Even in more reasonable temperatures that are actually fun for hiking, you'll dehydrate quickly, but it's not enough to carry and drink a lot of water. You also have to keep snacking to keep your electrolytes in balance. Failure to do so will result in heat exhaustion, which creeps up on you insidiously. Unless you or someone in your group recognizes the symptoms, you can become unable to hike. Unless treated, heat exhaustion progresses into heat stroke, where the body loses its temperature-regulating ability. Heat stroke is a life-threatening medical emergency requiring immediate evacuation to a hospital. It kills hikers every summer in Arizona, especially in the deserts around Phoenix and Tucson, and in the Grand Canyon.

So naturally one gets a bit obsessed with water, even on day hikes where you can carry all the water you should need. I'm always noting any water sources I pass. Each one gives me a clue to where the next water might be found, because most water in the desert is secretive, except for the few perennial streams and rivers like Oak Creek, Sycamore Canyon, and the Verde River.

Looking at the ramparts of the Verde Rim, you might think the place is bone dry. Not so. Often when flying past the Verde Rim and looking down from the air, I see the wink of water reflecting sunlight from some hidden pool deep in a canyon. I've even seen the flash of hidden water out of the corner of my eye when climbing up nearby Copper Canyon on I-17, when most of my attention has to be on the slow trucks ahead and the crazy drivers weaving in and out of traffic, desperately trying to get a car length ahead of everyone else.

When rain falls and snow melts in Arizona, much of it evaporates right back into the air. But some of it sinks into the ground and percolates slowly downward until it reaches the local water table. In moist climates the water table is usually pretty close to the surface, as anyone with a basement can tell you. But in the desert the water table can be hundreds or even thousands of feet down. For example, Flagstaff drills 2,000 feet to get a reliable water source for the city. At the south rim of the Grand Canyon, the water table is more than 4,000 feet down. Fortunately, in most of Arizona except the Colorado Plateau, the water table is closer to the surface.

If Arizona were flat, we'd only know about groundwater from drilling. But since the terrain is rugged, underground water often makes it to the surface. Underground

Coyotes are found from the deserts to the forests in the Sedona and Verde Valley areas.

water flows slowly through pores in the rock, moving downhill just as it does on the surface, unless stopped by an impervious rock layer. Sandstone and limestone can hold a lot of water, but rocks such as shale tend to block the downward flow so that water collects in the porous layers above. If a porous layer is exposed along the walls or bed of a canyon, water may appear at the surface in the form of a spring. Another way the water reaches the surface is along a fault. Sterling Spring, the source of Oak Creek, is a perfect example. The water table is about 1,000 feet below the surface of the plateau here, but the shattered rocks along the Oak Creek Fault allow water to move upward. North of Oak Creek Canyon, it doesn't reach the surface, but Flagstaff took advantage of the fault to drill its first deep wells in the 1950s. They were able to hit water about 800 feet down because of the upward flow.

Sterling Spring is just below the lower end of the switchbacks that bring Arizona 89A to the bottom of Oak Creek Canyon. Just below the spring, Sterling Fish Hatchery, operated by Arizona Fish and Game, takes advantage of the pure water of the spring. In contrast, Pumphouse Wash comes in from the northeast and doesn't align with the Oak Creek Fault, so there are no permanent springs along its length.

As Oak Creek cuts deeper and deeper into the rock layers as it follows the fault south, more water appears, some in named springs that flow a short distance to the main creek, including Pine Flat and Cave Springs. Most of the water added to the creek is in the form of springs in the bed of the creek itself. Midway through Oak Creek Canyon, the West Fork adds its own spring-fed flow to the main stream.

Springs vary from just a tiny seep that barely wets the rock to underground rivers bursting out of caves with a roar. Many springs are reliable, such as those that feed Oak and Sycamore Creeks, flowing year-round, even through the midsummer heat; others are seasonal, appearing only during the cool half of the year or after a wet winter or summer.

Water pockets are another natural source of water. Known by their Spanish name in southern Arizona, tinajas, water pockets are natural basins in bedrock that trap and hold rainwater. Like springs, some water pockets are large enough and sufficiently protected from sunlight that they hold water all year. Others dry up just hours after the rain that filled them. All are important sources of water in the desert.

The southernmost emigrant trail in the United States, El Camino del Diablo (the Devil's Highway) ran across the southwest desert of Arizona just north of the present-day Mexican border. The route was only possible because of deep, permanent tinajas in the foothills of the low desert ranges the trail crossed. You can drive the route today, through the Cabeza Prieta National Wildlife Refuge, and still see the stone graves that mark the final resting places of emigrants who didn't find a tinaja before it was too late.

Water pockets form in canyon bottoms where bedrock is exposed when floods scour out deep basins below pour-offs and waterfalls. The narrower the canyon and the deeper the water pocket, the more likely it is to retain water year-round. The other type of water pocket forms where large areas of sandstone are exposed on the surface, as around Sedona and especially in the canyon country of northern Arizona and southern Utah. Rainwater flowing across bare sandstone puddles in low spots, gradually dissolving the calcite that cements the sand grains together. When the water evaporates, wind blows the loose sand away. Over time, the depression deepens and a water pocket forms. Most water pockets hold water for only a few weeks after a rain, but some are so deep that they never go dry. A lot depends on the slope of the sandstone above and how effectively it collects and channels water into the water pockets.

The ability to locate a spring or a water pocket may save your life or that of someone in your party in an emergency, and it certainly will make your backcountry life more pleasant. Years ago, a friend and I were attempting to climb a few summits in the far eastern Grand Canyon. We were running low on water, and the only spring we knew of in the area was suspected of being poisonous. Sure enough, there was no animal or plant life around the spring, the classic danger sign. We loaded up with water just in case, but continued our hunt for water pockets as we climbed one of the peaks that day. We found just enough for camp that night in a side canyon, enabling us to bag our second summit the next day. That night, a storm rolled in and it rained for the next day and night. Yet, even after all that rain, there were no water pockets

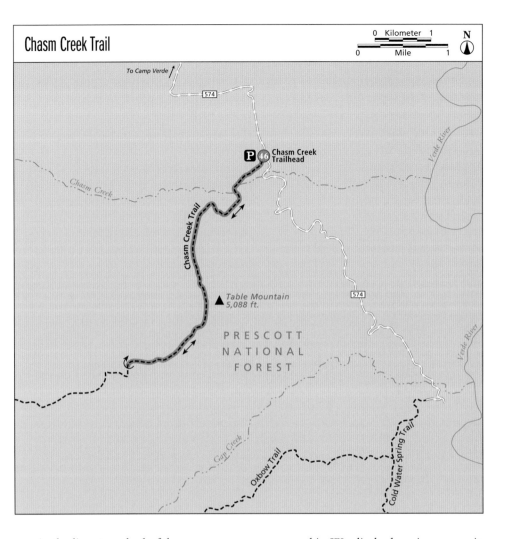

Chasm Creek Trail

0 Kilometer 1

0 Mile 1

N

To Camp Verde

574

P 46 Chasm Creek Trailhead

Chasm Creek

Chasm Creek Trail

▲ Table Mountain 5,088 ft.

574

Verde River

Verde River

PRESCOTT NATIONAL FOREST

Gap Creek

Oxbow Trail

Cold Water Spring Trail

in the limestone bed of the canyon we were camped in. We climbed a minor summit, and there below us, hundreds of water pockets winked in the morning sun, scattered across a few acres of sandstone that had just enough slope to create the perfect collection basin.

Miles and Directions

0.0 Start at the Chasm Creek Trailhead and go through the wire gate.

2.0 Traverse a saddle on Table Mountain.

3.4 Reach Verde Rim; return the way you came.

6.8 Arrive back at the trailhead.

47 Cold Water Spring Loop

This challenging hike in a remote area on rarely-used trails offers fine views of the Verde River canyon.

Distance: 14.4-mile loop
Hiking time: About 10 hours
Difficulty: Strenuous
Seasons: Spring and fall
Trail surface: Dirt and rocks
Water: Cold Water Spring
Other trail users: Horses
Canine compatibility: Dogs under control allowed

Land status: Cedar Bench Wilderness, Prescott National Forest
Fees and permits: None
Maps: Trails Illustrated Sycamore Canyon, Verde Valley; USGS Tule Mesa, Horner Mountain; Prescott National Forest
Trail contacts: Prescott National Forest, 344 S. Cortez St., Prescott 86303; (928) 443-8000; fs.usda.gov/prescott

Finding the trailhead: From Camp Verde, drive south on the General Crook Trail (FH 9), then turn right on paved CR 163. This turnoff is just before the Verde River bridge. Continue generally south and east 16.5 miles to a locked gate near the Brown Springs Ranch. The road becomes FR 574; it will change from paved to maintained gravel and then to unmaintained dirt but is passable to most cars with care. Trailhead parking is to the left of the ranch buildings in a clearing next to Gap Creek. GPS: N34 24.852' / W111 47.408'

The Hike

All the trails in this loop hike are little used and are faint in places. It will be necessary to watch for tree blazes, rock cairns, and even cut limbs on trees to stay on the trail. In difficult sections, don't leave the last cairn or blaze until you have located the next one. The trail is rocky, and some sections are brushy. Allow extra time for this hike. The reward for your efforts is a continuously changing view of the rugged Verde River canyon, the Mogollon Rim, and, in the distance, the San Francisco Peaks and Mazatzal Mountains.

Walk up the road past the locked gate about 200 yards, then turn right on a much rougher road that climbs steeply west up the ridge. After another 200 yards the road swings sharply left, and a small sign marks the beginning of Trail 163 (Oxbow Trail). Follow the trail another 200 yards to a gate in a saddle. Two fences cross at right angles here. Turn left (south) and go through the gate in the east–west fence. Do not go through the gate in the north–south fence. The trail becomes more distinct as it climbs south along the ridge. At Bear Grass Tank, about 1.0 mile from the trailhead, the unsigned Oxbow Trail goes right (west); this will be the return trail. Continue straight ahead (south) on the Cold Water Spring Trail. The trail climbs through an open forest of pinyon pine and juniper as it skirts the east slopes of Cedar Bench then climbs sharply up the headwaters of Cold Water Creek to reach Cold Water Spring.

The spring appears to be reliable, and there are numerous campsites for those who wish to do this loop as an overnight hike.

Turn right on Trail 162. (The Cold Water Spring Trail continues south another 2.0 miles and ends at FR 68G on the Verde Rim.) This junction is unsigned and difficult to find. Just above the spring, marked by an old water trough, turn right (northwest) and contour along the slope. Watch for a length of black plastic pipe and a series of cairns and blazes. After a short distance the trail becomes clearer but is still more difficult to follow than the Cold Water Spring Trail. The trail contours the steep slopes below the Verde Rim then climbs onto the upper slopes of Cedar Bench, clearly visible ahead. After crossing Cedar Bench the trail swings more to the west and crosses steep, brushy slopes that offer panoramic views of the Verde Valley to the north. About 4.0 miles from Cold Water Spring, the trail crosses through a broad, grassy saddle. Carefully follow the cairns about 0.5 mile to an unsigned trail junction at a fence. Turn right (north) and follow the cairned trail (Oxbow Trail) downhill to Oxbow Tank. Pass the tank on the left then continue on the trail as it descends the deepening canyon. Just above a cliff, the trail veers right and crosses the drainage then contours around the slope above the cliff, generally in a northeast direction. About 1.0 mile from the last trail junction, an unsigned trail forks left and descends into Gap Creek. (This trail goes to FR 5907M.) Continue straight ahead on the Oxbow Trail as it contours the north-facing slope for about 1.0 mile then comes out on a ridge and starts descending. The trail is distinct and well-marked with rock cairns. In another 1.0 mile the trails turns south, leaves the ridge, and crosses a series of drainages, then climbs slightly to reach the junction at Bear Grass Tank. Turn left and return to the trailhead, now 1.0 mile away.

Ranching and Stock Tanks

Raising cattle and sheep in the desert requires water. Lots of water. The ranch near this trailhead is named for the nearby springs that made the site usable for the early settlers, who didn't have the means to drill deep wells. Modern ranchers drill wells where they can, often marked by that man-made icon of the Southwest, the windmill. With their 30-foot steel tower and water tank at their base, windmills are still an important source of water in the desert. My mother grew up on a ranch west of Phoenix, and she and her friends often went swimming in the open-topped tanks that collect water from the windmill. On the vast Navajo Indian Reservation in the high desert of northeast Arizona and covering one-sixth of the state, water is very hard to come by. So the tribal government drills wells and installs windmills, each of which may serve dozens of nearby Navajo families raising sheep and cattle.

Ranchers also develop natural springs, usually by fencing the source to protect it from trampling and pollution and running a pipe down to a watering trough. The trough can be made of concrete, half a steel barrel, or even a hollowed-out log. These require maintenance because floods wipe out the pipe, and sometimes the spring shifts a bit so that the intake clogs or goes dry. The sound of water pouring out of a pipe into a trough is music to a desert hiker's ears.

Hidden springs were developed by the early settlers in the Verde Valley area and are still important sources of water.

I visited a spring in the Mazatzal Mountains south of Payson many times. The spring served an old rancher's line camp—the wood cabin was still there, complete with a giant centipede on the wall, the first time I camped there. Clear, cold, clean water came out of a plastic pipe and splashed into an upright 55-gallon drum. From there the water flowed to a wooden trough, and the overflow ran down the slope a short way before sinking into the bone-dry earth.

Once when I arrived tired and thirsty and ready to make my dinner, there was no water coming from the pipe. Usually the source spring is obvious, but not in this case. I followed the black plastic pipe up the slope, across the main trail, and on up the steeper slope above. There wasn't a drainage, just an open hillside, and no patch of green vegetation to mark the location of the spring. Luckily the pipe was only partly buried, so I was able to follow it several hundred feet to a small pool tucked into a little pocket of rocks. Talk about a secret spring; unless the flow was unusually high, you'd never spot it from the main trail. I had my bottles with me, so I filled them at the source and then fixed the intake. The spring was unusually low and the intake screen was clogged. By the time I got back down to camp, water was flowing merrily out of the pipe.

Another method ranchers use to increase the water available for their stock is to build "stock tanks" by bulldozing up an earthen dam in a drainage to collect runoff. You'll see several examples along this hike. Building a stock tank is an engineering exercise, of course, but also an art form. Build your stock tank in too small a drainage, and it never gets enough runoff to fill. Build it in too large a drainage, and the floods wipe out your dam. You also have to provide a spillway to safely divert water around the dam without destroying it. Some stock tanks get wiped out the first time it rains; others provide reliable water for years. Eventually, silt fills up the pond and it has to be dug out again.

Stock tank water is usually muddy and polluted by livestock, so it's not appealing. I would use stock tank water in an emergency, but only after filtering it and using a double dose of iodine or chlorine dioxide tablets.

When ranchers drill wells and build stock tanks, the water also benefits wildlife. But there's another man-made water source that is primarily created for wildlife, usually constructed by Arizona Fish and Game or the US Fish and Wildlife Service. These structures have various names—water-saver, trick tank—but they all work the same way, by collecting rainwater on a gently sloping collection area made from concrete, steel or aluminum roofing, or plastic and piping it to a metal, plastic, or concrete storage tank. Another pipe carries the water to a trough, where the flow is regulated with a float valve to keep from wasting water. If intended primarily for wildlife, the trough is fenced to keep domestic livestock out. Trick tanks can be found on public lands all over Arizona, especially in the various wildlife refuges. The only area where they aren't common is the White Mountains in eastern Arizona, which receives a lot of snow and summer rain and has the largest concentration of perennial streams in Arizona.

Trails and Highways—Crossing Arizona

Transportation has always been difficult in Arizona because of its rugged terrain. In most areas of the world, ground transportation corridors for roads, highways, and railroads tend to follow rivers and valleys, because these features offer the least-difficult terrain and the gentlest gradients—especially important for railroads. That doesn't work in Arizona, because our terrain is a mix of low desert with parallel low mountain ranges, high desert with high mountain ranges, mixed rugged mountains and canyons, and high plateaus with deep canyons.

I-17 from Phoenix to Flagstaff is a prime example. If you're using this book, you've probably driven it at least once if you're a visitor to Sedona, and many times if you're a resident of Sedona or Flagstaff. Leaving Phoenix northbound, I-17 crosses the Salt River Valley, which is basically a gently sloping plain with desert mountains sticking up here and there. So far so good, but then the freeway encounters the foothills of the Central Mountains and starts to wind its way through the rugged foothills. It drops down a bit and actually follows the New River for a few miles, but then veers away and crosses a few tributary canyons at right angles. After reaching the Agua Fria River, the river that drains the entire area, the freeway crosses it and, instead of following the river valley, climbs a 12 percent grade to the top of the plateau to the north. It crosses this plateau, passing the turnoff to Prescott, then crosses a much smaller Agua Fria River and plunges down Copper Canyon to the Verde Valley. It crosses the Verde River and then climbs up another steep grade to the Mogollon Rim, winding

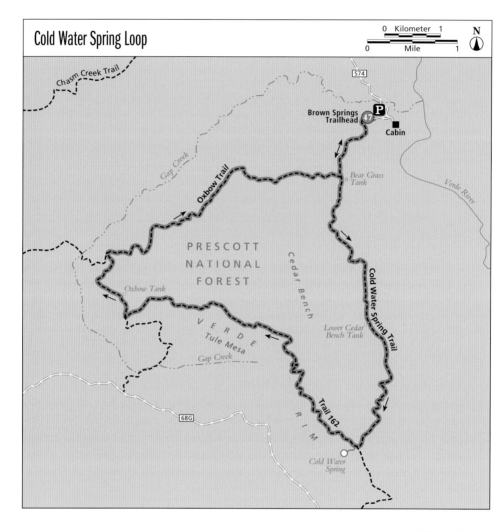

through ponderosa forest and crossing meadows before ending at I-40 and Flagstaff. It's the country's steepest interstate.

Why doesn't I-17 follow the rivers? Because they flow through deep canyons for much of their length. The section of the Agua Fria River that I-17 ignores runs through a 600-foot-deep canyon where construction would be far more expensive. And just downstream of the I-17 crossing, the Verde River enters a designated Wild and Scenic portion between the Mazatzal and Pine Mountain Wildernesses. Again, not a cheap place to build a road.

Northern Arizona is even worse. Because of the deep canyons that dissect the Colorado Plateau, highways take very indirect routes. For example, Grand Canyon Village on the south rim of the Grand Canyon is just 14 miles from North Rim Village, 21 miles by foot trail. But the drive is 212 miles and takes 4 hours. That's because there are two major canyons that must be skirted because they are too wide to bridge.

Trails for foot or pack travel have a lot more options for working with the terrain.

Miles and Directions

0.0 Start at the Brown Springs Ranch Trailhead.

1.0 Junction with the Oxbow Trail; continue straight on the Cold Water Spring Trail.

4.6 Reach Cold Water Spring; turn right on Trail 162.

9.2 Turn right onto the unsigned Oxbow Trail.

10.2 Turn right again at an unsigned junction to stay on the Oxbow Trail.

13.4 Turn left at an unsigned junction to stay on the Oxbow Trail.

14.4 Arrive back at the trailhead.

GREEN TIP

If you're an infrequent hiker or backpacker, you may want to borrow, rent, or share gear instead of owning. If you buy your own, buy top-quality equipment. It is cheaper in the long run because good equipment lasts so much longer than poorly made gear. Remember: In the backcountry, your life depends on your footgear, your pack, your tent, and your water bottles.

48 Towel Creek

This unique hike leads to the Verde River, one of only a few remaining free-flowing rivers in Arizona. It's also the lowest elevation hike in this book.

Distance: 14.2 miles out and back
Hiking time: About 8 hours
Difficulty: Moderate
Seasons: Fall through spring
Trail surface: Dirt and rocks
Water: Verde River
Other trail users: Mountain bikes and horses
Canine compatibility: Dogs under control allowed

Land status: Coconino National Forest
Fees and permits: None
Maps: Trails Illustrated Flagstaff and Sedona; USGS Hackberry Mountain, Horner Mountain; Coconino National Forest
Trail contacts: Coconino National Forest, 1824 S. Thompson St., Flagstaff 86001; (928) 527-3600; fs.usda.gov/coconino

Finding the trailhead: From Camp Verde, drive about 7.6 miles east on AZ 260, then turn right on FR 708. Continue 8 miles to the trailhead, on the right. GPS: N34 26.095' / W111 41.234'

The Hike

At first the trail heads south, nearly parallel to the road. It then climbs through a saddle and contours southwest across the slopes of Hackberry Mountain. The trail then swings west and crosses into the head of Towel Creek at Towel Tank. As you continue west, you'll pass a side canyon coming in from the south. A short spur trail leads to Towel Spring, which is in this side canyon. The main trail continues west, loosely following Towel Creek all the way to the Verde River.

Wild and Scenic Rivers and Desert Bald Eagles

The course of the Verde River south of Camp Verde to Horseshoe Lake flows through a series of deep, rugged canyons between the Cedar Bench and Pine Mountain wildernesses on the west and the isolated Mazatzal Wilderness on the east. This reach of the Verde River is Arizona's first designated and protected Wild and Scenic River. It's a popular float trip for kayakers, canoeists, and rafters, depending on water levels.

The river is also home to a nesting population of desert bald eagles. The only surviving desert bald eagles all live in Arizona, and one-third of them nest along this section of the Verde River. These majestic birds are classified as endangered under the Endangered Species Act, and the Verde River nesting area as well as the other nesting areas in Arizona are managed to restore the population of eagles to a viable level. In order to protect the eagles during nesting season, portions of the Verde River are closed from December 1 to June 30 each year. Boaters may float through on the river, but landing, stopping, and camping are prohibited.

Towel Creek

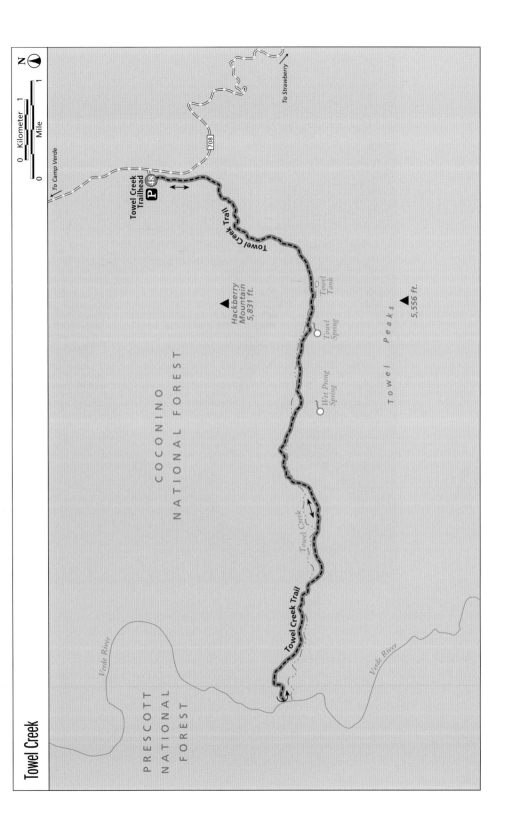

N

0 Kilometer 1
0 Mile 1

To Camp Verde

Towel Creek Trailhead
P 48

708

To Strawberry

Towel Creek Trail

COCONINO
NATIONAL FOREST

Hackberry
Mountain
5,831 ft.

Towel
Tank

Towel
Spring

Wet Prong
Spring

Towel   Peaks

5,556 ft.

Towel Creek

Towel Creek Trail

PRESCOTT
NATIONAL
FOREST

Verde River

Verde River

A Mexican poppy near Towel Creek. In wet years, wildflowers often form a stunning spring display.

It's important to distinguish nesting from wintering eagles. Eagles that nest in northern regions of the West come to Arizona for the winter, but they don't nest here.

Miles and Directions

- **0.0** Start at the Towel Creek Trailhead and head south.
- **0.8** Climb through a saddle.
- **2.3** Reach Towel Tank.
- **2.8** Come to the Towel Spring junction.
- **7.1** Reach the Verde River; return the way you came.
- **14.2** Arrive back at the trailhead.

Mogollon Rim

E ast of Oak Creek Canyon, the Mogollon Rim turns southeast to form the eastern boundary of the Verde Valley. At Fossil Creek, the rim resumes its general east-southeast orientation. A series of long, spectacular canyons cut into the Mogollon Rim; most are wild and remote and are protected as wilderness areas. Several of the following hikes are in these canyons; others are on the southeast portion of the Coconino Plateau.

49 Bell Trail

East of Oak summer hike along Wet Beaver Creek. The trail climbs to the Mogollon Rim for some good views.

Distance: 8.4 miles out and back
Hiking time: About 5 hours
Difficulty: Moderate
Seasons: Year-round
Trail surface: Dirt and rocks
Water: Wet Beaver Creek
Other trail users: Horses
Canine compatibility: Dogs under control allowed

Land status: Wet Beaver Creek Wilderness, Coconino National Forest
Fees and permits: None
Maps: Trails Illustrated Mogollon Rim, Munds Mountain; USGS Casner Butte ; Coconino National Forest
Trail contacts: Coconino National Forest, 1824 S. Thompson St., Flagstaff 86001; (928) 527-3600; fs.usda.gov/coconino

Finding the trailhead: From Sedona, drive about 14 miles southeast on AZ 179 and go under the I-17 interchange. Continue 2.1 miles on Beaver Creek Road (FR 618), then turn left into the Wet Beaver Creek Trailhead. GPS: N34 40.459' / W111 42.807'

The Hike

The trail stays along the north side of Wet Beaver Creek. Stands of Fremont cottonwood and other riparian vegetation crowd the creek, but there are several short side trails down to the water. One of several permanent streams flowing through the canyons below the Mogollon Rim, Wet Beaver Creek is very popular during the summer. As you continue up the canyon, notice how the slope to the left, which is sunnier and drier, features a nearly pure stand of juniper trees. On the other hand, the slope to the right faces north, is cooler and moister, and supports a mixed stand of juniper and pinyon. Evidently pinyon pines require just a bit more moisture, and possibly cooler temperatures, than the junipers. Very slight changes in climate can have a dramatic effect on plant and animal communities.

At 2.1 miles you'll pass the Apache Maid Trail. Continue east along the canyon on the Bell Trail. There are a number of good swimming holes along the creek, just below the trail. After another 1.0 mile the trail crosses the creek and climbs up a steep ridge to the Mogollon Rim. Although the trail continues to FR 214, this scenic spot makes a good turnaround point.

Option

You can also reach the rim via the Apache Maid Trail, which climbs the north slope of the canyon. The juniper forest is open, and the first section of the trail provides good views down Wet Beaver Creek. A series of switchbacks lead up to the base of Casner

Butte, then the trail crosses the drainage to the north and angles up to the Mogollon Rim. Here the view ranges from the San Francisco Peaks to the north to the Verde Valley to the west and southwest. Originally built for access to the Apache Maid fire tower, the remainder of the trail is faint and difficult to follow, so this is a good place to turn around. This option adds 2.8 miles round-trip and 1,050 feet of elevation gain to the main hike.

Fire Lookouts

The Apache Maid Trail was originally built for access to Apache Maid Lookout. Lookout towers are staffed during periods of high fire danger to provide early detection of wildfires. Early detection and rapid initial attack are critical to stop a fire before it becomes large and difficult to control.

The USDA Forest Service was created in 1905 to manage the nation's growing National Forest System. Among the new agency's many responsibilities was a requirement to control wildfires. Before a fire can be attacked and controlled, it first has to be detected. The obvious solution was to send forest rangers to hilltops and mountaintops to watch for fires. Some areas have high points with clear views, good for maintaining a watch, but others do not. Obviously this was a temporary solution, and not a comfortable one for the observer. In particular, there was no protection from lightning. The only option for the observer in the event of a thunderstorm was to seek lower ground.

On the Kaibab Plateau, north of Grand Canyon's north rim, early foresters turned tall ponderosa pines into ready-made lookout towers by putting a ladder or a series of spikes up the trunk, topping the crown, and installing an observer's platform with rails, a chair, and a fire finder. Lookout trees were used throughout the West from 1905 to 1920, and the Kaibab Plateau had at least a dozen. However, lookout trees were dangerous, uncomfortable, and deprived the forest of observers right when they were needed to observe lightning strikes.

This led to the construction of permanent wood or steel towers on mountaintops carefully selected for their viewshed. Ideally the viewsheds of adjacent towers would overlap, allowing the observers to locate smoke more accurately. The observer's cab, a small room with glass windows on all four sides, kept the observer out of the weather, and a system of lightning rods and ground wires kept the lookout safe from lightning strikes. Most lookouts had a wooden chair with glass insulators on its feet that the lookout would sit on when lightning was dangerously close.

Some lookouts on rocky summits don't actually need towers to obtain a good view; such lookouts are called ground cabs, but the lookout is still referred to as a lookout tower. By the 1930s, with the assistance of New Deal programs such as the Civilian Conservation Corps and several others, thousands of lookout towers were being built across the country, including many in state forests.

Lookouts didn't serve just for fire detection. Often, they were staffed by a husband-and-wife team. The woman was the primary lookout, relieved by her husband. When the team spotted a fire, the man would either ride to the fire on horseback or hike, depending on the terrain, and attack the fire with hand tools and backpack water bags. Because there were few roads in the early days of the national forests, many such combination lookout/fire guard stations were built to enable faster response to fires.

Numerous styles of towers were built, but two basic types are the most common. The observation tower has a small cab, usually about 7 feet square, with just enough room for the observer to move around all four sides of the fire-finder stand, and a stool to sit on. The lookout only occupied the tower when on duty, and generally lived in a small cabin at the base of the tower when off duty. The idea was that the lookout would have minimal distractions while looking for fires. In my opinion as a former lookout with four fire seasons under my belt, this policy was in error and was developed by people with no fire-observing experience. Watching for smoke is not a continuous job—if you stare at the landscape for too long, your eyes just glaze over and you don't notice what you're seeing.

Many fire managers realized this, and so a second style of tower cab became popular: the live-in tower. From 11 to 14 feet square, these cabs provided enough room for one or two people to live and move about comfortably. The larger tower cabs also had catwalks, which gave the observer a completely unobstructed view and allowed him or her to get some exercise, which helped keep the observer alert. One hundred and forty-four square feet doesn't sound like much, but when it's a glass house with 360-degree views, believe me, it's spacious.

As more roads were built throughout the national forests and there was no longer a need for observer/firefighter teams, many lookouts were abandoned, especially after 1950. The advent of aircraft for fire detection and observation also reduced the need for fire towers. The remaining towers became more valuable as more and more people used the national forests for recreation, and as urban interface fires became a serious problem due to people building homes next to national forests or inside the boundaries on private inholdings. For example, Mount Elden Lookout, 2,000 feet above Flagstaff just north of the city, detects the most fires in Region 3 (Southwestern) of the USDA Forest Service (Arizona and New Mexico) due to the extensive urban interface of this small city in the pines.

Many fire towers are still in use, especially in the Southwest, where early fire detection is critical, and some abandoned towers are being restored as fire managers realize that towers are a relatively cheap method of detection compared to aircraft and other means. Skilled observers can also immediately provide the initial attack crew with crucial information about the fire, such as size, rate of spread, intensity, fuel types, and threats to structures and other resources.

Aircraft are invaluable for observing and attacking fires, but an airplane or helicopter can only observe a small portion of the forest at a time, and it takes time for an aircraft to reach a growing fire.

The observer locates smokes (the firefighter term for a suspected new fire start) with an Osborne Fire Finder, a 2-foot-diameter circular brass platform mounted in

The Bell Trail follows Wet Beaver Creek, a rare permanent stream.

Bell Trail

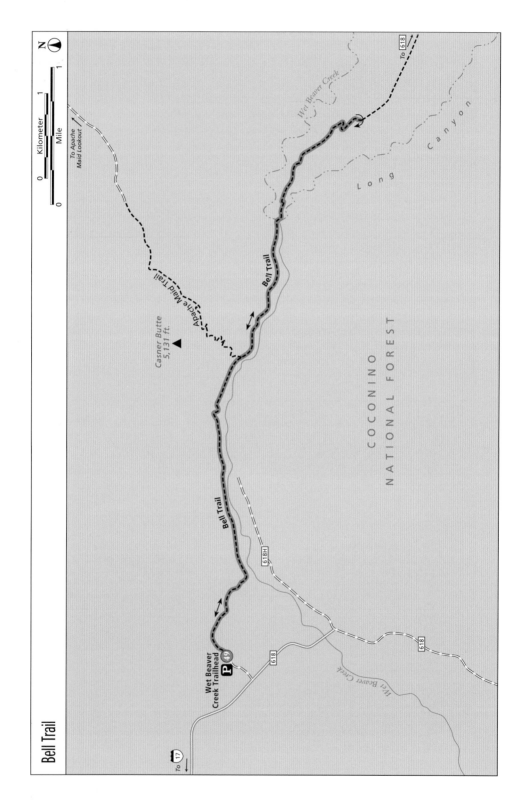

N

0 Kilometer 1

0 Mile 1

To Apache
Maid Lookout

Casner Butte
5,131 ft.

Apache Maid Trail

Bell Trail

Bell Trail

To 618

Wet Beaver Creek

Long Canyon

COCONINO
NATIONAL FOREST

618H

Wet Beaver
Creek Trailhead

P 49

618

Wet Beaver Creek

618

To 17

the center of the tower cab over a precisely surveyed point on the gro
rotating ring with a slit for the observer's eye on one side and horsehair cro.
the other is used to sight on the column of smoke and determine the azimut.
bearing) of the fire. The azimuth can be measured to 1 minute of arc (1/60th of a
degree); the elevation of the fire can also be measured in degrees if necessary. A forest
map is mounted on the disk of the fire finder, and a steel tape stretches between the
sights. The position of the fire tower is in the center of the map, so the smoke has to
be located along the tape between the center and the crosshairs.

There is no way to directly measure distance from a single lookout except by
using terrain features to locate the smoke on a topographic map. This doesn't work
on low-relief terrain such as the Kaibab Plateau or much of the Mogollon Rim, but a
skilled observer can locate a fire pretty accurately in more-mountainous terrain, such
as the Central Mountains of Arizona.

This is why fire towers have overlapping viewsheds. If a second observer can see
the same smoke, the bearing lines can be plotted on a large wall map in the dispatch
office and the fire located very accurately.

It takes a special type of person to work a fire tower for three or four months—
the isolation isn't for everyone, but for those of us who love it, our time spent on a
mountaintop is an unforgettable experience.

Miles and Directions

0.0 Start at the Wet Beaver Creek Trailhead.

2.1 Pass the Apache Maid Trail.

3.1 Cross Wet Beaver Creek.

4.2 Reach the Mogollon Rim; return the way you came.

8.4 Arrive back at the trailhead.

50 Walker Basin Trail

A hike on a little-used, historic trail to the Mogollon Rim.

Distance: 4.8 miles out and back
Hiking time: About 3 hours
Difficulty: Moderate
Seasons: Fall through spring
Trail surface: Dirt and rocks
Water: None
Other trail users: Mountain bikes and horses
Canine compatibility: Dogs under control allowed

Land status: Coconino National Forest
Fees and permits: None
Maps: Trails Illustrated Mogollon Rim, Munds Mountain; USGS Casner Butte; Coconino National Forest
Trail contacts: Coconino National Forest, 1824 S. Thompson St., Flagstaff 86001; (928) 527-3600; fs.usda.gov/coconino

Finding the trailhead: From Camp Verde, drive east about 5.7 miles on the General Crook Trail (FH 9), then turn left on maintained dirt FR 618. Continue about 9 miles; turn right and drive 0.8 mile to the Walker Basin Trailhead. Low-clearance vehicles may have to be left on FR 618. GPS: N34 38.189' / W111 42.589'

The Walker Basin Trail turnoff can also be reached from the north. Take the AZ 179 exit from I-17, then go southeast on FR 618, which is paved to the Beaver Creek Campground. The signed Walker Basin Trail turnoff is 5 miles from the interstate.

The Hike

The historic Walker Basin Trail, built to move stock between summer and winter pastures, starts out as an old, closed road, wandering northeast through juniper forest toward a slow ridge visible ahead. It climbs this gentle ridge along its crest, and the views start to open up. The trail starts to climb more steeply when you're just over 1.0 mile from the trailhead. The reward for this exertion is ever more sweeping views of the Verde Valley. The ridge merges with the steep slopes of a point that looms above, and the trail attacks the slope with steep, rocky switchbacks. The views are some of the best of the hike, plenty of excuses for rest stops. Most of the Verde Rim is visible, from Pine Mountain on the south to Mingus and Woodchute Mountains to the west. A large section of the western Mogollon Rim is visible as well, including the Sedona area and the San Francisco Peaks. At the top of the steep climb, the trail crosses the flat top of the point before making a short, final climb to the rim, at 5,350 feet. Our hike ends here, having covered the most scenic part of the trail.

Option
You can hike the remainder of the trail 3.5 miles to FR 214, adding 7.0 miles to the total distance.

Larkspur graces the desert after a wet winter.

Walker Basin Trail

Miles and Directions

0.0 Start at the Walker Basin Trailhead.

0.7 Start a steeper climb.

1.9 The climb moderates a bit.

2.4 Reach the Mogollon Rim; return the way you came.

4.8 Arrive back at the trailhead.

51 Buckhorn Trail

This hike takes you up a rarely used trail to the Mogollon Rim, with expansive views of the Verde Valley.

Distance: 4.6 miles out and back
Hiking time: About 3 hours
Difficulty: Moderate
Seasons: Fall through spring
Trail surface: Dirt and rocks
Water: None
Other trail users: Mountain bikes and horses
Canine compatibility: Dogs under control allowed

Land status: Coconino National Forest
Fees and permits: None
Maps: Trails Illustrated Mogollon Rim, Munds Mountain; USGS Walker Mountain; Coconino National Forest
Trail contacts: Coconino National Forest, 1824 S. Thompson St., Flagstaff 86001; (928) 527-3600; fs.usda.gov/coconino

Finding the trailhead: From Camp Verde, drive east about 5.7 miles on the General Crook Trail (FH 9), then turn left (north) on maintained dirt FR 618. Continue 6.1 miles; turn right (east) on FR 9201M. This unmaintained road is just past the sign for Wickiup Draw. Go 1.1 miles to the third closed road on the left (north). The trailhead is not signed, and there is minimal parking. GPS: N34 35.483' / W111 42.627'

FR 9201M can also be reached from the north. Take the AZ 179 exit from I-17, then go southeast on FR 618, which is paved to the Beaver Creek Campground. FR 9201M is 8.1 miles from the interstate, just before the Wickiup Draw sign.

The Hike

Initially, the Buckhorn Trail is an old jeep road the forest service has closed by bulldozing a pile of dirt at its beginning. The trail leads northeast across a flat then climbs onto a juniper-covered mesa. It is a pleasant walk about 1.3 miles to a fence line, where the trail turns southeast and starts to climb along a ridge crest. The view becomes wider as the ridge gains elevation and becomes narrower. Pinyon pines begin to compete with the junipers. Finally the ridge runs into the slopes below the Mogollon Rim, and the trail becomes very steep and rocky. Mercifully, this section is short, and the trail soon reaches a saddle on the ridge leading to Hollingshead Point. Above this saddle the trail becomes difficult to follow, so the hike ends here.

Option
You can continue 2.4 miles to the east end of the trail at FR 214, adding 4.8 miles to the total distance.

Apache Wars

The increasing numbers of settlers, miners, and ranchers coming into the Southwest in the 1860s soon created conflicts with the Native Americans, in particular the various Apache bands from Arizona to west Texas. After the American Civil War, the US Army was ordered to carry out a series of campaigns against the resisting Indians, which became known as the Apache Wars. Although it's popularly believed that the Apache Wars ended with the surrender of Geronimo's Chiricahua Apache band near the Chiricahua Mountains in southeast Arizona in 1886, Apache warriors carried out raids in Arizona as late as 1924, and in Mexico until 1933.

In the Verde Valley, conflicts arose in the 1860s with both the Tonto Apache and the valley's previous inhabitants, the Yavapai. The hostilities were actively fueled by a Confederate deserter, King Woolsey, who deceived, poisoned, and murdered the Apaches. In 1871 Lieutenant Colonel George Crook, a renowned Civil War veteran and leader of several previous successful campaigns against Indian tribes, was sent to Arizona to subdue the Apache. In order to conduct the Yavapai War, the US Army built Fort Verde, later renamed Camp Verde, in the lower Verde Valley. Part of a string of US Army forts from Fort Whipple at Prescott to Fort Apache in the White Mountains, Fort Verde was connected to Fort Apache by a wagon road that General Crook had built along the Mogollon Rim. Parts of the General Crook Trail survive today and can be followed by modern hikers as part of the historic Cabin Loop trail system. (See my FalconGuide *Hiking Northern Arizona* for more information.)

A trigger point in the Yavapai War was the Camp Grant Massacre, in which 150 Pinal and Aravaipa Apache who had surrendered to the US Army were killed by settlers and O'odham warriors. Some of the survivors fled north into the Tonto Basin to seek protection among their Tonto Apache and Yavapai allies.

General Crook and his troops fought some twenty skirmishes with the Yavapai and Apache, including the Battles of Salt River Canyon and Turret Peak. In the Battle of Salt River Canyon, General Crook, with 130 troops and 30 Apache scouts, located a Yavapai stronghold at Skeleton Cave above the Salt River. They surrounded the cave and completely surprised the Indians, who refused to surrender. The troops opened fire, deliberately shooting at the roof of the cave and rolling rocks down from above. The one-sided battle resulted in the death of seventy-six natives, including women and children.

In March 1873 a band of Tonto Apache attacked and killed three white men. Crook's men under the command of Captain George Randall tracked the Apache to the Yavapai stronghold at the top of Turret Peak and crept silently up the mountainside under cover of darkness. The Indians were totally surprised by the dawn attack, and many fell to their death in panic. Some resisted, but the fighting quickly ended. Fifty-seven natives were killed as well as several civilians held in the stronghold. The attack proved demoralizing to the Yavapai and Tonto Apache, and most soon surrendered to the US Army at Camp Verde.

You probably won't even notice hedgehog cactus—until it blooms in late spring.

Skirmishes continued until 1875, when the Yavapai and Tonto Apache were forcibly removed from their reservations and marched to San Carlos. Eventually, about 200 survivors were returned to the Camp Verde Reservation. Crook was promoted to general as a result of his success, a move that angered some officers who were senior to him.

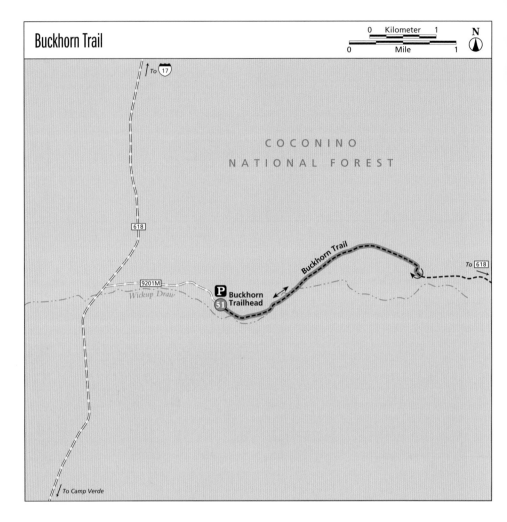

Buckhorn Trail

COCONINO
NATIONAL FOREST

To ⑰
618
9201M
Wickup Draw
Ⓟ Buckhorn
51 Trailhead
Buckhorn Trail
To 618
To Camp Verde

Miles and Directions

0.0 Start at the unsigned Buckhorn Trailhead.

1.3 Come to a fence line and turn southeast.

2.3 Reach the Mogollon Rim; return the way you came.

4.6 Arrive back at the trailhead.

52 Tramway Trail

This short trail provides easy access to the upper end of spectacular West Clear Creek.

Distance: 0.8 mile out and back
Hiking time: About 1.5 hours
Difficulty: Moderate
Seasons: Spring through fall
Trail surface: Dirt and rocks
Water: West Clear Creek
Other trail users: None
Canine compatibility: Dogs under control allowed

Land status: West Clear Creek Wilderness, Coconino National Forest
Fees and permits: None
Maps: Trails Illustrated Mogollon Rim, Munds Mountain; USGS Calloway Butte; Coconino National Forest
Trail contacts: Coconino National Forest, 1824 S. Thompson St., Flagstaff 86001; (928) 527-3600; fs.usda.gov/coconino

Finding the trailhead: From Camp Verde, drive about 30 miles east on the General Crook Trail (FH 9). Turn left (north) on AZ 87 and continue 11 miles, then turn left (northwest) on Lake Mary Road (FH 3). Go 7 miles, turn left on FR 81, and continue to the trailhead at the end of the road. GPS: N34 33.486' / W111 25.273'

The Hike

The short but spectacular trail descends into the gorge of West Clear Creek, affording fine views both up and down the canyon. It follows the route of an old aerial tramway. The Kaibab Limestone forms the rim. This fossil-rich layer was deposited in a shallow ocean and forms the edge of the Mogollon Rim in this area. Below the Kaibab Limestone, the cross-bedded Coconino Sandstone appears, with its layers of overlapping petrified sand dunes. The trail ends at the bottom of the canyon.

Options

One option is to hike cross-country upstream and climb out via the Maxwell Trail. Another is to hike and swim the entire 25-mile length of West Clear Creek downstream to the

The clear, cool waters of West Clear Creek, at the foot of the Tramway Trail, are always a delight.

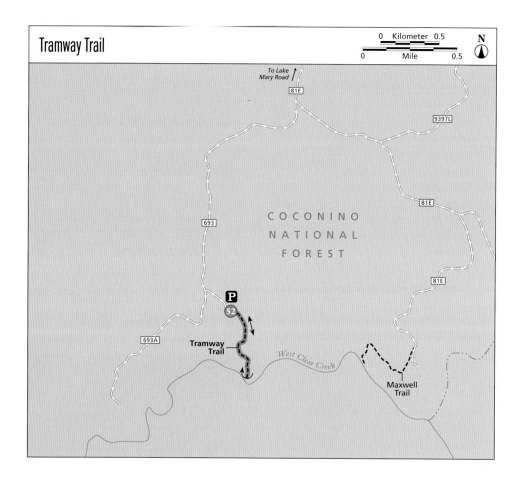

To Lake
Mary Road

81E

9397L

81E

C O C O N I N O
N A T I O N A L
F O R E S T

81E

693

P
52

693A

Tramway
Trail

West Clear Creek

Maxwell
Trail

Bull Pen Ranch Trailhead. This difficult, multiday backpack trip requires swimming and floating your pack across numerous pools. It should be attempted only in warm, stable weather by experienced canyon hikers.

Miles and Directions

0.0   Start at the trailhead and descend into the gorge.

0.4   Reach West Clear Creek; return the way you came.

0.8   Arrive back at the trailhead.

53 Maxwell Trail

Another short trail provides access to upper West Clear Creek.

Distance: 1.0 mile out and back
Hiking time: About 1.5 hours
Difficulty: Moderate
Seasons: Spring through fall
Trail surface: Dirt and rocks
Water: West Clear Creek
Other trail users: None
Canine compatibility: Dogs under control allowed

Land status: West Clear Creek Wilderness, Coconino National Forest
Fees and permits: None
Maps: Trails Illustrated Mogollon Rim, Munds Mountain; USGS Calloway Butte; Coconino National Forest
Trail contacts: Coconino National Forest, 1824 S. Thompson St., Flagstaff 86001; (928) 527-3600; fs.usda.gov/coconino

Finding the trailhead: From Camp Verde, drive about 30 miles east on the General Crook Trail (FH 9). Turn left (north) on AZ 87 and continue 11 miles, then turn left (northwest) on Lake Mary Road (FH 3). Go 7 miles, turn left on FR 81, and continue to the traihead at the end of the road. GPS: N34 33.508' / W111 24.258'

Relics and artifacts dating from the pioneer and prehistoric days are common in Arizona and should never be disturbed. They are protected by the American Antiquities Act as well as state law.

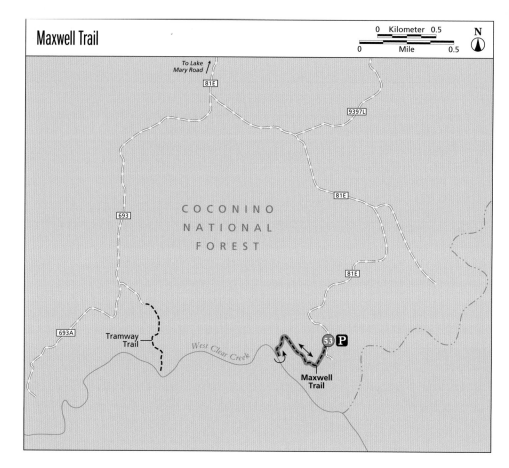

0   Kilometer 0.5

0   Mile   0.5

N

To Lake
Mary Road

81E

9397L

81E

693

C O C O N I N O

N A T I O N A L

F O R E S T

81E

693A

Tramway
Trail

West Clear Creek

53 P

81E

Maxwell
Trail

The Hike

The Maxwell Trail descends in a series of switchbacks, then traverses to the west for a
short distance before resuming the steep descent to the canyon bottom. At the creek,
which flows year round, a lush riparian habitat is encountered, a strong contrast with
the dry plateau at the trailhead.

Hiking with Your Dog

Most of the trails in this book are in the Coconino National Forest, and many are
within a wilderness area. Dogs are allowed, but the USDA Forest Service specifies
that dogs must be kept under control—either on-leash or under verbal command.
What does this mean? Well-trained dogs that always come when called and have been
taught to heel are under effective voice command. Dogs that run off, chase wildlife,
bark, and run up to other hikers—even in a friendly way—are not under control and
must be kept on a leash. Out-of-control dogs are hard on wildlife. And many people
have had bad experiences with dogs and don't appreciate being rushed by one, even

when its tail is wagging. Why give dog owners a bad name? Keep your dog on a leash, and if it's just not a good trail citizen, leave your dog at home and save the dog walks for your home neighborhood. That being said, dogs can be truly wonderful wilderness companions, as they delight in checking out every new and exciting scent. Just make certain your dog is as respectful of others as you are.

Miles and Directions

0.0 Start at the trailhead and descend on switchbacks.

0.5 Reach West Clear Creek; return the way you came.

1.0 Arrive back at the trailhead.

GREEN TIP
If you see someone littering, muster up
the courage to ask them not to.

54 Willow Crossing Trail

This trail follows the route of a historic crossing of Willow Valley, a tributary of West Clear Creek, and also takes you to a natural arch.

Distance: 2.4 miles out and back
Hiking time: About 2 hours
Difficulty: Easy
Seasons: Spring through fall
Trail surface: Dirt and rocks
Water: None
Other trail users: Mountain bikes and horses
Canine compatibility: Dogs under control allowed

Land status: Coconino National Forest
Fees and permits: None
Maps: Trails Illustrated Mogollon Rim, Munds Mountain; USGS Calloway Butte; Coconino National Forest
Trail contacts: Coconino National Forest, 1824 S. Thompson St., Flagstaff 86001; (928) 527-3600; fs.usda.gov/coconino

Finding the trailhead: From Camp Verde, drive about 30 miles east on AZ 260. Turn left (north) on AZ 87 and continue 11 miles, then turn left (northwest) on Lake Mary Road (FH 3). Go 3 miles and turn left (west) on FR 196. Continue 1,9 miles, then turn right on FR122A. Continue 2.6 miles to the unsigned trailhead at the end of the road. There are numerous side roads; make sure you stay on FR 122A. GPS: N34 35.036' / W111 22.710'

The Hike

The Willow Crossing Trail is not shown on the topographic map, but a sign marks the beginning of the trail. It follows the drainage in a gentle descent through tall ponderosa pines for about 0.4 mile. As the side canyon becomes steeper, the trail abandons it for the ridge to the west, and then stays on the ridge to the canyon bottom. Watch for poison ivy along the canyon floor. Here the trail turns north to cross the normally dry creek bed then climbs the west side of the canyon to reach the rim. It's an easy walk across the pine-covered flat to the end of the trail at FR 9366M. After retracing your steps to the bottom of Willow Valley, go downstream a few yards and you will spot the natural arch on the west wall. It is not easily seen from the trail.

Options

You can hike cross-country both up- and downstream. The experienced canyon hiker can walk downstream to West Clear Creek and the Maxwell Trail, a boulder-hopping distance of about 9.0 miles one way.

The natural arch along Willow Creek

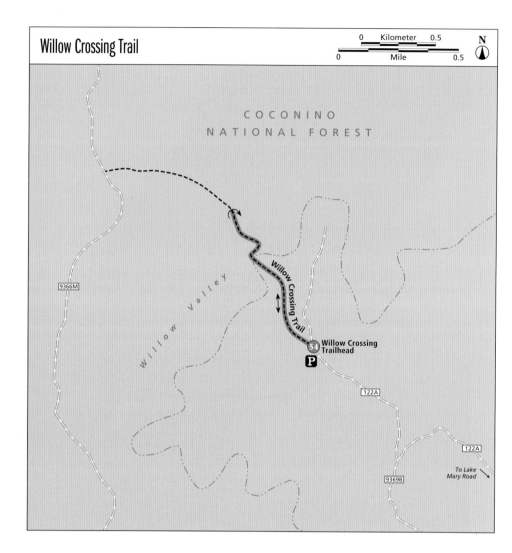

0   Kilometer   0.5

0   Mile   0.5

N

COCONINO
NATIONAL FOREST

9366M

Willow Valley

Willow Crossing Trail

54 Willow Crossing
Trailhead

P

122A

122A

To Lake
Mary Road

9369B

Early Days on the Mogollon Rim: The Crossings

Why is this trail called the Willow "Crossing" Trail? Crossings date from the early days
of settlement, logging, and ranching on the Mogollon Plateau, which is the forested
southernmost edge of the Colorado Plateau, just north of the Mogollon Rim. The
Mogollon Rim is the watershed divide east of Fossil Creek, so drainages north of
the rim flow generally to the north down the gently sloping plateau. There are several major canyons cut into the plateau, each with multiple tributaries, resulting in a
topography of long north–south, flat-topped forested ridges separated by steep-sided
canyons that are several hundred feet deep. This makes east–west travel difficult, so
the first east–west wagon road on the Mogollon Plateau was the General Crook Trail,
which followed the Mogollon Rim itself and so avoided the canyons to the north.

Wagon roads and trails were easy to build along the ridges, but inevitably the time came when people needed to connect the ridge roads. So trails and wagon roads were built at the easiest places to cross the canyons, and they became "crossings." Some of the old crossings survive as foot trails today; others are used by the modern forest road network. The names, however, survive—Jones Crossing, Kinder Crossing, Horse Crossing, Macks Crossing, and more.

Miles and Directions

0.0 Start at the signed Willow Crossing Trailhead and begin a gentle descent.

0.4 Reach the bottom of Willow Valley. (You'll visit a natural arch here on the way back.)

0.6 Arrive at the west rim.

1.2 The trail ends at FR 9366M; return the way you came. At the bottom of Willow Valley, walk a few yards downstream to the natural arch.

2.4 Arrive back at the trailhead.

GREEN TIP

Consider the packaging of any products you bring with you. It's best to properly dispose of bulky packaging at home before you hike and re-bag into reusable zipper bags. Anything you can carry in, you can carry out. In fact, if every hiker picked up a bit of someone else's litter, the trails would be very clean and we'd all get to feel very smug about our efforts.

55 Fossil Springs Trail

This trail takes you to Fossil Springs and a historic diversion dam on Fossil Creek.

Distance: 6.8 miles out and back
Hiking time: About 4 hours
Difficulty: Moderate
Seasons: Spring through fall
Trail surface: Dirt and rocks
Water: Fossil Springs
Other trail users: Horses
Canine compatibility: Dogs under control allowed
Land status: Fossil Springs Wilderness, Coconino National Forest

Fees and permits: Parking permit required by advance reservation Apr 1 through Oct 1. Day use only in the permit area. Camping and campfires are prohibited.
Maps: Trails Illustrated Mogollon Rim, Munds Mountain; USGS Strawberry; Coconino National Forest
Trail contacts: Tonto National Forest, 2324 E. McDowell Rd., Phoenix 85006; (602) 225-5200; fs.usda.gov/tonto. Coconino National Forest, 1824 S. Thompson St., Flagstaff 86001; (928) 527-3600; fs.usda.gov/coconino

Finding the trailhead: From Camp Verde, go east 31 miles on AZ 260, then turn left on AZ 87. Continue 7.7 miles to Strawberry and turn right on the Fossil Creek Road (the main road through town.) This road becomes FR 708, a maintained dirt road. Continue 4.7 miles; turn right and drive 0.4 mile to the Fossil Springs Trailhead. There is no access to the trailhead from the west on FR 708—the road is closed to motor vehicles between the Fossil Springs Trailhead west to the Waterfall Trailhead. GPS: N34 24.398' / W111 34.102'

The Hike

The trail follows the route of an old jeep road and descends northeast below the rim of the canyon. It soon turns northwest and continues its descent through pinyon-juniper woodland to reach Fossil Creek. Now turn left and hike downstream. Though upper Fossil Creek often flows, there's no mistaking the added volume when you reach Fossil Springs. These warm springs gush from the left bank of the creek. A short distance below the springs, you'll leave the wilderness area and reach the remnants of a concrete dam, the destination for our hike.

Option

You can hike upstream cross-country in Fossil Creek, from the point where the trail first reached the canyon bottom. The bulk of the wilderness lies upstream and encompasses two major side canyons, Calf Pen and Sandrock Canyons.

Ice in a side canyon during a winter cold snap—a contrast to Fossil Creek, which is fed by warm springs and never freezes

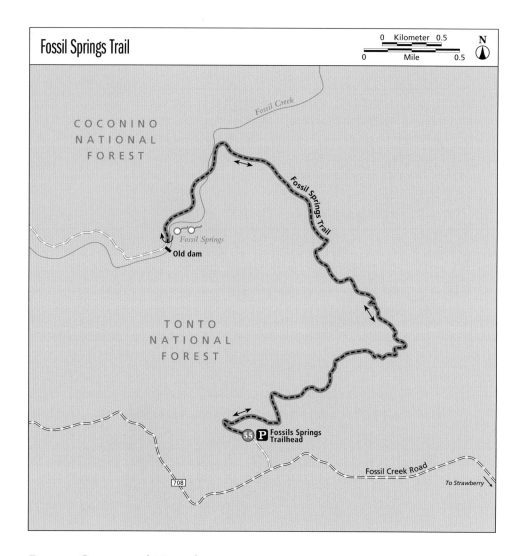

0   Kilometer 0.5

0   Mile   0.5

N

COCONINO
NATIONAL
FOREST

Fossil Creek

Fossil Springs Trail

Fossil Springs

Old dam

TONTO
NATIONAL
FOREST

55 P Fossils Springs
         Trailhead

Fossil Creek Road

To Strawberry

708

Dams—Concrete and Natural

The dam was constructed in 1916 to divert water into a flume. Several miles downstream, the water was used to spin the turbines at the Irving Power Plant. Another power plant, at the mouth of Fossil Creek on the Verde River, harnessed the power of Fossil Creek a second time. These facilities were among Arizona's first hydroelectric generators. By 2000 the power produced was minuscule, and Arizona Public Service realized that the goodwill to be gained by restoring the free flow of Fossil Creek far outweighed the benefits of power production. Both power plants and the flumes were decommissioned in 2005. The return of natural flow caused a spectacular return of wildlife and also resulted in Fossil Creek being designated as Arizona's second Wild and Scenic River, in 2009.

Fossil Springs produces water rich in calcium carbonate, which precipitates out as travertine to form small natural dams, cascades, and pour-offs. The travertine formations had all but disappeared due to the diversion of most of the water through the power plants, but restoration of the flow has caused the travertine formations to return surprisingly quickly. Today, Fossil Creek is such a popular destination that a permit is required for parking at any trailhead during the summer season.

Miles and Directions

0.0 Start at the Fossil Springs Trailhead.

2.8 Reach Fossil Creek.

3.4 Come to the old dam; return the way you came.

6.8 Arrive back at the trailhead.

About the Author

The author has a serious problem—he doesn't know what he wants to do when he grows up. Meanwhile he's done such things as wildland firefighting, running a mountain shop, flying airplanes, shooting photos, and writing books. He's a back-country skier, climber, figure skater, mountain biker, amateur radio operator, river runner, and sea kayaker—but the thing that really floats his boat is hiking and back-packing. No matter what else he tries, the author always come back to hiking, especially long, rough, cross-country trips in places like the Grand Canyon. Some people never learn. But what little he has learned, he's willing share with you—via his books, of course, but also via his website, blogs, and whatever works. His website is BruceGrubbs.com.

Other Titles by Bruce Grubbs

Hiking Nevada: A Guide to State's Greatest Hiking Adventures, 3rd edition

Best Easy Day Hikes Tucson, 2nd Edition

Hiking Arizona: A Guide to the State's Greatest Hiking Adventures, 4th edition

Basic Illustrated Using GPS, 3rd Edition

Hiking Arizona's Superstition and Mazatzal Country: A Guide to the Areas' Greatest Hikes, 2nd edition

Camping Arizona: A Comprehensive Guide to Public Tent and RV Campgrounds, 3rd edition

Camping Southern California: A Comprehensive Guide to Public Tent and RV Campgrounds, 2nd edition

Best Hikes Near Las Vegas

Backpacker Magazine's Using a GPS: Digital Trip Planning, Recording, and Sharing

Best Easy Day Hikes Palm Springs and Coachella Valley

Best Easy Day Hikes Las Vegas

Best Easy Day Hikes Albuquerque

Best Easy Day Hikes Sedona, 2nd edition

Best Easy Day Hikes Flagstaff, 2nd edition

Best Hikes Near Phoenix

Hiking Northern Arizona: A Guide to Northern Arizona's Greatest Hiking Adventures, 3rd edition

Grand Canyon National Park Pocket Guide

Explore! Joshua Tree National Park: A Guide to Exploring the Desert Trails and Roads

A FalconGuide to Saguaro National Park and the Santa Catalina Mountains